Why and Why Not to Invest in Real Estate

A Learn By Doing Book

Copyright © 2017 by Bruce M Firestone

All rights reserved, including the right to reproduce or transmit this book or portions thereof in any form whatsoever without written permission of the author and publisher.

For information, please contact:

Learn By Doing Publications

Ottawa Canada

Attention:
Ms Nina Brooks ninabooks@rogers.com
@ProfBruce www.brucemfirestone.com

How to Get Rich for Real Series

First Edition

Firestone, Bruce Murray, 1951—

This is the third in a series of Prof Bruce real estate investment mini books, which preferably should be read in this order:

> *Real Estate Investing Made Easy*
>
> *Retire Rich, Retire Early—How to retire at any age for real*
>
> *Why and Why Not to Invest in Real Estate*

You may also want to read by Bruce M Firestone:

> *Don't Back Down, the real story of the founding of the NHL's Ottawa Senators and why big leagues matter*
>
> *Entrepreneurs Handbook II*
>
> *Real Estate Handbook*
>
> *Quotes for Entrepreneurs—Great Quotes to Inspire, Guide and Motivate, For Real*
>
> *Quantum Entity Trilogy—We Are All One, American Spring, The Successors*
>
> *Jenna's Story*

Testimonials

I think I've learned more from Prof Bruce in the past year than I had in the entire decade prior. My collective rents are much higher (and my vacancy rate much lower) than when I first came to see Bruce. A lot of the credit goes to him for helping me focus, execute, and learn about how to differentiate my portfolio and animate it (add value) too. As a result, I've attracted better tenants who are paying higher rents, and enjoying my properties more as well...

Brian Dagenais
owner 32 doors
founder, BlackSheep development company

When I was first introduced to Prof Bruce, I was considering purchasing a property in Bells Corners for a development project. Bruce informed me of the multiple projects he had been involved with throughout Bells Corners. We viewed the property I was considering and he made alternate recommendations that had higher cap rates than my original option. At that point, I knew coaching with Bruce was the right move; we assessed my finances and situation, and created an amazing strategy based on it. Soon after, I purchased another property and created an incredible income stream from it, which Prof Bruce has actually used as an example at his seminars because of the extraordinary results I got with it. By the way, it also cost a lot less in terms of time and money than my original Bells Corners idea. Prof Bruce also helped me with my startup (CoHouse.ca)—we build coach houses in Ottawa. It'll be a huge business for us and it's changed my life. I can honestly say Bruce has been one of the biggest influences on my life, helping me not only with my real estate investments, but also business development as well as my personal development too.

Chris Long
contractor
investor

Real estate investment coaching with Bruce Firestone has been a great experience. When I first came to Bruce, I explained to him our current situation—that I was looking to expand my real estate portfolio. At that time, I was basically out of ideas—my wife and me had purchased triplex in Little Italy and it was doing ok, but I thought we could be doing better. I believed it was probably time to move on to a new investment but Prof Bruce opened my eyes to a new concept—one he calls "animation." Instead of immediately moving on to a new property, we examined my current rental property. How could we animate it? How could I add value? How could I boost revenues and cashflow? We looked at various options. In the end we ended up converting two of the three units into Airbnb suites. We've now increased our cashflow from that property by a factor of 10!

Dave Bush
technology worker, real estate investor
airbnb'ologist

I feel very fortunate to have found a real estate coach like you, Prof Bruce. Someone of your caliber and expertise could have chosen to remain a consultant solely to large corporations and governments, advising on multi-million dollar projects; but instead you also dedicate your time to coaching individual entrepreneurs, like me, to achieve her vision that anyone can build long-term wealth via real estate investment, developing a comfortable pension that way. I've certainly "upped my game" to a much higher level after taking your online training and completing your 9-month mentoring program. My horizons are wider and my senses are acutely attuned as a sophisticated real estate investor. This is not to mention the side benefits, such as the many real estate professionals you referred me to, many of whom are now part of my "dream team" in building my real estate investment portfolio. Despite your fame and success, I found you, Prof Bruce, to be a person who is down-to-earth and approachable, and sensitive even to the seemingly small needs of others. I sincerely THANK YOU for all your coaching, advice, referrals and care. I might come back for more when I'm ready to jump into commercial or land development.

Belinda Cheung
mother of five
owner 7 doors

Bruce Firestone hardly needs an introduction, let alone a recommendation, but it doesn't mean he doesn't deserve one. Anyone who spends a couple of minutes with him will be captivated by his speaking abilities combined with his in-depth knowledge in real estate, entrepreneurship among other topics. What is so admirable about Prof Bruce is that when he decides to take on a challenge, he immerses himself in it and doesn't give up until he masters it. Anything from personal to professional accomplishments he puts 110% in. He gives back more to the community than many others who are dedicated full time to that cause. It's a pleasure to work alongside Bruce on many initiatives—personal, professional and charitable, and I look forward to continuing to helping him in his ongoing efforts to make a difference in this world.

Brent Mondoux
technologist

I realize now that it was my fear holding me back and I'm glad that you helped me push through all that fear, because it has been a very great learning experience. I can't imagine my life without having done it… I would probably still be hoping and dreaming to do what I'm doing. It was a very important lesson to me that you've just got to push through, no matter what could be on the other side.

Paul Cairns
environmental engineer, real estate investor

Prof Bruce is the ultimate real estate coach; you don't only learn about real estate, you learn about life.

Gheorghe Adamche
real estate investor
air traffic control officer

Wow, I was just able to explain everything about a complex multi-residential deal I'm working on to an overseas buyer. Prof Bruce, I can't believe how much I've grown thanks to you!

Roman Monaenkov
Keller Williams realtor

For the past six months, Bruce M Firestone has been my real estate coach. With his guidance, I have accomplished more in that half year than in the previous five. Prof Bruce helped me refine my strategy, look in new development directions, and find property that was manageable, affordable and offers great returns. He assisted in selecting appropriate investments, negotiating favorable terms, and closing deals, overcoming potential roadblocks. He coached me to polish my presentation skills, and he is a constant source of positive encouragement. Moreover, Bruce helps me focus my energy on achievable objectives, and then holds me accountable. I highly recommend Bruce as a real estate investment coach and mentor so you can turn your ideas into reality.

Bob Wachna
real estate investor and developer

Prof Bruce taught me the skills I require to bring my real estate investing to another level. His coaching has given me the confidence I need to take on any challenge, including more complex ones and be successful.

Matthew Maxsom
owner, 21 doors

Dedication

Wondering where you should put your money after being disappointed with the performance of all your other investments? Look no further than real estate, still the single most dependable investment you can find in most cities and nations around the world.

I dedicate this booklet to all those people who, like me, have never found a better sector to invest in. In many ways real estate is unique. You can rent it to third parties who help you pay off your mortgage. It generally doesn't go out of fashion. Unlike ideas which are in infinite supply, real estate is not. When cities or your neighbors build new infrastructure around your property, it's likely to go up in value without you having to do a thing. These are just a few of real estate's unusual characteristics. Read on there's more.

Another thing I like about this industry is that business models built around real property are not usually as complex as, say, running Apple or Facebook let alone Alphabet or SpaceX. It's a *business model for dummies* of which I am one. In fact, my wife makes me carry around a piece of paper that says only this on it—

IT'S REAL ESTATE, STUPID.
IT'S REAL ESTATE, STUPID.
IT'S REAL ESTATE, STUPID.

Really.
Have you heard this one?
Question: "What's the second happiest day of your business life?"
Answer: "When you buy a National Hockey League franchise."
Question: "What's the happiest day of your business life?"
Answer: "When you sell a National Hockey League franchise."
Really.

So this mini book is dedicated to all those people like me who prefer simplicity over complexity, and rates of return that are usually 6, 8, 10, 12 or 14% pa not 0.99% on, say, your bank savings account, 1.5% on your t-bills or potentially negative rates on mutual and pension funds, stocks and bonds or catastrophic losses from owning an NHL franchise like someone I know….

Bruce M Firestone, PhD
Ottawa Senators founder
Real Estate Investment and Business coach
Century 21 Explorer Realty Inc broker
twitter.com/ProfBruce
profbruce.tumblr.com/archive
brucemfirestone.com
Ottawa, Canada
September 2017

MAKING IMPOSSIBLE POSSIBLE

Contents—Why and Why Not to Invest in Real Estate

Testimonials
Dedication
Contents

    Introduction, why invest in real estate
    If I were King (or Queen) of Exxon, I would....
    Real estate invention and animation/the "WOW" effect
    Three Ways to Boost Cap Rates and Increase Property Values
    Internal Rate of Return (IRR), Cap Rate (Capitalization Rate) and ROE (Return on Equity)
    Toronto real estate is out of control
    Why Not to Invest in Real Estate
    The problem with deposits
    Things to ask your contractor or renovator before you sign
    Why Real Estate is a Unique Asset Class
    Warren Buffett Methodology Applied to Real Estate Investing
    Flipping versus buy and hold
    What info you should have on each property you buy/every real estate project requires these steps
    How to value property
    How to Buy Low/What Not to Buy/What to Buy
    Canadian investment options
    How to become an equity lord
    Donald Trump and late capitalism
    How to really finance real estate
    Executive Travel Apartments—reducing your capital requirements, a form of bootstrapping
    Why use mortgage brokers
    The more leverage you take on early in your career, the less you will have later on
    Accretive finance
    15 reasons why most partnerships fail
    Trade-off between Property Management and ROI
    Staging your home and even your commercial space
    Every dollar you save is two you don't have to earn
    Highest and Best Use, HABU—What do Planners Mean When They Refer to Highest and Best Use?
    NIMBYs are Wrong to Oppose Mixed Use and Higher Densities, the annual cost of NIMBYism to the economies of the United States and Canada
    Approval of Coach Houses Opens the Way to Better Urban Design
    Negative Property Taxes—a Possible Response to NIMBY'itis
    Why Land Prices are Taking Off
    Over-Investment in Real Estate and Why You Should Treat Even Your Principal Residence as if it was a Rental Property
    Conclusion

ADDENDUM 1 Vertical Rent Curves
ADDENDUM 2 Real Estate Insiders
ADDENDUM 3 Raising Capital by Raising Scrip
ADDENDUM 4 Leisure is the New Infrastructure
ADDENDUM 5 How to Avoid Deal-Flopping Appraisals
ADDENDUM 6 Buying Residential Property? Don't be Lazy + Grasshoppers, Squirrels and Ants—a diversified financial strategy that makes sense
ADDENDUM 7 How to Use Garden Suites to Add Value to Your Home and Community
ADDENDUM 8 Urban Catalysts and Anti Catalysts
ADDENDUM 9 How a Behemoth Real Estate Developer Can Clobber You

ABOUT THE AUTHOR

Introduction: why invest in real estate

I tell most of my SMEE (Small and Medium Sized Enterprise) clients (and my students) that real estate investing is usually a good idea. Homeownership, some residential rentals and owning your own business premises makes sense to me in most cases. Why is that?

Well, I go into some detail on this subject below. So why do I think it is important for my readers to know my reasons? Why is it not sufficient for them to simply know that I believe investing in real estate is a good thing?

Because all of us are subjected to and influenced by fashion trends. Some years, day trading is the big thing; other years it's mutual funds or options trading. Maybe everyone is buying bank stocks or they are investing in gold. Or perhaps a life insurance salesperson has just left you dazed and confused about what the right thing to do for your family is.

Writing these real estate mini books gives me an opportunity to talk to a new audience about a subject I am passionate about—helping the great majority of Canadians and Americans and others not covered by defined benefit pensions plans provide independently for themselves and their families.

Twenty-five years ago, I had a plan that seemed likely to work. I had taken over a small real estate company, grown it from annual revenues of $350,000 to $120 million in nine years, bought an expansion team (the NHL's Ottawa Senators) for $85 million and built a 20,000-seat arena (now called Canadian Tire Centre) for $240 million, which was sitting on a square mile of land (600 acres) that was going up in value, fast. But the Canadian dollar decided to go from 90 cents US to 62 cents, and NHL payrolls went from $6.5 million CAD when we purchased the team (including its minor league affiliate) to $55 million USD (around $86 million CAD, excluding its minor league affiliate) a decade later. The team went bankrupt in 2003 and was sold to current owner, Eugene Melnyk, for $120 million awhile later. Oh yeah, and that included the arena plus $13 million in playoff revenues sitting nicely in cash on the team's balance sheet from a long playoff run.

This strategy is called buying high and selling low; it explains why I work as a real estate broker, keynote speaker, coach, mentor and author who will have to work 'til he dies. It also explains why as I said above I keep in my briefcase a note to self, which says, "IT'S REAL ESTATE, STUPID." Three times.

Every time I think about investing in professional sports, tech companies, sign companies, toy companies, low return CDs, GICs, RRSPs, TFSAs, t-bills, IPPs, mutual funds, life insurance, stocks, bonds, (all of which I have done and all of which turned out to be rubbish), my wife makes me read the note again, out loud.

I think wide and varied experience, successes and failures, have given me an opportunity to be an effective teacher/coach/mentor. At least, that is what people I coach tell me. Thank you for that.

In a recent Bank of Montreal poll, 34% of respondents said their retirement "plan" is to win the lottery. Some plan. Almost as good as my old plan.

I have a client (he's 72) who came to see me recently and said, "Bruce, I've done everything right, everything my financial advisor told me to do. I own my own home. It's worth $600,000. I've paid off the mortgage. I've saved for years so I've put $700,000 away in my RRSP. Now he tells me that when I turn it into a RIF (a retirement income fund, sort of a reverse RRSP) this year, my wife and I will have to live on $15,000 per annum because we both come from long-lived families (over 90 for men and women) and don't want to outlive our money. What can we do? My wife and I can't live on $1,250 a month."

Developed nations are basically divided into three classes today—people, mostly government workers, with defined benefit pension plans, which take all the risk out of their retirement (about 20% of the population fall into this category), the top 1% who in 2012 had a 19.3% share of US national income (up from just 7.7% in 1973) and everyone else (the remaining 80% or so of the population). The strategies I use help the "everyone else" group whether they are 25 or 75.

It is based on acquiring real estate assets in four categories—owning your own home, owning some residential rental property, owning some commercial property to diversify your portfolio, and owning some land. By the way, the 600 acres around the Canadian Tire Centre that I bought in the early

1990s for $7.2 million ($12,000 an acre) is now trading for $450,000 to $820,000 per acre, which translates into more than a quarter of a billion dollars. Unfortunately, it is now owned by someone other than my family and I since it went with the bankruptcy estate of the team. Oh well.

I did some research a few years ago and you know what I found? Out of the 100 richest families in Canada, 61 of them had all or substantially all of their wealth invested in real estate. What do the Holy Roman Catholic Church, Emperor of Nippon and House of Windsor share in common other than they are long-lived institutions? They all have the bulk of their wealth in real estate. (Their long institutional lives may also be partly explained by that correlation as well.)

A coaching client of mine, a former student from my time teaching at Carleton University's Azrieli School of Architecture & Urbanism, Erik Rossmann runs a successful architecture practice in downtown Gatineau, Quebec. He not only runs his own architecture practice, he also owns the building in which he and his nine employees work. It's beautifully renovated and maintained—ie, there is no deferred maintenance on this or any other building he owns.

Erik is living proof that understanding not only the cost side of his industry (cost to complete, architectural and engineering fees, development charges etc) but also comprehending the value created through design and animation helps immensely in terms of landing new and retaining existing clients. They hire Erik because he cannot only develop strong forms that function well but also deliver greater value/higher income streams for owners, landlords, tenants and, indeed, even the surrounding community.

He has become one of my most successful acolytes, at least in terms of animation and boosting return on investment for all stakeholders... including social returns.

He also coined this phrase, which he uses when it comes to his personal investing in real estate—

Prof Bruce, I prefer the 5Rs instead of the 3Rs. Remember the 3Rs are: reduce, reuse, and recycle. Well the 5Rs are: reduce, reuse, recycle, and retire rich.

He understands that what's good for the environment is also good for the triple bottom line. I mean using less materiality, producing less waste, using more local sourcing and other environmental protections boost efficiency and effectiveness. What's not to like about that?

Real estate is a business model for dummies, me included. Once you own a great building in a terrific location, no one else can (by definition) locate there. You've squeezed out your competition. If the city around you keeps growing, more people want your product and you didn't have to do anything. But it isn't work-free.

People often say they want to get involved because it's "passive income". That's incorrect. Every business, including real estate, requires care, attention, passion, patience, vision, differentiation, effort. If you are prepared to do the work though, put together a good team and get a mentor, real estate is for you, all of you, brothers and sisters.

To be fair, I include (later on) a section on some of the industry's pitfalls—the "why not to invest in real estate" part of the title of this mini book. But to begin with, here're my reasons *for* investing in real estate...

Forced Savings

Most people are really bad at saving so, if at a minimum, they own their own home or condo plus some residential rentals or (for entrepreneurs) their own business premises, every month that they make their mortgage payments, they are paying off (saving) some of the principal. This is a type of "wealth effect"—it creates equity on your personal balance sheet (which everyone should have—equity as well as a personal balance sheet[1]) or your corporate balance sheet. It is kind of a hidden part of your

---

[1] Even for people starting out, I strongly recommend putting this (a PBS, personal balance sheet) together and updating it at least twice a year. I update mine quarterly. It's the best way to know and control all your assets over a lifetime, and discover hidden wealth too. Hidden wealth? Sure. If you start a student pro painting franchise while you are in college or

ROE (Return on Equity) too. Even people who are pretty good at saving their money may eventually succumb to the temptation to *spend* their savings. I mean that new Tesla model 3 looks pretty cool, huh?

However, if their savings are tied up in bricks and mortar, they are going to have to do more than turn on their computers or boot up their smart phones to use internet banking to, say, buy that holiday or sailboat of their dreams. Getting at your real estate equity can be relatively straightforward using something like a home equity line of credit (HELOC) or re-mortgaging your house, condo or office building (or putting a "reverse" mortgage in place, something an elder might do, for example, if they are real estate rich but cash poor[2]) but, at least, it requires some effort and will give you time to reflect on whether this is really what you should be doing.

I ask my students every year, how many of you can save, say, $700 per month? Usually, one or, at most, two students raise their hands (out of 45 or 50). When I re-phrase the question and ask how many of them can pay rent of $700 per month, well, most of them can do that. So if you had a mortgage of $700 per month (on a very small flat), you would be "forced" to save a bit of money every month…

Oh, and one last thing, if you can, crank your amortization. Instead of a 35-year term, try 30 or 25 or maybe even 20 years instead. If your cashflow will allow it, turn up the amortization "heat." Some of my clients use very short amortization periods (11 years is the shortest I've seen so far) so they are not only paying off their mortgages way faster than most folks, they are also setting the stage either for early retirement (debt-free) or boosting their equity so they can refinance them later, pulling out cash (tax free) so they can buy more property.

It's the closest thing to a perpetual motion machine anywhere in the known universe… something Warren Buffett figured out a long time ago upon his return to the US after having served his nation in Korea in the 1950s. I'll talk more about the Warren Buffett methodology applied to real estate later on.

Get Rich, Slow

Real estate is not a get rich quick scheme. Let me repeat that: real estate is not a get rich quick scheme.

I realize that a lot of real estate training and trainers promise that, but it's not true. They'll tell you to put in 50 low-ball offers a month searching for a sucker (a seller) who'll foolishly part with their property at a fraction of its market value.

Then they'll tell you to add a lick of paint, and flip it for a fortune.

Is this a complete falsehood?

No, it is not.

It does happen. But the frequency is so low as to be an unsustainable.

You can't plan on winning the lottery. So depending on naive sellers as a business model simply won't work.

Everyone gets lucky at least once in a lifetime but you can't build a business on luck.

So I teach a build, hold, add value, manage well, drive up value, refinance, pass on to your heirs model that works… every time. Just add effort and smarts. You are the "effort" part of this equation; Prof Bruce is the "smarts" part. OK?

---

university, add the value of that franchise to your PBS. One of my former students did just that—he made $30k his first summer, and $65K his last summer as a student pro painter. He put a value on it of income divided by 10% (his cap rate) or $650,000. Then he walked into a bank and got a loan for $400,000 to build his first home. His custom homebuilding business now does $30,000,000 a year (18 years later).

[2] By the way, these reverse mortgages are usually a terrible idea. They tie up one of your principal assets and they're expensive. I asked my real estate broker of record at Century 21 Explorer Realty Inc where I work (Ralph Shaw) about this. We call Ralph an all-seeing-all-knowing broker for a reason. That guy knows more about this industry than anyone else I've ever met. He told me, "CHIP (reverse) mortgages have an effective rate of about 6.5% when you factor in all their fees and costs. Most of those people could get a home equity line of credit or mortgage at much lower cost, which are also much more flexible and easier to pay off/get rid of…"

Most cities and towns have some real estate inflation or, at a minimum, real estate markets don't usually sink as fast as say tech stocks did in the great bubble burst of the early 2000s.

So if general real estate inflation is say 1.5% per annum and you have 25% equity in the deal then you are adding an extra 6% pa to your ROE. Obviously, if general real estate inflation is higher than this, and it often is, this factor will play an even larger part in creating investor wealth.

Diversification of Risk

If you own your own business premises, you have a diversification of risk. I advise SMEEs that they should generally keep their real estate in a company or ownership separate from their operating company so that if something happens to their operating business, they can always sell or hold onto their real estate holdings and, hopefully, living to fight another day.

One of my tech clients needed more and better office space. We looked at leasing 15,000 square feet of class A office space for his cluster of companies. At that time in Ottawa, Canada, prime office space was leasing for $18 per square foot per annum triple net (which means that the tenant must pay all operating costs, utilities and property taxes in addition to basic minimum rent). Operating costs and property taxes and utilities were around $12 per square foot per annum at the time so 15,000 square feet of space would have cost his company in the order of $450,000 per year.

After Bill (not his real name) recovered from sticker shock, I convinced him to buy his own building. He bought a beautiful two storey, 15,000 square foot, class A office building for $100 per square foot. He put down $500,000 and got a seller take back mortgage (known as a STB—ie, his financing came from the seller not a bank or other lender) for the balance. His annual mortgage costs were about $85,000 per annum, and he took ownership of the building in a separate company.

I also convinced him to buy a house (he was renting up to that point) and to pay down both mortgages as fast as he could. Now, a few years later, Bill owns a beautiful $750,000 home and an office building worth over $3 million with almost no debt against either of them (and soon to be zero). So even if his tech company somehow goes away (which I doubt—he owns very profitable enterprises), Bill can always sell his real estate for $3.75 million[3] and therefore not have to eat cat food when he turns 65.

In many enterprises and especially technology and consulting companies, your key assets tend to walk out the door every night on their way home. In a fast changing global economy, your technology or key competitive advantage can become obsolete almost (and sometimes) overnight. Real estate doesn't usually go out of fashion as quickly. If you look at some of the longest lasting fortunes on the planet, they tend to be (at their core) real estate based—like, say, the House of Windsor, Emperor of Japan, Hudson's Bay Company, the old Canadian Pacific Railroad Company and the Holy Roman Catholic Church.

I remember a time in the 1980s when my dad got involved with a group who wanted to build roller disco emporiums and, boy, did they ever. I'll never forget one of the principals behind these developments telling me that Roller Disco (places where kids could boogie to disco music while on roller skates; they went round and round in a counter clockwise direction with lights flashing all over the place) was a "cash cow." Hey, when the kids got bored, they stopped the music, and then they went clockwise for awhile. I wanted to bale out of the operating company faster than if I was a paying passenger on the Titanic. We managed to exchange our interest in the operating business for the underlying real estate—and the Roller Disco operating entity went broke less than two years later—but we turned the real estate into cool office space for new high tech companies specializing in things like CAD systems, which were new at the time. Real estate has legs; roller disco was just a fad.

Canadian Pacific (CP) got huge real estate concessions in prime urban locations in return for the near-impossible job of laying railroad track over the Rockies to what was then a nothing town called Vancouver. Decades later the stock price for CP moved up when the company started selling off its real estate portfolio.

---

[3] Or better yet, refinance them with a low ltv (loan to value ratio) of say 50%, pulling out $1.875 million tax free. And guess what? He still owns them.

More about Forced Savings

If you own rental property or if part of your home of office is rented out, your tenants are helping you with your "forced savings" since they are paying off part of the principal on your mortgage every month for you. This in a way compounds the wealth effect. When someone else is paying off all or part of the principal on your mortgage, this benefit accrues to you. Now it's true that you can't use it for what my wife calls IGA[4] money (money you can touch, feel and spend on stuff) every month but when you sell the property (provided you sell it for what you paid for it or more) or refinance it, you will get the cash in your jeans from the pay down of your mortgage… Of course, if you follow the Warren Buffet school of real estate investing, you don't sell it; you re-mortgage your property and get the cash, tax-free that way.

Cash on Cash Return

Hopefully, your real estate portfolio is providing you with a cash-on-cash return too so that every month you are receiving some spending money.

I try to never to let my clients buy property that doesn't cashflow. The idea of buying property that loses money every month in the hope that real estate inflation will somehow bail you out is a losing proposition that Mr Buffet would also frown on I am sure.

And never buy something for tax loss purposes. Be proud to pay your taxes—it means you are making a profit—now that's a good thing.

Security of Tenure

You will have security of tenure—what you don't want is to have your landlord raise your rent every few years, especially if he or she knows you are doing well financially.

There seems to be a rule in life—costs always rise to whatever your income is. This is as true for a company as it is for an individual; landlords just have a sixth sense about these things and can keep on increasing your rent until you simply have to move.

Brand Equity from Great Locations

Brand equity—you do develop a kind of brand equity in your location over time and if you own the real estate, at least you are developing brand equity in your own property not someone else's. Brand equity is important because it helps you build up your credibility; credibility and trust are hugely important in sales—people like to buy from people they like and trust. The two things go together. Did you ever buy from someone you didn't like and didn't trust—not too often I'll bet…

That's why mega corporations spend so much money building their brand; it's so that when one of their salespeople is in the trenches competing for a sale, and trying to close a deal, they often get the nod over the competition because they are a known (read: trusted) commodity. Imagine if you were hearing an insurance pitch from somebody who worked for the "Pirate Insurance Company of Kinakuta" versus somebody who worked for Clarica[5] or Manulife. Which one would you be more likely to put your trust in and trust your family's future to?

Clarica's ads were funny and almost didn't mention that the company sold insurance—a typical ad had a man in a high end club needing to use the facilities. However, he was stymied by the fact that the signs identifying which bathroom was for men and which for women were so ambiguous, he had to cross his legs and wait 'til someone exited to know where he was supposed to go. Unfortunately, when someone finally does, s/he is so androgynous, that the guy is no further ahead at which point, a narrator

---

[4] Independent Grocers Association. Substitute your own favorite grocery store instead and say, "Whole Foods money" or whatever.
[5] An insurance company formed from two predecessors, and now absorbed by yet another insurance giant…

enters the scene from stage right and says something like, "Clarity is important." Then there is a subtext—Clarica for all your insurance needs.

These ads don't sell insurance, they build a brand, which builds trust (through humor in Clarica's case), which creates an opportunity for a sale in a separate sales process. Any time you meet someone whose biz card says, "VP, marketing and sales," you've just met someone who doesn't know what their job really is.

Companies spend money on marketing their brand not just so you can watch the Super Bowl on free TV—they spend money on ads so they can increase sales but not in the way most people think. By spending $$$ on TV ads to establish a new brand (like Clarica did in 2002 and 2003), they don't actually expect 100,000 people to suddenly dial their call center and order life insurance. They know better than that.

They understand that all the marketing in the world doesn't sell much, if anything—they need a separate process to *harvest* the goodwill that they have generated via their marketing blitz. All that their marketing does is increase the propensity-to-buy. The separate sales process involves a huge team of focused, Clarica salespeople—the sales team is like "facts on the ground" in military/political speak. They are in the trenches with consumers selling one customer at a time. Each in-the-trenches sales team member has a greater likelihood of making the sale because of the mass marketing that Clarica has done but that is all that marketing dollars can do—increase the probability of a sale and only if there is actual selling activity going on.

Buy Smart, Buy Great Locations, No Deferred Maintenance, Improve Curb Appeal, Add Differentiated Value/Animation, Manage Well, Build Brand Value Over and Above What Anyone Else is Doing, Drive up Value, Refinance tax free, rinse and repeat, pass on to your heirs...

Again, going back to our imaginary couple in the living room, if you tell them you work for the Pirate Insurance Company of Kinakuta[6], they are not likely to trust their future and their kids' futures to your firm. But if you say you work for Clarica, they'll say, "I saw your ads on TV! They were great," then focus on how you can help them prepare for the unexpected...

Credibility

Owning your own location instantly builds credibility with suppliers, bankers, lenders, employees and others whom you depend on too. What's the no 1 source for startup capital in the world? Home equity.

---

[6] This is the Sultanate of Kinakuta, a fictional island somewhere in the South Pacific, which featured as a data haven in Neal Stephenson's excellent 1999 novel, *Cyrptonomicon*.

Making Alterations

If you want to make any changes to the premises, you can without investing your money in someone else's building or having to ask permission.

Unearned Rent

Once you have paid off your mortgage, you can either continue to have the operating company pay rent and enjoy another income stream (in a commercial setting) or you can benefit from tax-free, unearned rent (on your principal residence). The latter is another type of wealth effect (which is also why you want to pay off your home mortgage as fast as you can pretty much everywhere in the world today except perhaps the US where mortgage interest on your personal home is tax deductible, which changes the calculations).

This wealth effect is quite real. Suppose you own your own building and the mortgage is fully paid off. Now you decide to reduce your rent to zero. Your operating company's net income goes up by an amount equal to the rent they paid in the last year of the mortgage, an amount equal to Y dollars. Now in Canada, related inter-company dividends are tax free so you could dividend out the equivalent amount to your real estate holding company. Whereas before you had income in the holding company (of course you had some offsetting expenses too), you now have inter-company, tax free dividends.

For your personal home, it works differently. Let's say you have a home worth $400,000 and you have finished paying off the mortgage. And let's say you could rent it out for $3,000 a month. If your marginal tax bracket is 50% say then you are left with $18k after tax less whatever costs you might have against this (for property taxes, insurance etc). But if you stay in the home yourself that means that you are enjoying the benefit of living there; that is, you are benefiting from an "unearned rent" (a British term) of $36k a year—which isn't taxed. Unearned rent is also sometimes referred to as "imputed rent."

Another way of looking at it is if you moved out of the home, rented it for $3k a month and rented another *exactly* equivalent house for yourself (you have to live somewhere after all) at $3k a month, you are gaining $18k in after tax income but paying $36k in after tax rent yourself so you end up actually *losing* $18k on the whole deal. It's weird but true—people who have paid off their principal residence mortgages may not understand the exact mechanics of this wealth effect but they sure feel it. They tell me things like: "I seem to have more money than I ever did when I was working. I just seem to have more cash around these days…"

Unearned rent is a concept derived from a British sensibility that owners of real property are somehow undeserving of a return on capital. No doubt this is a class-based concern. There have been attempts to tax homeowners who have no mortgages on their residences on their unearned rents—one attempt in Switzerland and one in Australia that I know of. Both were roundly hated by the populace, and were rescinded shortly after introduction in Switzerland and never actually implemented in Australia.

One also has to think that taxing unearned rents would work against thriftiness on the part of homeowners and against social order too. Evidence abounds that people who own their own homes tend to see themselves as having more of a stake in their societies—they tend to vote in civic elections, participate in volunteerism and form the bedrock of a civil society.

In addition, home equity and real estate equity more generally are the bedrock source of friendly capital for startups.

The work of Hernando De Soto in less developed countries, LDCs, has shown that until they: a) recognize private property rights in what used to be called "slums," now termed "informal settlements," b) give municipal addresses and clear legal title in real property to sitting owners, and c) develop a competitive market for financing of real property (a system of mortgage financing), they cannot unlock real estate capital for redeployment to productive, entrepreneurial uses.

Cheaper to Own

It is often cheaper to own than to rent especially in low interest rate countries like what Canada and the US are experiencing today.

No Partners

You should want to own your own real estate without partners if you can manage it. There are still: "Two chairs in heaven waiting for the first two partners to get there and still like each other."

But if you do take on a partner to acquire real estate, make sure that you both have the same financial incentives and goals.

In general, I prefer investors to partners—investors usually have little or no input in decision-making and are simply looking for a return. They don't get married to a project, have no emotional stake in it, and are often prepared to exit once the entrepreneur dangles enough cash in front of them.

In a bankruptcy of one of my dad's real estate partners, five properties jointly owned by Jack Firestone and his partner, Les (not his real name) were caught up in a significant court proceeding along with 75 other projects. A major, publicly traded real estate business wanted to buy all 80 properties out of bankruptcy including the halves of the 5 projects that Jack owned with Les.

Two things saved my dad—he had had the good sense to enter into first right of refusal agreements on all five properties with Les and he had me to negotiate with the major realty company, we'll call DevCo.

DevCo was buying Les' half of each of the 5 properties in question for $400,000. Our internal valuation carried these projects at $2.2m and that was just for our halves. Andy Jenkins (not his real name), VP for DevCo, told me that we had two choices—sell our half interests for $400,000 or stay in and become partners with DevCo. "Why not be partners with DevCo?" he asked. "We are a national company with a national network of leasing and operating executives." Why not, indeed.

Our concern was that DevCo had a lot of other vacant buildings near these properties—geez, they could actually make money by taking tenants out of our buildings (where they would own 50% and we would own 50%) and putting them in buildings where they owned 100%. After a couple of years, we might have been lucky to get an offer from DevCo for our half interests where we did not have to pay *them* for accumulated losses just to take our share of those buildings off our hands.

I don't like 50/50 partnerships anyway. No one is in charge; no one has final say; it's a recipe for stalemate and disaster. If you are going to have partners, at least have someone own 51% and you all know then where the buck stops.

So we exercised our rights of first refusal and offered to buy Les' halves for $400,000 (it's like a right to match). Jenkins and his boss went nuts. They told me they would "see us in court" where they would argue a "greater good" theory—ie, that the bankruptcy judge should override our rights because the greater good (ie, DevCo's greater good) demanded that all 80 properties be dealt with in one fell swoop.

A couple of days before the hearing, Jenkins asked me what we really wanted for our half interests. I told him $2.2m and he blanched. I argued that he was still getting a good deal—he had Les' half for $400k and ours for $2.2m for a total of $2.6m on buildings we valued at $4.4m so he was getting them for about 50% of their value anyway. He said again: "See ya in court."

Ten minutes before the hearing began; Jenkins asked again what we really wanted. I said "$2.2m." We dickered for a few minutes and settled at the courthouse door for... $2.1m[7].

This was one of the things that really got Terrace Investments Limited going—eight years later (in 1990) we acquired the Ottawa Senators franchise from the NHL for $50 million; some of DevCo's money was in that deal.

---

[7] I deal with this story in more detail in an Addendum, *How a Behemoth Real Estate Developer Can Clobber You.*

More Financial Flexibility

Owning your own real estate gives you more financial flexibility—borrowing based on real estate collateral is usually much easier than say using your IP to secure a loan. The financial markets are much more developed and flexible for real property (at least in NA) than for intellectual property. Home equity loans are generally readily available to homeowners if they have a good credit rating (and sometimes even if they don't). Home equity loans are still the largest single source of capital to start your own business. They are also used by homeowners if they get into financial trouble or lose their jobs.

By the way, appraisers are the gatekeepers to the mortgage system. Lenders both major institutional lenders (like chartered banks) and secondary lenders as well as most private lenders, base much of their loan decisions on two things—their LTV (Loan to Value ratio) and the appraised value, AV, of property.

The loan amount (LA) is determined using the following simple formula:

$$LA = LTV \times AV$$

So if the appraised value is equal to the purchase price, PP, of a property you just bought, the loan amount will be:

$$LA = LTV \times PP$$

However, appraisers tend to be conservative people, and, even though they are often being paid by you, they owe their first loyalty to lenders from whom they get much more work than they do from you....

To make matters worse for you, you have to select/use an appraiser from a lender-approved list.

So naturally they tend to look at things from a lender's point of view.

I find appraisals are often anywhere from 5% to 10% below FMV, fair market value. They do this to protect lenders—it disadvantages borrowers in the sense that they end up with lower overall mortgage loan amounts.

LTV ratios vary.

Most residential lenders will lend 75% to 80% of the AV. You can get mortgage loan insurance (in Canada from CMHC (Canada Mortgage and Housing Corp) or private firms), which reduces the amount of equity you require to as little as 5% (ie, increases LTV ratios to as high as 95%).

Commercial lenders are more conservative and their LTV ratios are typically 65% for office, commercial and industrial buildings and as low as 50% for land (if they will even do it at all).

Commercial lenders also may only loan against the quick sale value, QSV, of a project, which is often much less than the AV. The QSV is what they can get for your project in a power of sale or foreclosure.

Therefore, we find:

$$LA = QSV \times LTV, \text{ in some commercial projects}$$

Many of these projects may only get off the ground either with very large amounts of equity or secondary financings.

Secondary financings include second mortgages, mezzanine financings, cashflow financing and lines of credit as well as investor funding. Every form of secondary financing is really a form of equity; only the first mortgage is true debt. Secondary and tertiary financings (including structured equity) almost always have the right of redemption—which means that if the first mortgage goes into default, they have the right to cure the default and take possession of the property via foreclosure. Then they own it and can do whatever they want with it, including keep it/add it to their portfolio, or sell it. If they do well (ie, make more from its sale than you originally owed), they get to keep the extra dough in a foreclosure. In a power of sale, you would be entitled to any overage so foreclosure is often the best move for a lender or investor group than POS.

What you are typically hoping for in these circumstances is to build your project, get it off the ground, prove your revenue streams, drive its AV up so you can refinance the project and take out (often expensive) secondary financings or investors within a reasonable period of time.

Better Citizenship

Nations made up of homeowners and business owners who own their own real estate are usually more robust societies since ownership of real estate can convey a sense of permanence, social responsibility, and civic pride.

Stability

Buildings don't tend to run out on you—if you operate a consulting business, your assets go home each night. Your IP goes with them and they can always find alternate employment. If you own a tech business, your market position can melt away virtually overnight.

...

If I were King (or Queen) of Exxon, I would....

I wrote this part of *Why and Why Not to Invest in Real Estate* more than a decade ago when peak oil was a big topic on the world stage, but I thought it was worth including here to further emphasize why real estate is probably the only sustainable business model ever discovered...

I've edited it and added new material as well.

The title of this section today could easily have been "If I were King (or Queen) of *Apple*, I would..." or we could insert the word "Samsung," "Google," "Alphabet," or "Facebook" and it'd work just as well[8].

Back in 2005/06, no one thought these tech behemoths could rack up profits like an oil company—nearly $10 billion in a single quarter.

However, Samsung Electronics is set to report 13.29 trillion Korean won ($11.5 billion USD) in second quarter [2017] operating profit, while Apple, in the same period, will probably report $10.49 billion[9].

Google's parent, Alphabet, reported a not too shabby net income of $5.43 billion in the first quarter of 2017[10]. Facebook's net profit was $3.9 billion in the second quarter of 2017[11], and Facebook did it with many fewer employees than Google. In fact, right now, Facebook makes about four times more profit per employee[12]. Wowza.

It also wasn't too long ago that tech companies weren't much interested in owning real estate, choosing instead to focus on their core competencies. But large tech firms and smaller ones as well plus many, many tech execs have come to realize that for reasons such as diversification of risk as well as compelling financial considerations require them to reevaluate their position.

It's hard to ignore the $5 billion USD that Apple just spent on their new headquarters building in Cupertino (nicknamed "the Spaceship," the "Ring" or the "Death Star" but more properly referred to as "Apple Park")[13].

So if you were king or queen of [INSERT NAME HERE], here's what you just might consider doing in real estate...

INTRODUCTION

If you were King (or Queen) of Exxon, what would you do with the unprecedented gusher of profits accruing to that company over the last decade?

Here are a couple of excerpts written about Exxon from 2005 and 2006:

Exxon profits hit fresh US record
Exxon Mobil is the world's largest listed oil company. US oil giant Exxon Mobil posted a quarterly profit of $9.9bn (£5.55bn), the largest in US corporate history, on the back of record oil and gas prices. Profit was up 75% and revenue rose 32% to more than $100bn.

---

[8] But not "Amazon" because Jeff Bezos believes in growth and market share more than he does in profitability, at least, so far...
[9] Source: https://www.cnbc.com/2017/07/06/samsung-q2-earnings-preview-profit-apple.html.
[10] Source: http://www.reuters.com/article/us-alphabet-results-idUSKBN17T2ZZ.
[11] Source: http://www.myrepublica.com/news/25337/.
[12] Source: http://www.investopedia.com/news/facebook-makes-4-times-more-profit-employee-google/.
[13] Some folks have taken to referring to it as the "Spacesh*t." Staffers don't like its open floor plan (https://www.bizjournals.com/sanjose/news/2017/08/08/apple-park-employees-floor-plan-hq-spaceship-aapl.html) and Wired Magazine wrote this review, "You can't understand a building without looking at what's around it—its site, as the architects say. From that angle, Apple's new HQ is a retrograde, literally inward-looking building with contempt for the city where it lives and cities in general. People rightly credit Apple for defining the look and feel of the future; its computers and phones seem like science fiction. But by building a mega-headquarters straight out of the middle of the last century, Apple has exacerbated the already serious problems endemic to 21st-century suburbs like Cupertino—transportation, housing, and economics. Apple Park is an anachronism wrapped in glass, tucked into a neighborhood." Source: https://www.wired.com/story/apple-campus/.

Thursday 27 October 2005
(http://news.bbc.co.uk/1/hi/business/4383296.stm)

Exxon Mobil Posts $10.36 Billion Profit: Company Faces New Round of Criticism

Exxon Mobil Corp. said yesterday that its second-quarter earnings jumped 36 percent, to $10.36 billion, boosted by climbing oil prices and larger profits at its refineries.

The quarterly profit — the second largest in US history — brought forth a fresh round of criticism from consumer and environmental groups. Critics accused the Irving, Tex.-based company of getting rich at the expense of motorists — squeezed by $3-a-gallon gas prices — while distributing billions to shareholders through dividends and by buying back shares. The largest quarterly profit by an American company, $10.71 billion, was also posted by Exxon, in the fourth quarter of 2005.

Friday, July 28, 2006
(http://www.washingtonpost.com/wp-dyn/content/article/2006/07/27/AR2006072700383.html)

So what would you have done with all this munificence? You might have decided to:

a. re-invest it in more oil exploration;
b. buy other oil companies;
c. increase dividends for shareholders;
d. buy stock back from existing shareholders;
e. raise wages and salaries for employees;
f. reduce prices for consumers;
g. hire more Washington lobbyists to ward off a windfall profits tax;
h. shop for the next presidential candidate who would continue existing policies that have resulted in unprecedented gains for this company;
i. buy real estate.

I would guess that the CEO of Exxon was thinking about all of the above except for i. Now why would the King or Queen of Exxon consider buying real estate?

Well, the real question I was asking myself the other day is what would a person do if he or she wanted to create a lasting enterprise—one that would be around for several centuries or millennia?

This is a non-trivial problem. Think how few corporations make the age of 50 years let alone 100, 200 or more. Actually, think of how many make the age of five[14]!

But before tuning our minds to the idea of making Exxon a long, longterm play, let's just put in perspective what $10 billion in PROFITS mean each quarter. There are 52 weeks per year or 13 weeks per quarter on average. That means that Exxon made about $770,000,000 in profit each week. If you won $10 million in a mega bucks lottery, it would be like someone coming to your door 77 times a week with a cheque. That is, someone would ring your doorbell every two hours and 18 minutes, 24/7 holding a $10 million cheque. You would plead with them to stop coming after they had disturbed your sleep for a week or two!

Even baseball players don't make that much.

So if you wanted to create a sustainable enterprise, say one that would last as long as the Holy Roman Catholic Church (a couple of millennia so far), what would you do?

For readers of the popular business press who are older than 35, you will have realized by now that firms that they were raving about a few quarters ago are now treated like neighborhood lepers. Remember the celebrity CEO? He is in jail.

---

[14] The US Bureau of Labour Statistics, in a report in the May 2005 Monthly Labor Review, (http://www.bls.gov/opub/mlr/2005/05/ressum.pdf) showed that, across all sectors from March 1998 to March 2002, 66 percent of all establishments were still in existence after two years and 44 percent after four years, which of course means 56% didn't make it to their 4th birthday…

Companies have a birth, life and a death. They are subject to cycles. Great names like DEC, Arthur Anderson, Systemhouse, TWA, Pan Am, Enron, Sperry and Burroughs can disappear (to be replaced with yucky names like *Unisys*).

What do the House of Windsor, Emperor of Japan, Hudson's Bay Company, Canadian Pacific and the Holy Roman Catholic Church have in common other than they are all extraordinarily long-lived institutions? They all have significant ownership interests in real estate.

A DOZEN RULES FOR REAL ESTATE INVESTING

I think there is something fundamentally different about real estate from every other type of investment that humans might make. Here are a few things for the CEO of Exxon to consider if he or she wanted to make Exxon a long-lived real estate vehicle:

1. Ownership of real estate would become the chosen investment vehicle for their windfall profits (ie, their spare cash).
2. There would be little trading in real estate—it would be a longterm hold thereby minimizing capital gains taxes.
3. Properties would be rented or leased including the leasing (but not sale) of land (the Catholic Church has entered into longterm land leases for generations[15]).
4. Investment would be in jurisdictions where there is respect for rule of law, contracts, property, and human rights[16]. There can be no value created where war and violence are prevalent; where natural disasters are common (parts of Florida and hurricanes, Santa Cruz, California and earthquakes or Darwin, Australia and cyclones); where pestilence or disease decimates the population[17] (eg, Europe in the time of the Black Death or cities in Africa in the time of AIDS or Ebola); your property can be taken arbitrarily without due process or compensation.
5. Significant investment would be in the residential sector—it is less volatile than commercial real estate—people will always need a home.
6. Investment would favor high growth, desirable cities over low growth, less attractive ones. No one knows what will happen in major western industrialized nations including Japan where birth rates are far below replacement rates and immigration is low but surely, it won't be good for real estate values.
7. Careful consideration would be given to income tax and realty tax considerations. Once the Queen of England gave up her right to be income tax exempt in a colossal error in judgment, she unknowingly destroyed her family's future guarantee of lasting wealth.
8. There would be no leveraging of assets (after paydown of all debt; ie, no endless refinancings), no negative pledging or any other form of debt registered against the properties.
9. Properties would be self insured against loss. Insurance is a way for large companies to appropriate part of the value of your property each year without compensating you. If you are the US government, for example, you self-insure. Large property owners might do the same.
10. Property management is a core competency and would never be contracted out.
11. Investment would be in a maximum of maybe a dozen cities in a small number of countries—enough to give geographic and political diversity but not so many as to be unmanageable.

---

[15] One example in Ottawa, Canada might illuminate this a bit. A local church (St John's Anglican) in Kanata could have sold their 4 acres of land on March road for $135,000. Instead, they entered into a 65-year land lease with a housing co-op (later called Blue Heron Housing Cooperative) for around $45 per unit per month with an inflation hedge built in. The land lease is worth more than $6 million and, at the end of the lease term; the church still owns the land. They can do it again! For the co-op, they didn't have to budget for any land acquisition costs—future renters pick up the cost of their land lease.)
[16] Former prime minister Pierre Trudeau tried to get property rights entrenched in the Canadian constitution along with his Charter of Rights and Freedoms for individuals but failed. The provinces objected because of their fears that this would prevent them from managing and owing subterranean mineral rights as well as passing and approving municipal regulations such as zoning ordinances…
[17] Cities do disappear. Where is Troy now (destroyed by ancient Greeks). Where is Babylon…

12. Management would be highly centralized, conservative, and experienced in real estate. The portfolio would consist of existing income property, property to be developed (both greenfield and brownfield sites) and land with the bulk of the assets held in the income category.

These are a dozen "rules" that could apply to any large investor in the real estate sector. For smaller investors, they would inevitably amend the set of rules. For example, real estate is an intensely local business so it would make no sense for them to be in more than one or at most two or three markets.

In addition, small players (who want to get bigger) must by necessity use leverage to increase their ROE. They are almost certainly better off with four properties with 25% equity in each than one property with 100% equity. This assumes that they are not upside down on equity (ie, that their cost of borrowing is less than their ROE) and so leverage represents a positive gearing for their investments.

In addition, if they have four properties rented out and one becomes vacant, their vacancy rate is 25%. If they only have one and it becomes vacant, their vacancy rate is 100%. But we digress.

Therefore, if you were going to create a new state called Exxon Nation, you could do worse than follow the 12 rules above. But why is it that real estate appears to give enterprises such long life[18]?

WHY REAL ESTATE IS DIFFERENT

People, markets, weather, and sunspots are all subject to cycles. Real estate is subject to cycles too. But one thing about real estate—it generally doesn't go out of fashion. Since villages, towns and cities began to form about 10,000 years ago, real estate has generally tended to increase in value if we exclude factors such as war, famine, disease, pestilence, depopulation, and natural disasters.

Almost certainly, nations in Europe and Japan are going to face significant decreases in their populations. Russia's population is already imploding due to emigration and death from alcoholism, drugs, poverty, and crime. East Germany would have ended as a nation-state even without Glasnost—its population was dropping like a stone. Japan has very little immigration and Japanese women are having about the same number of babies as other women in developed nations—about half the replacement rate.

No one knows what will happen to real estate values in countries suffering from depopulation but overall, it can't be a good thing for real estate owners. Thus far, depopulation impacts have been reduced by other factors including:

a) a long trend toward lower dwelling occupancy rates which means that average household size has decreased and this has caused an increase in demand for residential accommodation even where populations are decreasing;

b) the amount of space per person in both residential and commercial settings has tended to increase, thereby offsetting some of the drop in demand;

c) migration from rural areas to urban areas has also caused prices to be more robust in cities than they otherwise would have been but there are many rural areas, villages, and towns where real estate is worth practically nothing.

It is strange that after the developed nations produced perhaps the greatest generation ever (one that faced two world wars, a great depression, a cold war and took the world from buggies to the moon), the next generation appears so self interested and so without core beliefs that having children is seen as more of a nuisance than anything else by many of them. Go figure.

...

---

[18] The oldest company in North America and one of the oldest anywhere is the Hudson's Bay Company, which was incorporated on May 2nd 1670. A Royal Charter from King Charles II granted the company a monopoly over the fur trade in the region where all rivers and streams flow into Hudson's Bay, an area of 3.9 million km² (ref: Wikipedia). The company has had significant real estate interests.

It served the purposes of the Catholic Church to own well-situated pieces of real estate in thousands of towns, villages, and cities. It makes sense for most people and companies to own their own real estate. I tell my students, as soon as you can, buy your own home and pay off your mortgage as quickly as possible. When you do that, you start to earn what the British term "unearned rent"—rents that you receive on your own home from yourself on which you are not taxed.

This sounds a bit far fetched but the effect is real enough. The way to understand it best is to imagine that you move out of your own home because someone has offered to rent it from you for $2,500 a month. But you still need a place to live so you go out and rent another home—guess what?

You end up paying $2,500 a month but this is not a zero sum game. You are paying your rent with *after* tax dollars and receiving rent that is *before* tax. So if you are in the 50% tax bracket and ignoring your cost of doing business for the moment, you end up with $1,250 a month from the rent you are collecting on your own house after tax and you are spending $2,500 per month on the home you are occupying so you are $1,250 per month *worse* off in this scenario...

This is a very tangible outcome—people who have paid off their mortgage will tell you that, somehow, they don't quite understand how or why, they seem to have way more spending money every month. It's true, they do[19].

As you have already learned, I also tell my tech clients to buy their own buildings. I realize that most tech companies are told to focus on their core businesses but surely, it doesn't hurt them to diversify their risks by owning their own premises. In many cases, it is also cheaper.

Remember the story of one of my Ottawa tech clients who needed 15,000 sf of triple A office space? When he found out that it cost $18 to $22 per sf per annum (circa 1999) to rent this type of space plus more than $12 per sf for operating costs (or more than $450,000 per year total), he wanted to look at alternatives.

We ended up selecting a 15,000 sf building in the south end of Ottawa, which he bought for $1.5 million. He ended up paying $85,000 per annum on his first mortgage and, a few years later, he sold it when they moved to a bigger space. He got $2.1 million for it and bought a 33,000 sf building for just over $3 million.

He paid off the mortgage on his newest acquisition within 5 years.

Below is a table that summarizes attributes of four different asset classes—

1. GOLD
2. FORTUNE 500 STOCK OWNERSHIP
3. OWNING YOUR OWN BUSINESS
4. HOLDING REAL ESTATE

	Gold	Fortune 500 Stock Ownership	Own Business	Real Estate
Interest	No*	No	Yes	Yes
Dividends	No	Yes	Yes	Yes
Capital Gain	Yes	Yes	Yes	Yes
Cost to Store	Yes	No	No	No
Rental income	No*	No	No	Yes
Concession/Franchise/Location	No	No	Yes	Yes
Volatility	Yes	Yes	Yes	Yes
Inflation Hedge	Yes**	No	No	No
Portability/Negotiability	High**	Moderate	Low	Low
Unearned Rent	No	No	No	Yes

---

[19] Note that this effect is diluted somewhat in the US because home mortgage interest is tax deductible there. However, principal residences in the US are subject to capital gains taxes when sold whereas in places like Canada, while you can't deduct your mortgage interest from your taxes at least your home is not subject to capital gains taxes when you sell it. If you are a homebuilder starting out, it makes sense to build, live in and sell a few homes early in your career—it's one of the few (legal) tax-free ways to make money in Canada.

Capital Gains Tax Exempt	No	No	Possibly	Possibly
Capital Cost Allowance	No	No	No	Yes
Transaction Costs	High	Low	High	Moderate
Financing Available	No	Yes	Yes	Yes
Wealth Effect	No	No	No	Yes
Externalities	No	No	No	Yes

(*Note some central banks will enter into gold leases to top up their mix of assets and pay a small rent.)

(**Also note that gold is a unique asset in that it generally increases when interest rates increase where interest rates are tracking inflation. Higher interest rates generally mean lower values for most stocks, most SMEs, and almost all real estate holdings, at least in the short run. Gold is also a holding against catastrophe; it is portable and easily negotiable in times of war.)

Notice that real estate has some unique attributes including:

a) you can rent real estate to third parties;

b) by renting to a third party you are benefiting from a "Wealth Effect"; every year a renter is paying off part of your mortgage for you—when you sell or refinance that property, that decrease in principal owing goes into your pocket (assuming that the price you sell for or refinance for is more than what you paid for the property plus transaction costs);

c) you receive unearned (and untaxed) rent on self-occupied property after your mortgage is retired;

d) when the city builds infrastructure around you, when your neighbors improve their properties, when the density and area of the city increases, demand for your property increases without you having done a thing—as a result your property value benefits from positive externalities;

e) in many countries, you are allowed to deduct a non-cash capital cost allowance against income—a significant tax advantage from holding real estate assets.

In addition, real estate offers you a unique opportunity to develop a sustainable business model even if you aren't a genius. Real estate develops a concession or franchise for its owners because once you own a particular location, by definition, no one else can own at that location. Everyone knows that real estate is all about LOCATION, LOCATION, LOCATION but perhaps people don't realize why that is so crucial. For you to have a business that will nurture you and your family for a long period of time, you need to have sustainable competitive advantage.

Imagine how difficult it is to run a company like Apple Computer or how difficult it is to paint like Rembrandt. Not everyone can be Steve Jobs or create artworks like Rembrandt Harmenszoon van Rijn. Real estate held in fee simple (the highest form of title ownership) gives you a franchise forever that tough competitors like Amazon can't take away from you—IT'S A BUSINESS MODEL FOR DUMMIES!

A friend of mine owns a great site at the corner of Woodroffe and Carling avenues in the city of Ottawa. He comes from a tech background but his chosen investment vehicle is real estate.

They built a new, high concept strip mall (not intended as an oxymoron) on top of the old foundation of a previous building and, because of its high traffic location, great visibility, extra storage space (in the old basement) and design features, they get rents that are about 1/3 higher than other nearby properties.

I mean how difficult can it be to own a great location and have people come up to you, one after the other, to offer you top dollar for your space?

So when you own a piece of real estate, by its very nature, you have now come to own a "concession" or a "franchise" that no one else can use without your permission, which usually involves some kind of transaction, meaning they end up paying you rent. Companies like Apple work hard to create walled-off environments in which network effects multiply and ripple throughout the economy.

You buy an iPhone then an iPad then start using iCloud, iTunes, and their app store. The more people who use their services, the more developers want to build apps for the Apple universe, which, in turn means more people buy their products so they can access these applications. It's a virtuous (from Apple's point of view) circle. It also makes leaving the Apple world much more difficult, not only because all those purchases may become obsolete, you'll also have to learn how to use a new set of tools and software.

Amazon, Facebook, and Google do pretty much the same thing, and Microsoft and IBM in their day engaged in this type of monopolistic behavior.

It works… garnering a huge percentage of national economic gains in the hands of a small number of companies, whose employees also benefit handsomely via perks such as—free lunches, dry-cleaning, massages, egg freezing and fertility treatments[20], volunteer time off, paid parental leave, sports club memberships, on-site acupuncture and improv classes[21], cooking classes, life coaching[22], and breast milk shipping[23]. [Source, https://www.inc.com/zoe-henry/glassdoor-top-companies-employee-benefits.html]

It may be good for these firms and their workers but monopoly power inevitably shortchanges the rest of the economy—starving it of capital and talent plus limiting wage hikes everywhere else.

Warren Buffett calls network effects that create these economic bonanzas "competitive moats." I'm sure he's out there right now looking for them on behalf of Berkshire Hathaway shareholders.

Having said all this, guess what? Look no further than a great intersection or neighborhood in your town, and then go buy a ton of real estate there[24]. City planners, NIMBYs and politicians, you can be sure, are digging a competitive moat around the area to keep competitors at bay so now you've secured a lifetime (or multiple lifetimes) of income without having to work as hard or be as smart as Thomas Watson Sr, Bill Gates, Larry Page and Sergey Brin, Mark Zuckerberg or Jeff Bezos.

LEVERAGE AND REAL ESTATE PURCHASING

The messaging to my students is: buy your own home, buy your own business premises, buy some investment real estate, and pay off your mortgages as quickly as possible.

This message is meant to convey the importance, in my view, of being debt-free and being (relatively) creditor proof. Having said this, most of us end up with significant mortgages and it usually takes a long time to pay these off. It turns out that more leverage can mean faster paydown of larger mortgages later. Huh?

Take the example of an investor who wants to buy one townhouse or condominium to rent out. Say it costs $200,000 and she has 25% down. So her 50 grand buys one townhouse that produces rent of $2,050 a month. After paying property taxes and other expenses, she is left with $1,450. If she has a 25 year mortgage at 6%, her NOI (Net Operating Income) is $5,665.99, which gives her a ROE (Return on her Equity of $50,000) of 11.3% per annum. See the table below.

Townhouse or Condo Purchase—One Unit Using 25% Down

Purchase Price $200,000
Down Payment 25% $50,000

---

[20] I'm not joking—Spotify offers this service.
[21] Twitter.
[22] Asana.
[23] Zillow.
[24] Former Ottawa Senators president Cyril Leeder was the first to point out to me that every time Terrace Investments Limited (the first parent company of the Sens) did a project, land value in the neighborhood tended to increase. So he suggested, "The next time we do a project, Bruce, let's buy more land and buildings than we need so we can benefit from our own hard work." It's a theory that we put to work when we built the Palladium (now Canadian Tire Centre). We bought 600 acres even though we only needed 100 acres for the new arena. Did it work? Judge for yourself. We bought 600 acres in the early 1990s for $12,000 per acre (on average). A recent sale (in 2015) saw Cabela's (a group of outfitting stores) buy approximately 10 acres for development of a new emporium at $832,000 an acre. That represents a 19.32% pa compound return over 24 years. #Fabulous. It also means the lands we owned went from $7.2 million in value to nearly a half billion dollars in a single generation, and, ironically, it also means that if Rod Bryden (the Sens second owner after me) had managed to keep the parent company going through the early and mid 2000s, it wouldn't have been bankrupt after all… #Rats.

Mortgage 75% $150,000
Interest Rate 6%
Amortization 25 years
Mortgage ($11,734.01) per annum
Rent $2,050 per month
Property Taxes and Other ($600) per month
Net Rent $1,450 per month
Net Rent $17,400 per annum
NOI $5,665.99
ROE 11.3% per annum
Real Estate Inflation 1.25% on building value => 5.00% per annum on equity
Wealth Effect $6,000 12.0% per annum
Total ROE 28.3% per annum

Now in addition to her cash on cash return of 11.3%, she is also benefiting from general real estate inflation. In the example shown here, I assumed an average 1.25% increase in real estate values per year; this implies a 5% ROE from general real estate inflation (1.25%/.25, where .25 is the equity she has in the deal).

For greater clarity, think of it this way. She owns a $200,000 building that is increasing in value (on a compounded basis) by 1.25% pa or $2,500 in the first year. However, her ROE (return on equity) is $2,500 on $50,000 (her investment) or 5% pa.

However, real estate gives you something else—a wealth effect. Her tenants are paying off her mortgage for her. That means, over a period of 25 years, they are paying an *average* of $6,000 down on her principal ($150,000 mortgage amount divided by the amortization period of 25 years). This adds another 12% ROE so her total ROE is actually more than 28%. Now that is a pretty good investment and we have ignored any tax advantages from things like sheltering income using CCA (capital cost allowance).

Now these calculations are approximate and practitioners are advised to use IRR (Internal Rate of Return) analysis for more precise measurement of actual returns on investment in real estate. Nevertheless, it gives a first order of approximation, which is all we require here to demonstrate the fundamentals of real estate investing.

Now imagine our investor deciding instead to buy three places with her $50,000 instead of one; she puts down $16,667 on each one. What happens to her ROE?

Townhouse or Condo Purchase—Three Units Using 8.333% Down

Purchase Price $200,000
Down Payment 8.3% $16,667
Mortgage 91.7% $183,333
Interest Rate 6%
Amortization 25 years
Mortgage ($14,341.57) per annum
Rent $2,050 per month
Property Taxes and Other ($600) per month
Net Rent $1,450 per month
Net Rent $17,400 per annum
NOI $3,058.43
ROE 18.4% per annum
Real Estate Inflation 1.25% 15.00% per annum
Wealth Effect $7,333 44.0% per annum
Total ROE 77.4% per annum

It goes up. She is now getting a 77.4% total ROE—all three types of returns have increased. Her cash on cash return has gone up because her equity investment went down faster than her NOI. Her mortgage has gone up which means her tenants are paying more of her principal down for her each year. And lastly, her property is going up at the same absolute rate each year but because she has less equity in each deal, she is getting relatively more benefit from real estate inflation. Also, if one of her units becomes vacant, she has an occupancy ratio of .667 rather than 0.000, which would be the case if she just invested in one unit.

But interestingly, the increase in leverage also means that she can pay off her mortgages faster if she so chooses. In the first case, she has $5,665.99 cash left over at the end of each year. In the second example, she has $3,058.43 left over from each unit or a total of $9,175.30. So if she chose to pay down her mortgage each year with her cash on cash return, she would pay them off a lot *faster* in the case where she bought three units instead of just one using more leverage.

HOW TO BUY REAL ESTATE WITH LITTLE MONEY DOWN

A student called me recently to advise him on how to buy a commercial property for $600,000. He has no money but he does have two important things:

a) a tenant lined up;
b) his own credibility.

Actually, he has a language-training contract with the GOC (government of Canada) worth about $20k a month. For his $600,000, he gets an existing building and a ton of beautiful property in a scenic setting less than 20 minutes from the Parliamentary Precinct.

So here is what I told him not to do:

a) spend zero time raising money from VCs—most of them aren't interested in real estate;
b) spend zero time looking for angel investors— most of them aren't interested in real estate;
c) don't take on a partner.

And here is what I told him to do:

a) get a commercial appraisal that hopefully shows the property is worth at least $600,000;
b) arrange a first mortgage for 65 to 75% of the appraised value with an interest rate of around 7%;
c) arrange a second mortgage to bring you up to 85% of the appraised value of the property—this will cost him in the order of 10 to 12%;
d) get a line of credit (LOC) based on your own credit rating and the property for the balance plus some transaction costs and some working capital.

Now this is expensive and risky. No one wants to pay 12% interest on a second mortgage but I told him—debt is way cheaper than equity. If he could get someone to co-invest with him, trust me, they will want returns on their equity of at least 20% and probably 30%. And I don't like partners in most instances anyway.

It's risky because, if he doesn't make it work, he is on the hook for any shortfall in the equity financings part of the equation and maybe even for the first mortgage too. (Any secondary financing is considered a form of equity financing because they are paid out of the equity in the deal after the first mortgage is paid off.)

So I told him not to do it unless he was very confident that the GOC contract would get him past the first two years. The downside though isn't really too bad.

Most likely, I told him, if he fails, he would end up selling the property for at least what he paid for it and maybe he is only on the hook personally for the LOC.

Then I told him, he would have to get a JOB and pay it off.

Entrepreneurs who are successful don't let a little thing like failure get in their way. However, it is way better to make your first few deals successful.

After two years, he should be able to go get another appraisal and between the increase in value of the real estate and the now successful language-training centre, he should be able to refinance the deal to: 1. take out his secondary financing and 2. renegotiate the LOC, maybe without his personal guarantee.

The way I look at finance is different from most people. I believe if you need to use expensive financing to get into the game, that's an acceptable risk as long as you have a plan to replace it within a short period of time (1 to 3 years).

Let's say you are a first time homebuyer and you don't want to wait until you have saved enough for a downpayment because, for example, you are worried that inflation in your real estate market will move prices upwards faster than you can save so, in fact, you'll never actually be able to afford to own your own home, a real issue for many millennials today.

It's as if the market is a helicopter that is moving upwards and away from you. But wait—there's good news. The crew is lowering a rope ladder so you can grab/mount the first rung but you have to do it right now or even though there's a ladder, it'll be out of reach soon.

More good news—your family is willing to give you a loan but they want some interest on it, a lot it turns out, 15% pa to be exact.

So here's what your transaction might look like:

First Time Homebuyer Finance

Pp (purchase price)	$350,000			
Ltt (land transfer tax)	$3,725	https://www.ratehub.ca/land-transfer-tax		
legals	$1,200			
total	$354,925			
first mortgage	$315,000	90%	3.25% interest	25 yrs amortization
equity	$39,925			
family loan	$30,000		15% interest	15 yrs amortization
equity	$9,925			
first mortgage	($18,597.39)	pmt		
family loan	($5,130.51)	pmt		
	($23,727.90)	pa		
	($1,977.32)	per mth		
inflation	3.50%	pa		

		ppmt	first mortgage	
		1	($8,359.89)	
		2	($8,631.58)	
		3	($8,912.11)	
total			($25,903.58)	

		ppmt	family loan	
		1	(630.51)	
		2	(725.09)	
		3	(833.85)	
total			(2,189.45)	

total debt	$345,000	
total principal paydown during period	($28,093)	

total principal owing at end of period		$316,907		
value of home at end of period	$	393,511.69		
refi	$	354,160.52	90%	new first mortgage
less total principal owing at end of period		($316,907)		
cash out at end of period due to refi	$	37,253.56		
less total principal owing at end of period		($27,810.55)		on second mortgage
cash out at end of period due to refi	$	9,443.01		
pmt		($5,130.51)	pa	family loan
pmt		($15,391.53)		total over period
ppmt		(2,189.45)		total over period
interest		($13,202.08)		total over period
QED				

You buy a $350,000 home with 10% down. You also have to pay some closing costs (in Ontario that would be land transfer tax and legal costs/title insurance and so forth). This means you have to come up with about $40,000. However, you've only saved 10 grand.

But rich uncle Buck is willing to lend you $30,000 for three years at 15% pa. He tells you, "Don't worry about amortization, I'll make it interest only."

Quick question: how long does it take to pay off an interest only mortgage?"

That's right. Forever.

Uncle Buck didn't get rich because he's stupid. Interest only is good for him, not so much for you. Sure, he'll tell you it'll lower your monthly payments, but you've read one of Prof Bruce's real estate mini books so you know that you *want* to include amortization on all your loans if at all possible so you will one day be debt-free.

As a result, you tell Buck that you want an aggressive amortization (ie, a short amortization period) on your family loan/2nd mortgage of just 15 years.

Now principal and interest on both your mortgages is a big number—$1,977.32 a month. You wonder if you can afford it. But intrepid you decides to have two roommates live with you in your new 3-bedroom house, and they each pay you $650 monthly so your out-of-pocket cost is actually reduced to $677.32, which, phew, you can afford.

Life is good.

However, wait a second; you get a call from the mortgage underwriter a few days before closing to ask if you plan to rent any part of your home. Being an honest person, you answer, "Yes, I'm going to have a couple of my college pals live with me."

Guess what happens next?

They yank your mortgage, and you can't close.

This actually happened to a client of mine—a young engineer (I'll call him Peter) buying his first home. He called me up in tears.

"What am I going to do?" he asked.

"We'll fix it," I answered.

How did we do that?

Well, first of all, we asked and got a 10-day extension from the seller. He had to pay for that—$50 a day for every day he didn't close.

I mean what are they going to do? Sue him? Maybe, but most sellers will wait a few days if you run into an unfortunate situation like this.

Next, he had to take down his Kijiji/Craigslist ads searching for roommates. Hey, underwriters know how to use Google too, and they will look at your social media profiles as well. These days, they want to know more about whom they are lending to...

Then we found another lender for him.

Now I'll admit I didn't know that you are not allowed (by most lenders) to rent any part of your home; this is in the fine print of most mortgage terms, you know, the stuff that runs on for many pages in 8-point type that no one ever reads.

Got an extra bedroom you plan to put on Airbnb?

Going to have a roommate or three?

Thinking of adding a basement flat to your principal residence?

Not allowed.

It's atrocious but true.

Plus you are going to have to sign an affidavit swearing that you won't rent any part of your house.

My client was rightly uncomfortable signing something he knew was not accurate.

What finally convinced him to do so was that it was technically correct on the day he completed his transaction. A month later? Not so much.

This leads me to a point that I probably shouldn't make here but I will anyway.

I did an interview with a tech blog. They asked me, "What major trends do you see happening in real estate in the next ten years?"

I'm sure they expected me to talk about the Jetsons—you know, there'll be drones flying in special drone doors to stock your fridge with milk. Or everyone will have a Roomba that not only vacuums your place; it walks your dog and babysits your kids too.

Instead, I said, "The min trend I see over the next ten years in real estate is... CIVIL DISOBEDIENCE."

"Huh?" they said. "You'll have to explain that."

Hey, they're tech guys[25].

Yourdictionary.com defines it this way:

The definition of civil disobedience refers to the practice of breaking laws, usually in a non-violent way, as part of a protest because the laws are believed to be unfair or a violation of fundamental and inalienable human rights.

An example of civil disobedience is when American Rosa Parks refused to move to the back of the bus where African Americans were supposed to sit prior to the civil rights movement.

Henry David Thoreau put it more succinctly in his work entitled *Civil Disobedience*[26]:

"It is not desirable to cultivate a respect for the law, so much as for the right."

I personally believe that when ethics and the law part ways, ethics should prevail but don't tell that to most lawyers. They will not agree with you.

To my mind, when Peter rents to a couple of roommates, I believe it only strengthens his ability to service his debt.

---

[25] You can see the interview on YouTube at, https://youtu.be/w-qvpadXc4I. It's a rough outtake. So production values are... well there are no production values. We videoed it using Zoom.us, a great conferencing service that puts Skype to shame in my opinion. But I think you might find it interesting except it's 39 minutes 41 seconds l o n g.

[26] "Henry David Thoreau's *Civil Disobedience* was originally published in 1849 as *Resistance to Civil Government*. Thoreau wrote this classic essay to advocate public resistance to the laws and acts of government that he considered unjust. The practical application of Civil Disobedience was largely ignored until the twentieth century when, at different times, Mohandas Ghandi, Martin Luther King, Jr and anti-Vietnam War activists applied Thoreau's principles." Source: https://www.goodreads.com/book/show/18626866-civil-disobedience.

Lenders do *not* feel the same way. They say to themselves, "What happens if Peter can't find any roommates? Maybe he can't service his mortgage by himself. Maybe the very fact that he is looking for roommates in the first place is an indictor, *prima facie*, that he can't."

So his first offer of a mortgage got pulled despite the twin realities that he had a very good job (with the GOC, government of Canada) and his credit score was over 800 (which is, frankly, fantastic).

All this to say that while I can't counsel readers or clients to break any laws or tell any untruths, I certainly understand that it may be that folks, both young and old, will do and say what they need to do to take care of themselves and their families including lease to roommates, add basement apartments, build coach houses in their backyards, run businesses from their homes, and a zillion other things that mortgage lenders and zoners might not approve of. Too bad, so sad.

I mean who you gonna call? The government when you are too poor to visit a dentist with a toothache? Or are you going to rent out your extra room for 650 bucks a month—a nice recurring revenue stream?

Statistics Canada has some cool data (from their 2011 census) on household numbers and average sizes. See below.

There were approximately 7.33 million single detached houses in Canada in that year with an average dwelling occupancy rate of 2.8 persons. If each of those households decided to take in one roommate or one immigrant (Canada is a nation of immigrants taking in 300,000 people in 2017[27]), that is, rent out one room in their house, that's 7,329,150 rooms rented at $650 a month for a total of $4,763,947,500 *monthly* extra income. Multiply that by 12 and you get an income boost of $57.2 billion annually.

That buys your dentist a nice new addition to his/her cottage[28] and a lot more besides.

Put another way, Justin Trudeau (Canada's current prime minister for life) plans federal spending of $330.2 billion in 2017 and to run a deficit of $28.5 billion[29]. It'd be a tough sell to ask him to please send an extra 650 bucks to Prof Bruce and every other homeowner in Canada every month so they can afford to get a tooth pulled from time to time given that the average CPP (Canada Pension Plan) payout is just $550 a month[30]. If, however, JT could be persuaded to part with our money, this would increase Canada's annual deficit to an unprecedented $85.7 billion a year; so it wouldn't be long before the IMF (International Monetary Fund) would come knocking on the prime minister's door saying, "Sorry, I thought for a moment we were in Greece?"

Total households	13,320,610
Total persons in households	32,856,975 people
Average number of persons in household	2.5 persons
Single-detached house	7,329,150 units
Total persons in households	20,330,230 people
Average number of persons in household	2.8 persons
Apartment, five or more storeys	1,234,770 units
Total persons in households	2,229,695 people
Average number of persons in household	1.8 persons
Movable dwelling1	183,510 units
Total persons in households	394,630 people
Average number of persons in household	2.2 persons
Other dwelling2	4,573,185 units
Total persons in households	9,902,420 people

---

[27] Source: https://www.theguardian.com/world/2016/oct/31/canada-immigration-quota-2017.
[28] I used to ask our dentist for details about his cottage life, which question he always seemed happy to answer, seeing no irony whatsoever in the fact that the work he did on fixing our three daughters' teeth paid for a substantial part of his then lifestyle. Our two boys, I am sorry to say, never got/needed braces.
[29] Source: http://www.cbc.ca/news/politics/federal-budget-highlights-2017-1.4032898.
[30] "In March 2016, average monthly benefits for new retirement pension (taken at age 65) was just over $550.00 per month and the maximum amount was $1,092.50." Source: https://en.wikipedia.org/wiki/Canada_Pension_Plan.

Average number of persons in household   2.2 persons

1. Includes mobile homes and other movable dwellings such as houseboats and railroad cars.
2. The category 'Other dwelling' is a subtotal of the following categories: semi-detached house, row house, apartment or flat in a duplex, apartment in a building that has fewer than five storeys and other single-attached house.
Source: Statistics Canada, 2011 Census of Population, and Statistics Canada catalogue no 98-313-XCB.

The last word on this topic goes to Thoreau who said it better than I ever could:

"There will never be a really free and enlightened state until the state comes to recognize the individual as a higher and independent power, from which all its own power and authority are derived."

...

Now back to our example of expensive-looking family finance for our first time homebuyer. If you look closely at the above spreadsheet, you can see that over three years, the first timer spends a lot on interest paid to rich uncle Buck—a total of $13,202.08. Egad, that looks bad.
But wait.
The house is increasing in value (3.5% pa in this example). Who gets that raise? The bank? Uncle Buck?
No, our first time homebuyer.
How much is that?
$38,586.69
Frig, that's decent.
In addition, how much principal is paid down on the first and second mortgages?
$28,093
Man, it's hard to save $28,093 but, darn it, our first time homebuyer did it (with help from his or her two roommates).
Now if s/he refinances the place at the end of three years, it turns out that between inflation in the home's value over that period and principal paydown, they have enough to repay Uncle Buck ($27,810.55 still owing) and pull some cash out too ($9,443.01)... enough to pay for a nice winter vacay in the DR (Dominican Republic) say $3,500 (for two people for a week) and buy 6.6 grey iPad Pros (9.7" 128 GB with wi-fi) from Best Buy Canada ($903.99 including tax (HST) on sale until August 24th, 2017) or they could save it and buy a rental property next.

...

I just can't seem to explain to most Canuckleheads (who are much more conservative than the Americans I coach) that spending a *one-time* interest premium in the amount of $13,202.08 to unlock $66,679.69 in value makes sense. It makes financial sense to me. And it gets you on the first rung of the real estate ownership before the helicopter (the one with all the goodies aboard a civil society like Canada and the US have to offer) flies out of reach.
They've read in the popular press that you can get mortgage loans as low as 2% today.

SO WHY WOULD ANYONE EVER PAY 15%?
THAT'S CRAZY.
I'D BE A SUCKER TO PAY 15%.
EVERYONE WILL LAUGH AT ME.
MY MOM WILL TELL ME SHE RAISED AN IDIOT.
MY BANK MANAGER WILL TELL ME TO HAVE PATIENCE.

MY FINANCIAL ADVISER WILL INSIST I TAKE OUT INSURANCE THROUGH HIM AND INVEST IN HIS MUTUAL FUNDS.

ETC ETC ETC

BUT PROF BRUCE SAYS IT'S SOMETIMES OK, SO MAYBE I'D BETTER RE-EXAMINE MY ASSUMPTIONS

Right on, brothers and sisters.

...

So now out first timer is ready to move on to purchase her/his first rental.

What does that look like?

I've worked that out for you; see below.

You buy a place for $350,000 and add, say a basement apartment for $85,000.

You put in place an 80% ltv (loan to value) conventional first mortgage and you get (through your intrepid and entrepreneurial mortgage broker) a second mortgage for 15% of pp (purchase price), again at 15% pa.

Therefore, s/he needs a total of $44,925 to complete this transaction.

Nevertheless, here's the nub of it—where do you get the extra $85,000 you need to renovate the place? That's a lot of iPad Pros.

In this model, I kept it simple—I assumed s/he found it in their couch. But realistically, they probably financed it in any number of ways—via an RRSP (or 401(k)) self-directed mortgage, through a unsecured LOC (line of credit) at their bank, via a HELOC (home equity line of credit on their principal residence), through a first mortgage that provides cashback on closing and/or a 10% bump up for renovations, by borrowing again from uncle Buck or by getting an investor (via a technique I call Mad River financing dealt with elsewhere in this mini book, which, hmm, is getting longer by the minute as I "proof read" it and at the same time find myself adding more sections for you, dear reader, to labor[31] over) involved. These are just some of the clever ways real estate entrepreneurs work these things out. BTW, it's only astute if it works; that is, you don't go bankrupt.

But if s/he found a way, the good news is that, again after three years, they can refi the place and pay out all their expensive financing or get their dough back… so that they only have $52,318.52 of their equity in the building at this point not $159,925, which means they can (eventually) buy 2.06 more rental buildings to add to their growing flock of investment properties.

They're essentially recycling their money… very green.

First Time Rental Acquisition Finance

pp	$350,000				
ltt	$3,725	https://www.ratehub.ca/land-transfer-tax			
legals	$1,200				
total	$354,925				
renovation budget	$85,000	to add basement apartment			
total	$439,925				
first mortgage	$280,000	80%	3.25%	25	yrs
equity	$74,925				

---

[31] I use American spellings these days, not I must admit because of my readership in that great nation, but because they tend to be shorter ("labor" versus "labour") and I have serious issues with RSI (repeated stress injury) in my arms from way too much keyboarding. Apologies to my Canadian, British, Indian, New Zealand, and Aussie readers.

renovation budget		$85,000				
equity		$159,925	$439,925	check		
2nd mortgage		$30,000		15%	15	yrs
equity		$129,925				
first mortgage		($16,531.01)	pmt			
2nd mortgage		($5,130.51)	pmt			
		($21,661.52)	pa			
		($1,805.13)	per mth			
inflation		3.50%	pa			
ppmt		first mortgage				
	1	($7,431.01)				
	2	($7,672.52)				
	3	($7,921.88)				
total		($23,025.41)				
ppmt		2nd mortgage				
	1	(630.51)				
	2	(725.09)				
	3	(833.85)				
total		(2,189.45)				
total debt		$310,000				
total principal paydown during period		($25,215)				
total principal owing at end of period		$284,785				
value of home at end of period	$	487,752.71				
refi	$	390,202.17		80%	new first mortgage	
less total principal owing at end of period		($284,785)				
cash out at end of period due to refi	$	105,417.03				
less total principal owing at end of period		($27,810.55)			on second mortgage	
cash out at end of period due to refi	$	77,606.48				
equity		$52,318.52				
pmt		($5,130.51)	pa	2nd mortgage		
pmt		($15,391.53)		total over period		
ppmt		(2,189.45)		total over period		
interest		($13,202.08)		total over period		
QED						

E&OE

...

THERE'S ALSO NO BUSINESS LIKE THE OIL BUSINESS

Is there any business like the oil business? It's unique too. Where else could so many large firms apparently collude on prices and get away with it?

Petrol station owners get up to ten *phone calls* a day—no email record or fax record—telling them what price to charge. It just coincidentally matches to the tenth of a cent what every other station at every other oil company is charging in the area. Sheesh.

If you had left for Mars on the day Bill Clinton left the Oval Office and returned six years later to find that prices at the pump had gone from 45 cents per liter to $1.05 per liter, you could probably conclude with a high degree of confidence that the oil business had a friend in the White House whose last name rhymes with "Tush."

How long does it take a barrel of oil to jump out of the ground, into a pipeline, to get into a ship, to get into a refinery, to be refined into gasoline, to get into a tanker truck, to get driven to the local gas station, to wait for you to come along and pump some of it into your tank? Apparently, it's practically instantaneous. Another war in the Mideast can cause that barrel to traverse the distance from the desert to your fuel tank in the time it takes for a phone call from head office to the local gas station owner to raise prices by a quarter.

I feel sorry for the poor saps in Canada and the US who are caught for price fixing—not that colluding on prices should ever be tolerated, mind you. However, if a couple of slugs at a few construction companies decide to do a little bid rigging, it's as if they have committed a crime against humanity. They get their photos on the front page of the local newspaper and are totally disgraced.

There certainly appears to be one set of rules for the power elite and a separate one for the rest of us...

...

Real estate invention and animation/the "WOW" Effect

I work with several hundred real estate investors to determine their residential or commercial property's HABU, highest and best use, how to differentiate themselves from their competition, how to boost cap rates and ROI, how to get tenants to pay more of the share of the costs of running a building, how to provide more paid services to tenants, how to densify and intensify their properties...

I call this process: "how to *animate* your properties and your real estate portfolio."

Therefore, I've just given myself a promotion—I am now a "certified property animator," which is just as essential as a building inspection, plumbing inspection and structural inspection IMHO.

If you would like me to help you with any property you already own or, better, yet, assist you with a plan before you buy something, please let me know!

I'll not only provide you with a plan on how to improve your ROI, return on investment, from your newest acquisition, I'll also give you some design tips, help you focus in on your target rental market, and send you a spreadsheet laying out what you have to do to achieve your desired cap rate and IRR, internal rate of return. I'll give you plenty of pointers.

Here's a bit more detail about what I look at:

-determining highest and best use, HABU, for each property
-adding in-home suites
-adding coach houses
-adding garage offices
-adding sheds and workshops/maker spaces
-adding tech packages/home automation
-adding airbnb
-adding backyard games, natural gardens, fruit trees, mini forests, nature ponds[32]
-adding micro suites (currently the hottest trend in real estate[33])
-adding additional frontyard parking (using where possible grass parking mesh like this[34])

---

[32] In Ontario, I've found that if a pond is deeper than eight feet and if it's at least half an acre, you can populate it with large mouth bass, which are not only hardy fish, they'll keep your pond clean (by eating mosquitoes and bloodsuckers) plus they're mighty tasty.

[33] Microsuites are tiny; from 175 sq ft to 375 sq ft. They often have their own ingress/egress to the outside. The reason they're so popular is that in addition to being more affordable, they're also yours and yours alone. Do you remember what it's like to share a house/have roommates? You come home to find someone's eaten your pizza or drunk your beer. Next you argue over whose turn it is to clean the bathroom. They're also much easier to manage than rooming houses, attract a better class of tenant (often young professionals or an elder on her own), they stay longer with less churn, there is less damage to your buildings as well as less cost to prepare units for tenant changeover, you get higher rents and better cap rates too.

[34] You can blow snow off these surfaces too no problem. They're also easier on a city's storm drainage system—they allow water to infiltrate into the ground rather than overwhelming storm drains during a high volume event.

-use natural planting instead of grass (no weeding, seeding, fertilizing, watering, cutting needed)
-adding differentiated value (ie, creating a personal signature or a personal brand) like standup desks, bench seating with storage underneath… something that every one of your projects has
-adding more ingress/egress to the street from the building
-adding walkout basements
-adding loft beds

-adding beds underneath workspace

-adding light tubes

Light tube and soda pop bottle light bulbs

-deleting corridors like old farmhouses used to do[35]
-adding a w/c that is accessible from both the outside and inside
-making residential leases more like commercial ones (so that tenants pay more of the costs of running a rental property; eg, admin fee, property management fee)
-getting professional management
-selling more services to tenants like food services, events, tutoring… virtu car
-leasing to roommates
-energy saving LED lites and implementing other green for real options
-adding micro retail

---

[35] Typically, you would enter one bedroom to get to another bedroom, essentially using the first one as a "corridor" to get to the second one. The first one was usually reserved for the boys on a farm; the second for your girls. It was intended to give the girls more privacy. It was also a huge space saver…

-back to back freehold towns infill
-severance possibilities
-refinancing
-proper appraisals
-CMAs based on not only comps but also cost to complete less depreciation and income basis
-decks, privacy fences, front porches to give as many tenants as possible their own outdoor space
-outdoor kitchens
-outdoor TVs
-theming (I'm big on this—if you theme[36] a subdivision, your sell through will be faster in my experience and your prices too)
-wall plaques identifying building name
-tagline (I used to own a mini storage company called Blue Heron Storage; its tagline was, *Outta Site*)
-advertising local businesses to tenants as part of your tech package/multi media package
-home elevators
-backyard tribal council ring
-carports
-walkway covers
-organized street tree planting
-street parties
-outdoor lighting
-0-step entry
-step-in or roll-in shower
-accessible bedroom on main floor
-target renter market
-best marketing platforms to use to get to target market
-follow building code to make sure your buildings are safe
-taking advantage of vertical rent gradients, eg two story "towns" at the base of a condo tower with own private outdoor space and access
-more wow, "window on the world" like Canadian Tire Centre (see below)
-double loaded corridors
-present buildings at + 3 feet to the street
-making 2nd floor walkup space like ground floor retail space with own access at grade
-adding doors or subtracting them to make functional program change over time—similar to Villager IV and Theodora designs (see subsequent section where these designs are shown)
-exploiting subterranean rights right to property line/one and two and even three levels below grade
-name your buildings, eg, "the Palladium"
-home elevators
-street parties
-outdoor lighting
-agritainment
-farm stay networks
-communal backyards

---

[36] What type of theming are we talking about here? Architectural style is part of it. Say you like an American craftsman style. Well ok, everything in your subdivision will be a modified craftsman home. Other styles you might look at include: modern, Georgian, Victorian, Italianate, revivalism, Tudor, postmodern, Edwardian, American Colonial, Federal architecture, Dutch Colonial, art nouveau, contemporary, Renaissance, Beaux Arts or even Greek Revival and Classical architecture. But theming can go way past this though. You can apply it to street names, light standards, street furniture, roadways, all aspects of the built form… I have to say that I would add environmental covenants too as well as make commitments to energy efficiency, self-sufficiency, sustainability, grow local as well as natural planting.

-branded housing (towns with garden levels, maker homes with backyard sheds, etc)
-trail systems/conservation subdivision design
-malls connected to thousands of residential units, office towers, maker space, co-working spaces, learning and entertainment spaces
-push the envelope when it comes to zoning bylaws and ordinances so you can optimize returns from each property, and get as close to reaching its HABU—highest and best use—as possible.

If you would like to become a certified property animator yourself, ask me about my courses—I'll teach you all you have to know to do this for yourself and for others…

…

The "WOW" Effect

Every time you open up your building at grade with a penetration (doors/windows), you create additional value for both tenant and landlord. This is just as true for a residential apartment as it is for an office building or an arena.

I mean where would you rather live? In an apartment at grade that has its own doorway directly leading to the outside and maybe a little private patio or one that relies on an internal corridor and central access point for all apartments…

[photo by author]

Imagine if every ground floor apartment in the above complex had its own ingress/egress. The building would produce higher rents, tenants would have a better experience (especially if they have children) and neighborhoods would be safer—more eyes on the street mean more life and more personal safety for all.

This is a principle we put to use at Canadian Tire Centre more than 20 years ago. We sank the arena half into the ground—first, to make the building more human scale, second, to divide internal pedestrian traffic flows into two components (one goes up, one goes down) and third, to place the main concourse at grade so stores could be double loaded.

That means we could have restaurants, services and stores at grade that had their own window on the world (piercings at grade) plus they would face into the concourse. In this way, they can be busy even on dark days (periods when there is nothing going on inside the arena) and super busy serving the public and attendees on event days.

Here are a few pictures of CTC I took that demonstrate the WOW concept—

[photos by author]

You have to admit, it's better to have many building envelope piercings than more blank walls like this:

A blank wall

...

Can even a parking lot be animated?

By the way, I think I figured out how to animate even a humongous parking lot like the one at Canadian Tire Centre that holds more than 7,000 vehicles but which looks forlorn and empty most of the time… here is how—

So I asked myself, "What could you do, cost effectively, to animate (reanimate actually) Ottawa's CTC, Canadian Tire Centre's parking lot?"

The existing one. Not the new one never to be built at (possibly) their new downtown site at LeBreton Flats.

Here is a picture of CTC as it exists today:

This is their parking lot plan:

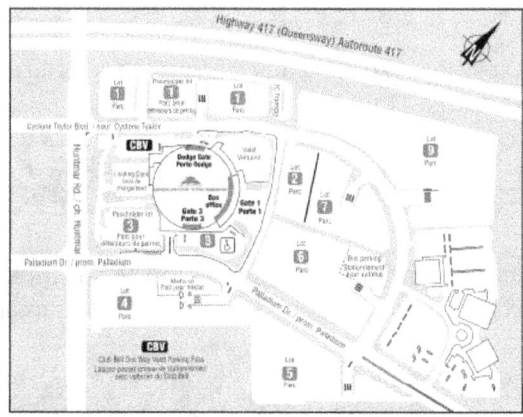

Hmm, let me see.

-you have a 7,000-vehicle parking lot
-empty most of the time

I know!
How about building a series of pop up stores for rent?
Remember "Field of Dreams?"
How about field of pop-up store dreams?
For shopaholics naturally.
Imagine if you added a dozen tiny pop up stores that could not only be used on game days or event days but also during times when the arena itself is dark.
Let's see, how about an HBO *Game of Thrones* container store[37] or a Beatles double-decker pop up (from New York City)[38]?

---

[37] CC BY-SA 3.0, https://commons.wikimedia.org/w/index.php?curid=32052087.
[38] CC BY-SA 3.0, https://commons.wikimedia.org/w/index.php?curid=22699979.

So animation is not something that applies just to residential use but commercial, institutional, industrial, and retail situations as well.

...

Animation is not a new idea; I've tried to apply these concepts throughout my real estate career, which began in 1983. The reason I got interested in the subject initially was because I found that most developers and investors, architects and constructors, city councilors and planners as well as economic development officers are mostly interested in the cost side of the industry's equation—how to reduce the cost of an architect's fees, the cost to install new infrastructure, the cost of a new building…?

It is always "cut, cut, cut."

I thought this was shortsighted—and at least some attention had to be paid to the revenue side of the business—as in, how do we create more value with our investments, boost our returns and the productivity of our efforts?

I carried this focus with me into teaching. At Carleton's Azrieli School of Architecture & Urbanism, I reinvented a core course called Design Economics. Its intent was to teach your architects to talk more about the value they create through design and less about the cost of the fees they charge their clients. My goal was to even up the playing field between architects and developers by giving architects a basic understanding of spreadsheet use, ROI calculations, cap rates, and IRRs so that they could talk to/bargain/negotiate with their clients on a more equal footing.

What does it matter if you're going to pay an architect's firm an extra $50,000 in fees and spend an extra $5,000,000 on a project if the marginal ROI on that spend is higher (often much higher) than the average for the project as a whole.

You see it's usually the last few percentage points you invest in a project that people (eventual users of the space) actually see and appreciate. Too often, we quit (run out of money, especially in capital-starved places like Canada less so in the US) before we spend this last crucial amount.

I can't believe how many developers and investors do that.

A friend of mine (Nick Lambros) wanted to open a restaurant in a location (in Bells Corners, a tiny enclave in westend Ottawa) that had seen three or four restaurants already fail there. In fact, the place had such a terrible reputation that Toronto-based Prime Restaurants (now part of Cara Operations)—their real estate group—nixed the deal.

I asked the president of Prime to come to Ottawa and sit with the prospective owner (of a new Darcy McGee's franchise) and me in the abandoned restaurant that had already closed.

He did and we told him, "Look, there are 10,000 tech employees down the road from here[39], and 120,000 residents living within a few minutes, it's a natural for a pub."

He still wasn't convinced so I added, "My take on it is that restaurateurs are spending $750,000 inside their buildings on these unbelievable fitups[40] but doing nothing outside to indicate to their

---

[39] It was a few kilometers from Nortel's headquarters, back when there was a Nortel.
[40] This was almost 30 years ago. Today's fitups can easily be double this or more. Former Ottawa Senators defenseman Chris Phillips spent more than $5 million opening his first Big Rig pub, which included a microbrewery. But don't feel

potential customers 24/7/365 what's going on/happening inside. So what I want Nick here to do is spend $750k on his fitup but keep $100,000 for the outside of the building."

"Isn't that the landlord's responsibility[41]?" *el presidente* asked.

"Yeah, but they won't do what needs to be done like I think it should be done so you guys should do it yourselves."

"But they'll pay for it, right?"

"Maybe," I answered.

It's not unusual in commercial settings to ask for free rent and/or a leasing inducement to help you pay for your fitup, which we did.

I wanted Nick and Prime to paint the outside of the building, to add fantastic lighting, signage, and murals, to build a huge new patio that doubled as an outside room with a vast canopy over it with flower beds enclosing it and infrared heaters making it useable for a greater part of the year.

I also suggested that they add an outdoor pool or beach volleyball court or paddle tennis court (which today would be a pickleball court no doubt) or something for active use. That was a bridge too far but a few weeks later, Prime gave Nick the go-ahead.

The results have been fantastic.

That place has made Nick and his family wealthy, provided employment to hundreds of young people (my middle daughter Miriam is a server there), satisfied more than 4,500,000[42] hungry/thirsty people over the 30 years or so it's been open…

It's now called the Brew Table and looks like this on Google's street view:

sorry for him—first year sales were in excess of $6 million before settling in at a run rate of $5.5 million a year just for that original location…

[41] The restaurant podium was attached to a Days Inn hotel owned by a super smart Ismaili family.

[42] I'm guessing here. I used 3,000 customers a week (around 428 per day) for 30 years, which gave me 4,679,999 persons served that I rounded down to four and a half million. Hey, it adds up…

And here's Miss Miriam:

So animation works in a commercial setting too.

...

More recently, I've been working with a group to help them resuscitate a failing office complex. What are some of the things they are contemplating?
Well, here's our list so far:

-adding solar power to its roof and other surfaces (luckily, the complex has a high capacity transformer right on site) so the complex is self sufficient and tenants can be assured that all their power needs are met in a 100% sustainable way
-repurposing its vast atrium to house not one but two pubs
-adding a coffee, tea and muffin shop to a floating platform in what will be left of its atrium
-constructing pedestrian linkages between all buildings on-site (at a second story height) so they act as one structure from a services point of view
-making better use of an existing feature stair to increase collisionable hours
-adding a residential tower (possibly two)
-adding some outdoor play space together with food truck(s)[43]
-making better use of signage opportunities including adding video capability to existing pylon signs, and billboard

...

And just to prove it to you that "animation" is not a new word in my vocabulary, I'll tell you one last anecdote.
In 1991, just as design of the new Palladium building (now Canadian Tire Centre) was gathering steam, Ottawa's city council decided to demolish a national historic site of Canada—a fabulous, Meccano-style exhibition hall called the Aberdeen Pavilion (nicknamed the "cattle castle" because of all the agricultural fairs hosted there over the years since it opened in 1898). It was the last of the Victorian halls in existence in Canada.
City council had decided it was better to spend $350,000 tearing down this treasure (which had more than 40,000 square feet of clear (ie, column-free) event space) rather than invest $5.5 million preserving it. Recall what I said about the misplaced focus on spending rather than ROI, right?
So I called then mayor Holzman and said this, "Jackie, how about if I save the city $350,000."
"How would you do that, Bruce?" she asked.
"Well, I'll send a crew to Lansdowne Park and take down the Aberdeen Pavilion myself. No charge."

---

[43] Remember, "Leisure is the new infrastructure," said Eric Kuhne.

"Huh? Why would you do that?"

"Because I visited it this morning and I think we can letter and number every member, every barn board, every sheet of tin, take it apart—piece by piece—and reassemble it next to the Palladium. Can you imagine how cool it would be to have the old and the new juxtaposed one with the other? We'll add a breezeway connection so the two buildings will work as one and we'll add over an acre of fabulous event space to our new arena."

"Can you send me a letter stating all this?" Ms Holzman asked.

"You bet."

...

So I did, and you know what? I got roasted it for it by the media and some councilors. Things like:

FIRESTONE TRYING TO STEAL CITY HERITAGE
FIRESTONE TAKING ADVANTAGE OF NAÏVE CITY COUNCIL
RAPACIOUS DEVELOPER TO DEMOLISH HERITAGE BUILDING

So in the end, council reversed itself and ponied up the dough to save the cattle castle. Just so you know, they (the city) got such a good deal that the contractor who bid on the renovation went broke because of that job and the Palladium missed out on a great opportunity to have its built form animated but—good news—I saved that damn structure for future generations.

From Wikipedia, here's what it looked in 1903[44]:

And what it shamefully looked like in 1991[45]:

---

[44] Photo by William James Topley; image available from Library and Archives Canada under reproduction reference number PA-009125 and under MIKAN ID number 3318760.

[45] Photo by Lars Plougmann, originally posted to Flickr as 00097_n_7ab88k78v003, CC BY-SA 2.0, https://commons.wikimedia.org/w/index.php?curid=11756739.

And what it looks like more recently[46]:

Finally, here's a shot of its impressive interior[47]:

...

Just so you don't think I'm a complete poser, I did later on get to move a miniature version of the Aberdeen Pavilion.

A developer by the name of John Galetta was getting ready to build a new subdivision in Kanata, Ontario.

During a casual conversation (the best kind, the ones that develop because of a chance collisionable encounter ☺), he mentioned that his old Amish-style barn was going to be demolished to make way for a new road and a bunch more (humongous, useless, costly, over-priced, unsustainable, highly-taxed) houses on 2-acre lots, each with its own septic field and well requiring future homeowners to become experts in proper sh*t disposal and safe drinking water provision instead of using conservation subdivision principles[48] together with collectively-owned, small bore sewer and water systems. However, I digress.

---

[46] Original uploader, SimonP, transferred from en.wikipedia to commons by Skeezix1000 using CommonsHelper, CC BY-SA 3.0, https://commons.wikimedia.org/w/index.php?curid=4542425.

[47] Photo by Ddeyell, transferred from en.wikipedia to Commons by Skeezix1000 using CommonsHelper, Public Domain, https://commons.wikimedia.org/w/index.php?curid=4542460.

[48] "A conservation subdivision typically conserves up to sixty to seventy percent of land in a parcel that is slated for development (Arendt, 1994). The conserved land might consist of forests, fields, marshes, or pre-existing agricultural land. This land is then commonly owned and managed by all of the landowners within the development... This common land in conservation subdivisions may incorporate amenities like trail networks and playgrounds or may be used for shared, onsite wastewater management systems (and water wells, ed). Even though conservation subdivisions use less land for development purposes, lots are smaller and developers can produce the same number of lots as in a conventional subdivision. The difference, however, is that conservation subdivisions require less land to be graded, fewer pipes, and fewer roads, as more compact built forms are possible. Studies from the United States show that developing land as

I made the same pitch to him as I did to Ottawa's mayor and, this time, the deal was accepted and he stuck to it...

So my crew and I removed it from John's lands and rebuilt on a property I owned about 12 kilometers to the north, viz:

[photo by author]

I even found my old plans:

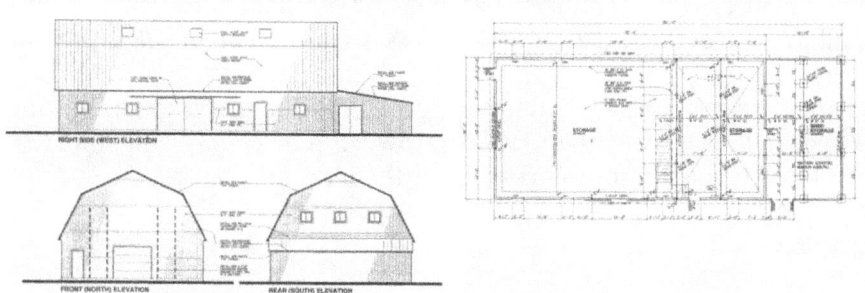

It was a party place for my kids and their friends even before it was finished:

...

---

conservation subdivisions costs less than conventional subdivisions and that lots sell faster and for more money (Mohamed, 2006). When neighboring residents are concerned about a loss of rural charm and open space, they may be more inclined to accept conservation subdivisions. They are a win for planners, developers, residents, and homebuyers," Alex Henderson and Lloyd Talbot, *Conservation Subdivisions, a win-win form of rural residential development*, Case in Point, 2013, https://umanitoba.ca/faculties/architecture/media/CIP_2013_Alex_Henderson.pdf. (It should also be pointed out that this form of development also allows freer wildlife migration especially when adjacent conserved lands are conjoined. Unfortunately, despite more than 30 years of lobbying, this type of development is still banned in Ontario. Why? Because Ontario's ministry of environment is afraid that these pocket communal systems will fail or the communities or businesses that operate them will fold, and they will be left with the cost of fixing them/operating them/connecting them to main sewer lines. This excuse is a tissue given that Ontario has more than 50 years of experience dealing with and making building condominium corporations work properly with registration, reserve funds, boards of directors, reporting requirements etc. Why not have a condominium corp own wastewater and water systems too? Ed.)

Three Ways to Boost Cap Rates and Increase Property Values

"Animating," as you already know, is a BIG word in my vocabulary these days—making properties and neighborhoods...

Livelier
More exciting, and
Highly differentiated

All of which can boost cap rates substantially and improve the surrounding economy as well as cityscape and community.

How to go about creating sustainable local economies is something I am passionate about, and something that I speak about not only in Canada but in other nations as well.

The challenge is the same whether you live in rural Saskatchewan or on the Greek island of Crete—how to keep your most valuable resource—your children—at home or get them to return?

The answer is the same all over—*nothing is sustainable unless it's also economically sustainable.* Or so say I.

Maybe your kids prefer the bright lights of the city at age 18, but before they're 30, they'll be thinking of having their own progeny... and your town, village, township or county will start looking a lot more attractive, especially if there is economic opportunity for them to come back to.

1) Coach Houses/Garden Suites

The city of Ottawa legalized coach houses[49]—granny flats or garden suites—in your backyard, above your detached garage, wherever you can fit it in.

Are they doing it because they want you to improve your ROI on your home or in your rental portfolio?

Not really.

They are doing it because a provincial policy statement mandates more affordable housing...

And one of the fastest ways of achieving that objective is by permitting, as of right, these types of infill projects.

It also has the happy consequence of boosting your ROI and cap rate, if you are a homeowner or landlord, as well as both densifying and intensifying existing residential areas.

Moreover, it will make them more socially diverse and interesting especially if they legalize micro retail too.

So one day soon, you may walk to your neighbor's place to get a freshly baked chocolate-covered croissant each morning...

2) Tech Packages

There are many such things we can do to make our urban areas livelier while at the same time improving individual economic circumstances by permitting a proliferation of choice in the built form and their uses in our towns, villages, and cities.

---

[49] In November 2016, coach houses became a legal part of the Ottawa's official plan and bylaws everywhere in the city except for the tony village of Rockcliffe Park, where a lot of rich dudes and many world ambassadors live. I suppose they either don't need the marginal income from granny flats or they fear that riff-raff will move into their sacrosanct neighborhood or maybe both. Hmm, I guess I should disclose that I grew up in Rockcliffe Park, *mea culpa*.

There are some things you can do almost everywhere without waiting on your town's council for approval.

It has always amazed me that small and large landlords don't sell more stuff to a captive audience—their tenants—not just to boost their own bottom lines, but also to increase tenant satisfaction.

How long does it take the average person these days to get reliable internet service hooked up and make all their tech work?

How long to get Netflix or Spotify operational?

To get a large screen TV, wall-mounted?

To hassle around with your local company to get basic cable working?

To get a net phone going?

I encourage property owners—large scale and small[50]—to offer these services to their tenants so that the day they move in, everything works.

Landlords can buy these services wholesale and resell them to their tenants at less than an individual client could contract for them directly, and still the property owner makes decent money[51].

Here's a project we did in Kanata, a high tech western suburb of Ottawa.

The owner created a lovely 2-bedroom apartment in the basement with its own entrance. The upstairs was a 3-bedroom, 2 and ½-bath place with sunroom.

Here's a shot of the lower level interior:

Front elevation:

---

[50] Both residential *and* commercial property owners should offer tech/multi-media packages to their clients in my view.

[51] From a tenant's point of view, buying these services from a landlord at about the same price they'd pay to service providers like Bell, Telus, Rogers, Verizon, AT&T, Sprint, T-Mobile… and having them work the first day they move in is not only a big time and hassle saver, it also helps them avoid having to pay large deposits to providers if they're first time customers. A few of my clients tell me that their clients (tenants) sometimes don't want these multimedia packages; that sounds suspiciously like an excuse to me to not bother with them. However, I've found that these things are very popular (once you properly explain the advantages to renters) so I refuse to lease to folks who decline to take our tech packages saying, "Hey, you don't have to sign up for this. No problem at all. But I'm not going to rent the place to you then." How come? Because, these days, everyone needs internet and, if they don't, that's a signal to me that they're probably not going to be decent, rent-paying tenants. I have roofers, laborers, carpenters, pipe fitters, boilermakers (one of those) and others I or one of my clients rent to who are great folks, great. They may have a few visible tattoos and throw a party here or there but they pay their rent, take care of our real estate, and are very independent people—if their toilet backs up, sink gets plugged up or there are a few ants marching though the place on their way to a nest, they'll fix it themselves likely as not. Plus they know how to use the internet almost as well as I do. In the units we manage, only a couple of really old ladies (in their 90s) are let off the hook; ie, don't have to take (full) tech packages but they still pay for basic cable, net phone and Netflix, which they adore. ☺

Tech package controls (using an iPad):

And finally, here's the ROI on his tech package investment. Note that it's higher because he ended up with not only two apartments but also a workshop (maker) space and a coach house in his (humongous) backyard, which means he sold four tech packages not two...

His ROI?

An insane 147.9% pa.

Remember real estate is get rich... slow and every penny counts so while his total annual profit/cashflow ($4,092) is not huge in and of itself, it pays for another 4.5 new iPad Pros *every* year. I mean how cool is that?

	Tech Package ROI	Kanata	
capital costs			
large screen wall-mounted TVs	$1,860	$465	4
basic fiber cabling	$445		
high speed internet, wi-fi routers, boosters, modems	$165		
Magic Jack phone	$0		
subtotal	$2,470	installed	
contingencies	$296	12%	
total cost	$2,766		
operating costs			
Netflix	$12	per mth	
basic fiber	$100		
high speed internet, wi-fi routers, boosters, modems	$0		
Spotify	$12		
Magic Jack phone	$10	$2.50	4
admin and management fee	$35		
total cost	$169	per mth	
upstairs charge--main house	$135	per mth	
lower level	$125		
coach house	$125		
backyard workshop	$125		
total income	$510	per mth	
NOI	$341	per mth	
	$4,092	pa	
cap rate	147.9%	pa	
E&OE			

Just for the heck of it, I recalculated this as if he only had the two apartments (that is, no backyard workshop or coach house). His cost to install and set up his multi media offerings decreases but his ROI on tech packages also drops from 147.9% pa to still healthy 74.4%.

Kanata: no workshop, no coach house	Tech Package ROI		
capital costs			
large screen wall-mounted TVs	$930	$465	2
basic fiber cabling	$335		
high speed internet, wi-fi routers, boosters, modems	$118		
Magic Jack phone	$0		
subtotal	$1,383	installed	
contingencies	$166	12%	
total cost	$1,548		
operating costs			
Netflix	$12	per mth	
basic fiber	$100		
high speed internet, wi-fi routers, boosters, modems	$0		
Spotify	$12		
Magic Jack phone	$5	$2.50	2
admin and management fee	$35		
total cost	$164	per mth	
upstairs charge--main house	$135	per mth	
lower level	$125	per mth	
coach house	$0		
backyard workshop	$0		
total income	$260	per mth	
NOI	$96	per mth	
	$1,152	pa	
cap rate	74.4%	pa	

E&OE

    I should point out that under Ottawa's new rules; you are not permitted to have both an in-home suite and a coach house. But here's the thing… that's a mistake in my view.

    And while you are entitled to have a home-based business in many jurisdictions these days, you are not (usually) allowed to rent a garage office, micro retail space, maker space or workshop to a third party, that is, someone not actually living in the home.

    And it looks like it's only a matter of time before idiot politicians pushed by hotel industry lobbyists will seek to curtail Airbnb use in their areas.

    I recently read a Guardian article (https://www.theguardian.com/world/2017/aug/10/no-cooking-in-kitchen-disbelief-amsterdam-rental-flat-rules) wherein critics lay the blame for skyrocketing housing prices and rental rates in Amsterdam predominantly at the feet of property owners who have taken their units out of the general rental market and into the Airbnb marketplace.

    As evidence, they cite this stupendously stupid ad (which has (after the Guardian published their article) been taken down by the realtor who wrote it):

    Huis Tuinstraat in Amsterdam
    1015 NX Amsterdam (Noord-Holland)
    €1.000 35m² 2 kamers *(rooms, ed)*
    Huurprijs *(monthly rent, ed)*

    This studio apartment on the first floor has a private bathroom and private kitchen. The kitchen is fully equipped, except for a cooking plate. *Cooking is explicitly not allowed* (italics mine, ed) in this apartment due to regulations. However, the apartment has a microwave. Water heater, How many followers are allowed (sic). Maximum 2 people at all times.

Notice anything weird? I mean besides the facts that despite the place having its own private kitchen you are not actually allowed to cook there because of some unknowable and nincompoopish "regulations" and you can't have more than two people in it at any one time?

Well, it isn't an Airbnb listing. It's a regular rental.

Polish*tans[52], planners, zoners and regulators should look at the real underlying causes of home price and rental increases rather than lynching a (new) favorite whipping boy (Airbnb) or resorting to that other old faithful standby—rent control—that only hurts the people it is alleged to help.

Do you think that in a rent controlled environment where *affordable unit* is an oxymoronic term, landlords will prefer to rent to single moms and their kids, other young people, folks with pets, the recently unemployed or homeless, visible minorities, people with religions different from their own, the disabled, elderly on fixed incomes or other vulnerable groups? They will not.

Do you think in rent-controlled environments, there is extra incentive for investors and developers to create more rental stock? Nope.

Do you believe that in such circumstances, there will be an increase in illegal rent gouging, an increase in soliciting by not only property owners but also by tenants who are exiting to ask the next occupant for key money[53], and that there will be much more civil disobedience? Of course you do.

Do you think landlords will have a bigger incentive to keep their properties up, to make them safe for occupancy, and to ensure that there are no deferred maintenance issues? No, you do not believe in fairytales either.

Do you believe that government is the answer—that they're just waiting in the wings with bags of *your* money to fill a huge and growing gap in affordable rental housing? More fairytales, I am afraid.

Even if governments were willing to step into the housing market in a big way, do you really think they'd do a better job at running affordable housing and developing public housing complexes than the private sector? Nope.

Do you think that, no matter what, clever property owners and their advisers will find ways around stupid government regulations and end up making more money with lower vacancy rates and higher rents anyway? I assure you they will.

I'm not anti-government. I actually believe there is a role for government to play—to keep the peace, to create a level playing field (of opportunity for all), to curb excesses, to ensure the provision of public goods and provide their nation with the right signals, not only price signals but to lead with moral authority. But governments, at least in my worldview, are bad at the actual *doing* of anything. That they should leave up to the rest of us.

So why are house prices exploding in certain urban areas?

Well, some of the reasons are, for all practical purposes, beyond government control such as in-migration from rural to urban areas, international flows of migrants (who prefer, for the most part, to settle in major urban areas near relatives or others from their original homeplaces), and secular increases in costs of construction for materials and labor.

However, there are a ton of things that governments could do that most of them have avoided because they are afraid of NIMBY pushback and ballot box suicide.

These include—allowing more density and intensity of use, relaxing zoning standards such as decreasing sideyard/frontyard/backyard setbacks, increasing building height limits, reducing road

---

[52] Jenna McConnell's term for "politicians" not mine.

[53] Investopedia defines it this way: key money is paid by a prospective tenant to a property owner or manager in the hopes of securing a rental contract in a particular property. In certain circumstances, key money can be considered a bribe to ensure that a property coming up for rent is secured by the payer of the key money, and as such, the transaction is conducted in an unofficial manner. In my experience, landlords and property managers may never see any key money because shrewd tenants who are, say, being transferred to another city will intercept it; that is, they'll sublet to a favored friend who, in all probability, looks, acts and comes from the same racial and social class as they do. Compounding the problem, sometimes the tenants who is leaving "levies" one key money payment, the property manager levies (and pockets) another and, finally, the property owner asks for a third installment. Most probably all of them in cash meaning no income or value added taxes get paid either. So who exactly benefits from rent control? Most certainly not any renters I know.

rights of way widths, permitting more on-street parking, reducing the number of parking spots developers are required to build, lowering building permit costs and development charges, reducing the minimum allowable size of units, allowing folks to live in tiny houses[54] if they so choose to (parked in someone's backyard or for that matter on a public street), and (above all else) increasing the supply of development land by expanding their urban areas/boundaries and the services that go with it, which will permit the construction of more housing.

I could go on for pages but this "mini" book is already too long; anywho, you get my drift...

...

Investors and homeowners[55], as I have said elsewhere, have no one to really rely on except themselves. Therefore, they are engaging in widespread civil disobedience, doing what they need to, to take care of themselves and their families.

If cities and towns, villages and townships, counties and provinces or states decide to curtail these activities/uses of the built form of their communities because of wrongly-placed fears of over-densifying, NIMBY/public backlash, dropping property values (and hence, ultimately, decreasing property/realty tax revenues) or breakdown of civic order, don't be surprised when there is near-universal disobedience amongst a savvy population of desperate property owners and the elderly, who are the new poor.

3) Mini Storage

Another simple thing to add? Backyard mini-storage.

In most jurisdictions, you can install a shed of 10 square meters or less *without* a building permit.

Now what does it cost to rent a 10' by 10' storage shed these days?

In most cities and towns, it's somewhere between $100 per month and $135. If it's indoors and heated, it's more like $155 to $185.

So why not offer your tenants the opportunity to rent a storage shed in their own backyards for, say, $99.95 or even $85 a month, instead of having to get in their vehicle and drive to a remote storage location only to have to pay more?

One of my clients, who owns 75 units in 30 locations, is currently doing just that.

His current capitalization rate on his existing portfolio is a not bad 8.75% per annum.

He can add a full percentage point to that by reselling tech packages (which he is doing with alacrity) and he can boost it further by installing 60 sheds.

The economics look like something this:

Mini-Storage Animation   (New line of business)

Owner's portfolio	30	Buildings 2.5	Doors per building (avg) 75 units
Sheds	60	2	Sheds per building
Cost per shed	$3,000		
Cost of gravel base	$300		
Patio stones	$1,120		
Labor for base prep	$240		
Subtotal	$4,660		
Contingencies	$839	18%	

---

[54] Which governments will probably never agree to because, at least in Ontario, structures on wheels cannot be assessed for property taxes since they are plated as "homemade RVs." What do politicians like best? Money and power, and those two things are connected so if the flow of money ever stops, so too does power. Jose Canseco is rumored to have put it this way, "The only thing politicians ever truly stand for is reelection."

[55] Even tenants are getting into the act as discussed elsewhere by me... for example; they'll sublet an extra bedroom on Airbnb to help them pay their rent.

Total cost per shed	$5,499
Grand total	$329,928
Income (per shed)	$99.95 per mth
	$5,997 per mth
	$71,964 per yr
Vacancy	($5,757) 8%
NOI	$66,207 per yr
Cap rate	20.1% per annum
Payback period	4.98 yrs
E&OE	

With 60 storage sheds (!), he's now really in the mini storage business as well as the landlord business and the "providing-my-tenants-better-service" business.

If you look at the cap rate on his mini storage enterprise, it's a terrific 20.1% per annum so, for sure, his portfolio's overall ROI is going to go up, which is nice.

But here's the thing: if tenants are taking advantage of loosening city regulations to establish what I call PB4Ls (personal businesses for life), why right out their back doors, they can store all the ingredients they'll need to make their new micro enterprises a success. Moreover, what if one day, my client decides to build workshops too?

Now that's progress!

...

After my client had about 30 sheds installed, he called me to let me know something strange—ie, not anticipated by either of us—was taking place. He was getting calls from neighbors (not his tenants, third parties) asking if they could also rent them a shed too.

He asked me, "Is that even legal?"

My answer was, "Probably not."

You can only rent a shed (in most cities) to someone who lives on-site. But you know what I said about civil disobedience above, right?

I cannot advise anyone to engage in it but I sure understand the motivation.

...

Now one last point about sheds/workshops.

Here's one my wife bought for our backyard from a large company whose name rhymes with "Rows."

It was what my spouse, Dawn MacMillan, and I refer to as a "$3 rake." You know the kind where the head falls off less than ten minutes after you start raking your leaves in the fall and where the tines started to bend, break, come loose, and fall out a few minutes before that.

Well, it only cost us $800 to buy this POS (piece of crap) from *Rows*, but it took two men a week to put it together (it shipped flat like an IKEA POS, you know, the ones that come with indecipherable instructions on how to put it together along with an unpronounceable name.)

That (their labor) cost us $2,000.

And then it only had 6-foot headroom at its peak. The doorway is worse—it's a head-banging 5'4" with each side exactly the same.

Oh well, I thought, *at least it's something.*

But during that first winter, the roof looked suspiciously vulnerable to snow load collapse so your hero (moi) had to go out from time to time to shovel the darn thing off.

It did no good. The roof knuckled after a snowstorm followed by sleet and rain, followed by a titanic freeze, which makes things really heavy and *unshovelable*. One thing about Ottawa, it is *guaranteed* to have horrible weather. The only capital worse off? Mongolia's Ulaanbaatar. I'm not kidding.

When my girlfriend (who is also my wife) went back to "Rows," they told her, "Oh yeah, we've had a bunch of complaints about that. You shoulda originally bought the roof strengthener kit with it. That'll cost you extra…"

Of course, it's our fault that the store is selling sheds with collapsible roofs in a northern shelf, snowbound city without their customers somehow knowing/suspecting it in the first place. Naturally.

Anyway, now we buy our sheds from the Amish… wood-framed with metal roof. And, by the way, they'll last more than 40 winters. They look like this and cost around $2,500 (CAD):

Moreover, when we want a backyard workshop, we buy things that look like these from an excellent Quebec-based manufacturer:

So there.

…

Internal Rate of Return (IRR), Cap Rate (Capitalization Rate) and ROE (Return on Equity)

Calculating your ROE is not really a simple thing. Almost certainly the best way to calculate it is to use an IRR (internal rate of return). This takes into account the time based value of money and can produce a fairly accurate rate of return for the overall project, your equity portion of the financing and the sub-debt position (first mortgage, second mortgage financing, STB (seller take back) financing, debenture financing and/or mezzanine financing… if any).

I show how to calculate the IRR for a duplex and retail plaza on my Prof Bruce youtube channel at:
https://www.youtube.com/watch?v=AX0l3DU4qWY&t=1233s&index=54&list=PLd3QdcBlEm9-b9B3sAnGd86s79M8ib_P3

IRR on your equity is highly sensitive to leverage. In one of the duplexes I built years ago (called the Villager IV model, see below), a 25% down payment yielded an IRR of 22.1% pa. But if I could have built it with just 5% down, it would have jumped to a whopping 56.4%.

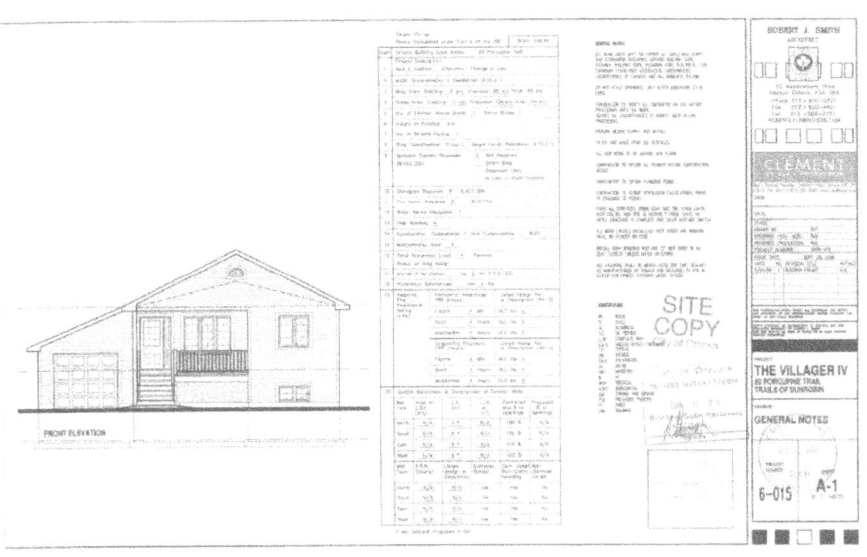

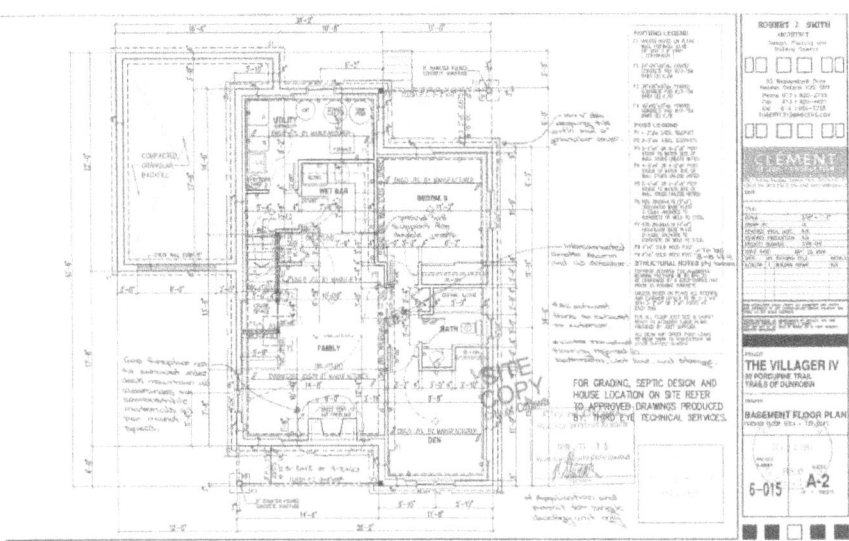

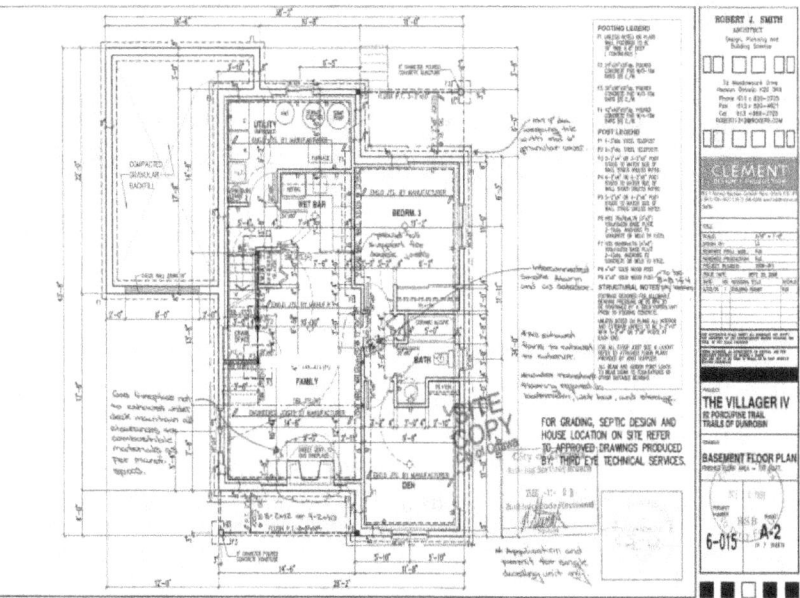

If instead of using your 25% equity to purchase one house, you used it to buy five homes with 5% down; you will end up with a much larger cash-on-cash return than if you just had one property. For one investment property with 25% equity in it, cash returned over 5 years was $89k. But for five investment properties with 5% equity in each of them, cash returned over 5 years ballooned to $254k.

It doesn't take many units before you can turn your real estate portfolio into a "perpetual motion machine"—this model answers the question: "How many rental homes do you need to buy (or build) and how much of your mortgages do you need to pay off before the system produces enough free cashflow that will then allow you to buy (or build) more rental properties without pumping in any more cash equity?"

Minto Construction, a large Ottawa-based company, is living proof that this model works after a fashion. One of the founders of the company, Irving Greenberg, once told me that the best day in his business life was when the government of Ontario under (conservative) premier Bill Davis introduced rent control in Ontario circa the 1970s.

After the introduction of rent control, Irving made more money than ever from his residential rental property portfolio. First, there was less competition as builders, developers and investors (foolishly) fled the market and, as a result, vacancy rates, including Minto's, fell. Second, Irving was able to buy out his competitors cheaply, thereby, speedily and substantially adding to his portfolio. Third, he was able to pass on rent increases every year since such increases were now "government approved" and tenants had nowhere else to go anyway. Fourthly, he could be picky about his tenants and damage to his units and maintenance costs went down as did churn rate—tenants stayed longer and his cost of preparing his units for the next tenant went down... a lot. Fiftly, he could pass on the costs of upgrades, repairs and maintenance to his tenants, again in additional, government-approved rent hikes every year.

Rent control was a travesty in my view—it certainly didn't help those who most needed help, aka the poor who are disproportionately single mothers and elders.

Minto ended up with tens of thousands of rental units in Ottawa, Toronto and Florida and tens of millions of dollars in free cashflow too... every month.

Cap Rate

Most real estate professionals do not use IRR calculations—they use cap (capitalization) rates to compare one project with another. The cap rate is an approximate estimate of ROI, return on investment, as all financial measures are anyway. But they are more approximate than the IRR is, in my view. Nevertheless, it's a handy first order of magnitude measure. The cap rate can be determined by simply dividing the net operating income, NOI, of a property by its sale price, purchase price, or fair market value.

One way to look at the inverse of cap rate is that it is an approximation for the number of years it will take you to earn back your capital. It is widely used especially in the commercial real estate sector and to evaluate residential rentals. The higher the cap rate, the better it is for a buyer and the worse for a seller.

Another way to look at the cap rate is that it is a rough measure of your rate of return on the project—it measures the rate of cash return on the overall project not your equity (unless you finance 100% of the property with equity).

Cap rates are calculated this way.

Cap rate = NOI/FMV

Where FMV = the fair market value of the building and NOI = gross income for the entire project less operating costs, property taxes, utilities, repairs, maintenance, insurance and other landlord costs *but before mortgage and debt payment*

Here's an example for an apartment building (based on a real case study):

	109 Any street	E&OE
pp	$6,200,000	
units	72	
unit price	$86,111.11	per door
INCOME		
rental income	$ 691,788.00	
laundry income	$ 22,000.00	
TOTAL ANNUAL INCOME	$ 713,788.00	pa
EXPENSE		
Property Taxes	$ 101,065.00	
Hydro	$ 118,000.00	
Insurance	$ 6,370.00	
Water	$ 26,934.00	
Management	$ 20,000.00	
Other	$ 26,398.00	
TOTAL ANNUAL EXPENSES	$ 298,767.00	pa
NET OPERATING INCOME, NOI	$ 415,021.00	pa
CAP RATE	6.7%	pa

The easiest way to understand a cap rate is this—pretend you are a rich dude for a moment and you bought 109 Any street for $6.2 million *in cash*... ie, you didn't need a loan. You found the millions you needed to buy this 72 unit building in your couch.

After paying all your costs, you end up with $415,000 every year to spend on whatever you want. It's your cash-on-cash ROI.

"Hmm," you say, "not all that impressive."

But what if you had saved up that $6.2 million and instead you had invested it in your bank at say 1.5% pa? Well, you'd only have $93,000 a year to spend.

Skill testing question—which is better? $93,000 a year or $415,000?

But your cap rate does not include all the different types of returns from real estate—there is no allowance for paydown of your mortgage[56] (the wealth effect I talked about above) or real estate inflation.

You don't get any inflation protection from having your cash in the bank but you do (in most cities and towns) when you own real property.

In Ottawa, house prices in 2016 accelerated by around 2%[57], in Toronto, by a crazy 20%[58], and in many cities across North America by anywhere from 1% to, well, Toronto-style numbers (particularly in desirable places to live and work like Boston, Seattle, Portland, San Francisco and Vancouver.)

Anyway, let's use 5% for real estate inflation, which means you also get an increase in fair market value each year of around $310,000 on your 109 Any street building. Now that buys you a lot of eggrolls if and when you refinance your building and take out some *tax-free* cash.

The cap rate does *not* take into account all the different types of return you can make in real estate, which is why professional investors use IRRs. Think of the IRR as a kind of weighted average of cash on cash return, principal paydown, and real estate inflation.

Here's the IRR calculations we did to evaluate the purchase of 109 Any street:

pp		$6,200,000				
ltt, land transfer tax		$120,475				
legals		$8,500				
total		$6,328,975				
equity		$1,582,244		25%	ltv, loan to	value
debt		$4,746,731		3.75%	25	yrs
mortgage payment		($295,871.78)	pa			
profit		$ 119,149.22	pa			
equity		$1,582,244				
ROE, return on equity		7.5%	pa			
IRR, internal rate of return						
	0	($1,582,244)				
	1	$ 119,149.22				
	2	$ 119,149.22				
	3	$ 119,149.22				
	4	$ 119,149.22				
	5	$4,085,208.70				
irr		25.7%	pa			
increase in value		5.00%	pa			
value at end of term		$8,077,554.10				
principal payments						
	1	($117,869.35)				

---

[56] There would be no wealth effect (principal paydown, effectively by your tenants) in the example I'm using here since you didn't "need" a mortgage to buy 109 Any street…

[57] *Thinking of buying a home in Ottawa in 2017?* Here's a price comparison, http://www.cbc.ca/news/canada/ottawa/ottawa-home-price-forecast-2017-comparison-1.3887110.

[58] *Average GTA home price jumped 20% in 2016*, Toronto Real Estate Board credits strong economy and low interest rates for climb in sales, https://www.thestar.com/business/2017/01/05/average-gta-home-price-jumped-20-in-2016.html.

2	($122,289.46)
3	($126,875.31)
4	($131,633.13)
5	($136,569.38)
total	($635,236.63)
mortgage at end of term	$4,111,494.62

E&OE (errors and omissions excepted)

...

You should remember that you make money in real estate when you buy not when you sell, so buy smart.

That means you buy when everybody else is selling (ie, when cap rates are high and interest rates are usually at their highest as well so it's a buyer's market) and sell when everyone else is buying (ie, when cap rates are lowest and interest rates typically lowest too). A simpler way to put it is: "Buy low, sell high."

In places like northern shelf cities like Ottawa, there is an ebb and flow of deals within the calendar year. The best time to buy is November, December, January and February when days are short and it's brutally cold. Canadians get depressed at that time of the year, DOM (days on market, a key variable) tends to increase, and sellers get more desperate. It can make as much as a 3% difference in purchase price, sometimes much more.

Now this is easier said than done. People are very sheep-like. We like to buy when everyone else is buying and what everyone else is buying. Ever bought a suit and had the salesperson tell you: "This is really in this season—everyone who is anyone is buying this." They tell you this because it works.

It's hard to buy real estate when no one else is and interest rates are high. Or when the weather is bad—everyone will tell you to wait 'til spring.

During recessions, everyone—your CFO, your auditor, your bank, your spouse, your BOD (board of directors), your CAO, COO, even your CTO (chief techie), your buddies at the gym, will tell you this is a bad time to buy/expand—she or he will want more dough for their department instead—it'll have a better ROI, or so they will tell you. But you are the CEO (of your own life) and, at the end of the day, the decision is yours.

The best deals I ever did[59] were when real estate markets were depressed. I bought some land in Ottawa near a major, east-end shopping centre in 1983 when interest rates approached 18%. The land cost me $1 per square foot for ten acres. In 1984, I got an offer for the land at 50 cents a square foot—I thought I was in real trouble. But I went to my dad and he reminded me about rule number 1—buy low/sell high so I declined the offer.

By 1985/86, interest rates were down by half and I sold four acres for $10 per square foot to an auto dealer and the other six acres to an industrial (roofing and truss manufacturing) company for $12. We made about $4m in three years on an investment of $450k; you don't need to do an IRR or ROE calculation on deals like this—they are good deals. (That money too later found its way into the Ottawa Senators and the Palladium, now Canadian Tire Centre. Money in NHL hockey circles only seems to go in one direction—in, never out.)

By 1994, the real estate biz was again in a slump. These down cycles seem to come about every seven years and real estate tends to lead a national economy into a recession and lag it coming out,

---

[59] If only I'd stuck to real estate and not gotten into NHL hockey and other involvements… I'd be a LOT richer ☹ Focus on what you do best and treat everything else as a hobby is what my experience suggests.

which means it usually lasts longer than a general recession. But when real estate bounces up, it bounces in a hurry and you have to start selling right away if you want to time the market.

Anyway, in 1994 I bought 60 acres of industrial land in Kanata (a west end suburb of Ottawa) for just 15 cents a square foot. I couldn't believe it—people were just giving the stuff away—prices were lower than at any time since the Great Depression of the 1930s for goodness sake.

But by 1999, in a subsequent tech boom, serviced industrial land in Kanata started selling for $6 to $8 per square foot, if you could find it. Imagine going from 15 cents to around $7 a square foot on 60 acres in five years? Now that's real dough. Again, you don't have to bother with IRRs when you do deals like that. The returns are fantastic.

The problem is that most entrepreneurs (guilty!) can't hang on to their gains; they're always onto the next BIG thing.

I remember seeing a bumper sticker on a trip to LA after the tech bust of the early 2000s that said:

PLEASE GOD GIVE ME ONE MORE REAL ESTATE BOOM AND THIS TIME I PROMISE NOT TO F**K IT UP

I LOL thinking, *Frig that's me.*

One of the reasons I make a good real estate investment and business coach I think is that if there's a mistake out there I haven't already made, it must reside in an orbit somewhere beyond Pluto, making it hard for me to bump into it.

...

A client of mine decided to follow some Prof Bruce advice—that is to own his own real estate. He was looking at what I'll call the "Soda Pop" building, which was selling for $4.8m. His biz would occupy about half the premises and the other half he would rent out. The cap rate for his acquisition was a healthy 12.8%.

From his point of view (as buyer), this looks decent. Cap rates for industrial property at the time (another recession so a good time to buy, right?) had climbed to 9, 10, 11, 12 or even more, which meant a much lower cost of acquisition for Paul (not his real name).

Remember, another way to look at the inverse of a cap rate is that it is a rough measure of how long it takes you to get your money back. So Paul's new project will take about 7.8 years to return all of its capital back to Paul (assuming he pays cash for the building.) That is pretty fast if you think about the average homeowner taking 20, 25, 30 or even 35 years to pay off their home mortgage, which many actually never accomplish.

But Paul should be much more interested in when he gets his equity back, assuming he is using some debt for part of his acquisition—this means he can turn around and do something else with his cash—buy more real estate, buy more equipment for his packing supplies biz, go on a nice holiday, buy a boat, whatever.

You get an approximate time for Paul to get his money back by simply dividing his equity by the NOI less whatever his debt payments are. This worked out to $1.2m divided by $301,736 or roughly 4 years. The IRR is a much more precise tool but it seems that many in the real estate industry are just much more comfortable with (rule of thumb) cap rates.

Paul bought that building and it worked out... especially since he later had some serious health problems, his operating company went bust, but he and his family were able to hold onto the building, rent it out and survive what otherwise could have been a devastating financial crunch.

...

Now let's look at the cap rate for a small investment property. Let's use as an example, a multi-residential building I'll call "Langlier Place," which has 12, 1-bedroom units and 36, 2-bedroom units.

Cap rates use net operating income where NOI is found by subtracting operating costs that the owner must pay from revenues received. Operating costs do not include either depreciation or mortgage interest and principal. This is because cap rates remove from their calculation the debt structure of the owner. Obviously, a large, well-funded REIT (real estate investment trust), penfund (pension fund), pubco (publicly traded company), bank or insurance company will have a lower COF (cost of funds)[60] than a typical private investor so, in a way, cap rates remove institutional bias.

In other words, cap rates can be useful to compare one possible investment with another similar one (similar in terms of quality, location, age, type of use, etc)—they remove the impact of different capital structures.

Langlier Place—Owner's Pro Forma—Appraiser's Pro Forma

Revenues

	YEAR 1	YEAR 2	YEAR 3
Rent	$688,000	$694,000	$698,000
Parking and Laundry	$ 24,000	$ 24,800	$ 26,400
Total	$712,000	$718,800	$724,400

Expenses

Realty taxes..	$ 52,800
Water..	$ 9,800
Hydro...	nil*
Insurance..	$ 7,800
Maintenance and Repairs.......................................	$ 5,500
Painting..	$12,000
Supplies..	$ 1,300
Elevator maintenance...	$ 1,100
Accounting and Legal...	$ 3,000
Superintendent...	$ 22,000
Mortgage Payments** (Principal and Interest)............	$404,186
Total Operating Costs and Mortgage Payments..........	$519,486

Potential Gross Income

12, 1-bedroom units @ market rent of $900 each...........	$129,600
36, 2-bedroom units @ market rent of $1,325 each......	$572,400
Sub-total..	$702,000

---

[60] Large well-capitalized firms are today able to borrow large amounts (often denominated in Euros) at negative interest rates. On July 19th 2017, CBC news reported that the CIBC (Canadian Imperial Back of Commerce) had issued 1.25 billion Euros of debt at a negative rate; ie, borrowers paid the bank to take and hold onto their money. Now if I gave you 1.25 billion Euros with a negative interest rate, do you think you could build a successful real estate investment portfolio? Of course, you could. Which is also why, as a private investor, you have to stay out of the way of these behemoths otherwise it's like you challenging Usain Bolt to a 100-meter race, one you are *guaranteed* to lose. This is why most individuals can't buy regional shopping centers, large office complexes, or enormous residential rental portfolios… they are competing with institutions that can make sense of cap rates as low as 2.75%, 3.25%, 3.75% pa. For my clients, we aim to buy property these days with not less than 6% cap rates and often much more, especially in smaller towns and in the commercial/industrial space.

Additional Income

Parking, 42 spaces @ $55 per month...................	$ 27,720
Laundry, 5 w/d @ $30 per month.........................	$ 1,800
Total Potential Gross Income.....................................	$731,520
Less vacancy allowance of 6%..................................	-$ 43,912
Effective Gross Income...	$687,628

Operating Costs

Realty taxes..	$ 52,800
Water...	$ 9,800
Hydro...	nil*
Insurance..	$ 7,800
Maintenance and Repairs..	$ 5,500
Painting..	$12,000
Supplies..	$ 1,300
Elevator maintenance...	$ 1,100
Accounting and Legal...	$ 3,000
Superintendent...	$ 22,000
Property Management (3% of Effective Gross Income)........	$ 20,629
Total Operating Costs...	$135,929
Net Operating Income.............................	$551,699
Selling Price...	$6,500,000
Cap Rate..	8.49% pa

(* Paid by tenants.)
(** Mortgage is a Canadian mortgage of $4.2 million with an interest rate of 7.25% and amortization period of 20 years.)

You will note that the cap rate for Langlier Place is calculated using a semi-net operating income. This shows how difficult and seat-of-the-pants cap rates can be. But as long as you know how the cap rate you are being quoted was calculated, it's a useful way to compare one property with another. But what if someone is using NOI and someone else is using a semi-net number and someone else is using gross income? Use cap rates carefully.

ROE[61]

Another simple (and very approximate) way to measure returns is as follows:

Total ROE = ROE (cash-on-cash return) + ROE (general real property inflation) + ROE (average principal repaid) + ROE (tax advantage on unearned rents)

Here is an example taken from some work I did for a client of mine who bought an 80,000 square foot industrial building, in part for their own use and in part to lease out to third parties (most of whom are in their supply chain so that there were some operational synergies that don't show up in these calculations). I have changed the numbers a bit to protect their identity.

---

[61] ROE (return on equity) can be different from ROI (return on investment). If an investor puts $100,000 into a project, and, say, one quarter of that is in the form of equity and the balance is debt, while an entrepreneur invests $25,000 (all as equity), the investor will be most interested in his or her ROI, the entrepreneur, ROE.

Sample Calculation of Approximate ROE for Acquisition of Soda Pop HQ

Cost to Acquire Soda Pop HQ Building 80,000 sf $60.00 per sf	$4,800,000
Equity 25%	$1,200,000
First Mortgage 75%	$3,600,000
Annual Payment 6% 20 year amortization	($313,864.41) per year
Total Rent 80,000 sf $9 per sf per year triple net[62]	$720,000 per year
less vacancy allowance 10%	($72,000) per year
less real estate commission on rents 5.00%	($32,400) per year
Total Net, Net, Net Rent[63]	$615,600 per year
Total NOI	$615,600 per year (same as triple next rent)
Cap rate	12.825% pa
less annual payment of mortgage	($313,864.41) per year
Total cash-on-cash return	$301,736 per year
Cash on cash ROE	25.14% per year
plus approximate Annual Inflation in Building Value 0.75% pa	3% per year
plus wealth effect of AVERAGE annual principal repayments	15% per year ($180,000 per year)
Total approximate ROE	43% per year

This is an arithmetic sum of all the different types or return on real estate and tends to be higher than IRR, which is, as I've already said, is more like a weighted average. IRR is the preferred method of calculation of returns by investment professionals.

...

---

[62] Triple net rents were "invented" in the 1980s as a way to put more of the burden of owning and operating commercial and industrial properties squarely on the shoulders of tenants in these buildings. It protected landlords from inflationary costs. Remember, inflation topped out in the US and Canada at 14.76 % in April 1980 (source, https://inflationdata.com/articles/inflation-cpi-consumer-price-index-1980-1989/) so if you were a commercial property owner and all your tenants were on gross leases, it wouldn't take many years of double digit inflation to find that you are paying your tenants to rent your space. Net, net, net leases mean that commercial tenants pay, in addition to basic (minimum) rent, landlord operating costs, utilities, and property taxes. Property owners also sometimes retail utilities and other services like tech packages to their tenants as well as put in allowances for administrative costs, vacancy costs (making their tenant base pay for the cost of all common areas no matter how much vacancy the building has), property management, repairs to building systems, even structural elements and re-roofing. They can also charge percentage rents (especially on retail/restaurant space) where landlords get a share of tenant revenues. These commercial leases are often long-winded, multi-page contracts heavily weighted in favor of property owners who pay real estate lawyers a lot of money to concoct these largely indecipherable documents.

[63] Note, once you know what the triple net rent is, you also know the property's NOI, net operating income; ie, they're the same because commercial/industrial tenants pay all other costs, save and except the landlord's mortgage.

Toronto real estate is out of control

Any time a client is thinking of purchasing a 6-plex in downtown Toronto based on these numbers, you can be pretty sure a property bubble has formed:

downtown Toronto 6-plex cap rate calculation			
rental income	$	194,412.00 pa	
vacancy allowance		($2,916.18)	1.50%
rental expenses		($52,325)	
property management		($15,552.96)	8%
NOI, net operating income	$	123,617.86 pa	
list price		$7,349,000	
cap rate		1.7% pa	
E&OE			

A 1.7% cap rate is far below what is needed to make this property cashflow.

The only reason I can think of why someone might buy this is the greater fool theory, which works along these lines:

> *It's like when you played musical chairs as a little girl or boy—there was always someone left without a chair when the music stopped. It's called the greater fool theory because you believe (irrationally) that there is **always** someone stupider than you who'll buy it for **more** next year... until, of course, there isn't, ie, you run out of fools.*

Even with animations (clever revenue enhancements), the cap rate only creeps up to 2.2%, viz:

animations				
parking	$9,000 pa	$125 per mth		
tech packages	$9,720 pa	$135 per mth	revenue	
tech packages	($2,400) pa		cost	
admin fee	$7,848.75 pa	15%		
property management fee	$15,552.96 pa			
total	$39,722 pa			
NOI, net operating income $	163,339.57 pa			
list price	$7,349,000			
cap rate	2.2% pa	with animations		

Still completely unacceptable.

So what *should* someone actually pay for this place?

Well, if your target cap rate is, say, 6.4% pa (which is about where it should be or, at a minimum, above 5%), this is easy to calculate—

desired cap rate	6.4% pa
suggested purchase price	$2,552,180.78

So a purchase price of around $2.5 million for this 6-plex makes sense.

$7.349 million?

Not so much.

...

More on the Greater Fool Theory

We've been seeing a lot of this in overheated markets like Vancouver, Toronto[64], and San Francisco, but when you start seeing it in small Ontario communities; you know markets are becoming really stupid.

You should NEVER buy property that doesn't cashflow from day 1 or at least in year 1.

Even break-even is a bad idea. MAKING MONEY is always a good financial strategy. Always.

If your properties cashflow and the market turns down, you can ignore these cycles like Warren Buffett does from his home in Omaha Nebraska.

If you are investing in rural or smaller markets look for cap rates of at least 9% and preferably 10% to 12% pa. These markets probably won't have the same real estate inflation as bigger, more dynamic cities so as a real estate investor you have to make up for that with higher cashflow…

Even in large cities, look for 5.5% to 8.5%. Anything less can spell trouble if vacancies climb, interest rates increase, or property values fall.

…

---

[64] TREB, the Toronto Real Estate Board, reported in early August 2017 that year-over-year sales had declined by 40% and prices by 19% in TO so you see—irrational exuberance has its limits aided, of course, by the government of Ontario's imposition of a 15% LTT (Land Transfer Tax) on foreign-based buyers of Toronto real estate. But even a 19% decline is not enough, not nearly enough, to bridge the gap between the asking price for that 6-plex discussed above ($7.35 million) and what I would consider a reasonable acquisition at $2.55 million…

Why Not to Invest in Real Estate

I realize the title of this section can be read in two ways—why not invest in real estate or why not to invest in real estate. I wish to address the latter here.

What are the negatives of investing in real estate?

I put this section in here because some of the folks I coach are very risk averse and I get asked this question... a lot.

There are risks—real estate investing is not all rosy. So here're a few pitfalls to watch for:

a) Transaction costs are significant especially if you trade frequently. Transaction costs may include: legal fees on completion, accounting fees/consultations (especially if you are selling, you'll want to know what your income or capital gains tax liability might be), land transfer taxes, adjustments on closing (eg, for pre-paid realty taxes or deposits/pre-paid rent), HST (Goods and Services Taxes, Harmonized Sales Taxes in Canada on certain types of real estate like residential rentals and almost all commercial property), withholding taxes for non-residents (income tax withholdings), realtor fees, title insurance, property insurance, mortgage insurance (on highly leveraged transactions), mortgage broker fees, appraisal fee, land survey fee, utility hook-up fees, special assessments (on condo purchases), prepaid utilities (like for a full oil tank), new home warranty enrollment fee, sales taxes on chattels purchased, interest adjustments, mortgage penalties (if you're a seller and your mortgage is closed), building inspection fees, septic inspections and well testing (for rural property) and so forth.

b) Lack of liquidity—real estate sales and closings can take a long time. Widely-held stocks, for example, can be sold in a few minutes or hours.

c) Bad tenants and difficulties with rent control and other forms of regulation (eg, the RTA, Residential Tenancies Act, in Ontario).

d) Cost overruns on construction or renovation as well deficiencies in their work.

e) Storms, floods, earthquakes, forest fires, and other natural disasters.

f) Vacancies.

g) Outdated design, floor plans, uses (eg, a few years ago, everyone wanted to build server farms until they realized that servers are small and getting smaller and more powerful all the time and, hence, don't take up a lot of floor space).

h) Delays in completion of new construction or renovation.

i) Long planning cycles made more difficult by NIMBY (Not In My Back Yard) behavior/protests/delays.

j) Long delays in acquiring building permits or other development permissions.

k) Low appraisals and low loan-to-value ratios for mortgage purposes.

l) Degradation of the neighborhood/bad neighbors.

m) Increased costs—electricity and insurance especially.

n) Surprise maintenance and costs from deferred maintenance.

o) Dishonest property managers[65].

p) Down cycles in the market.

q) Being upside down on equity (where, because of a downturn in the local marketplace, your mortgage principal becomes greater than the FMV of your property).

r) Negative changes in tax regimes like increasing capital gains taxes, reductions in allowable Capital Cost Allowance deductions against income and other income, rapid increases in realty taxes and gross leases where higher costs cannot easily be passed on to tenants, surprise government levies like special taxes levied on foreign buyers in Vancouver and Toronto or new regulation of real estate services such as Airbnb.

---

[65] It is surprising how much residential rent is still collected in cash. A dishonest superintendent who runs off with one or two months rent from your tenants can bankrupt you in a hurry.

s) Real estate is an intensely local business; success by you in one market does not necessarily translate into success in another.

t) Trouble getting appropriate insurance at affordable prices.

u) Political risk, civil unrest, and war directly impact real estate values.

v) Deflation.

w) As the population ages, more competition from retirement homes for tenants.

x) More tenants buying their own property.

y) Population decrease, changing tastes, increases in dwelling occupancy rates (eg, millennials staying with parents longer).

z) RISING INTEREST RATES.

So there are risks in owning real estate, and there is no way to avoid these entirely. One way to improve your odds is, of course, to buy low, which we have already talked about above. A good friend of mine, Barry Lett, a real estate veteran and a survivor of many real estate down cycles, once told me: "You don't make money when you sell real estate; you make it when you buy." If you buy low enough, it makes up for many sins later on.

Now there are a few other things you can do to somewhat de-risk the process—you can invest in more than one building, in more than one type of real estate, in more than one neighborhood and in more than one city as well as perhaps more than one country.

One last note. Former chief justice of the SCC (Supreme Court of Canada) Bora Laskin once said that insurance companies are larger firms that exist solely for the purpose of taking advantage of smaller companies and individuals. He obviously took a dim view of the industry.

I have always wondered why more real estate investors don't self-insure. This would only apply to large sophisticated investors, of course. But if you owned 50 or 100 or 1,000 separate buildings in say a couple of cities, perhaps it would make sense to only have liability insurance on them, and maybe not even liability coverage. I mean what is the chance that all 50 of them will burn down at the same time? You would need to do some careful analysis but you might well be better off paying property insurance to yourself—ie, build your own sinking fund and self insure. After 15 or 20 years, I am guessing you would have quite a sizeable fund that if you ever did decide to sell your portfolio, guess what? It belongs to you.

...

The problem with deposits

Sometimes it doesn't matter if your realtor is Moses, sellers can be unreasonable.

For example, in a recent case, sellers wanted a deposit of $75,000 on the purchase of a small shopping plaza. This is a terrible idea for any buyer because today no brokerage can release a deposit without BOTH the seller and buyer agreeing to sign a mutual release and termination.

Which means an unreasonable seller can simply decide not to sign the mutual release and termination simply because "they don't feel like it."

So then how does a buyer get his or her money back?

They don't.

What the heck?

Nope. It sits in the real estate brokerage's trust account 'til the sun burns itself out unless the buyer sues the sellers in court, is successful, and gets a COURT ORDER forcing the brokerage to release the darn deposit. Or they negotiate from a weak position, made weaker because of this one-sided regulatory rule.

I had a client in Toronto who had to give up half (half!) her deposit to the sellers to get (part of) her money back because the sellers said, "We don't think she tried hard enough to fulfill her conditions," even though the agreement said it was up to her in her "sole and absolute discretion."

As long as you make reasonable efforts to fulfill your conditions, you should be able to get out of any agreement.

For example, suppose you have a financing condition. And you get an offer to finance the deal at say an interest rate of 4.99%. The fact that you got an offer, any offer, is not by itself sufficient. You might not like 4.99% because you were hoping for 2.99%. So in your *sole and absolute* judgment, this offer (of finance) was unacceptable because, maybe, you cannot afford 4.99%; that is, you had budgeted for 2.99% instead.

But to unreasonable sellers, they can say (incorrectly) that because you got any offer of finance, in their opinion, you should have waived your condition/provided them with a notice of fulfillment of condition.

In litigation, no matter how "right" you think you are, there is always a risk of a judge finding against you.

It's a terrible, lopsided system, weighted in favor of sellers.

If I had my druthers, I would write in deposits of $2 on all my agreements... because of this.

What's the solution?

Well, I told my Toronto client NOT to sue; instead she had her attorney register her notice of termination and mutual release on title as well as her APS (agreement of purchase and sale) at a cost of about $150 in legal fees so the sellers could not sell or remortgage their property without first dealing with this "lien."

Sure enough, they sold their property a few months later, and, when their lawyer discovered this issue on title, and after a temper tantrum, the sellers were more willing to negotiate. Still, my client lost half her deposit having done nothing wrong.

The moral of this story?

BE CAREFUL BUT BE SMART.

And then on to the next thing!

...

Things to ask your contractor or renovator before you sign

Some of the biggest issues in the real estate investment business are—cost overruns and delay during construction as well as dealing with deficiencies from construction and renovation *post project*, securing proper and sufficient financing then getting decent appraisals and loan to value ratios upon completion.

Before you sign on with any contractor or renovator, here's my checklist of items to go over with them:

1. Start Date
2. Expected Completion Date
3. Initial Deposit Required
4. Progress Payments Expected/payment schedule/plan
5. Performance Measurements/meeting milestones/joint monitoring project schedule/critical path analysis
6. Gross Max Price, GMP/Costing/Bonding
7. Contingency allowance... to be used for quality assurance
8. Cost and time savings incentives/sharing
9. References including former clients/experience with projects similar to this
10. Safety record/daily clean up
11. Person(s) in charge/communications with client/after hours emergency contact
12. Dealing with change orders
13. Termination
14. Choice of designer/architect
15. Acquisition of building permit/responsibility
16. Union Participation (mostly for commercial jobs)
17. Choice of sub-trades
18. Sub-trade contribution to project sponsorship (mostly for commercial jobs)
19. Contractor contribution to project sponsorship/other project support and influence (mostly for commercial jobs)
20. Financing—intros to lenders, investors, penfunds, funders (mostly for commercial jobs)
21. Financial Guarantees (mostly for commercial jobs)
22. Process for and cost of dealing with post-project deficiencies
23. Future Business

WIP, work-in-progress/next steps

Finally, lay out next steps and who is doing what/when over the:

-next 30 days
-next 60-90 days
-beyond 90 days

Make sure you ask for and receive a complete project schedule and, if possible, ask them to play it out using critical path scheduling software.

I show what that might look like in a youtube video, *critical path methodology & scheduling explained*, which you can find on the Prof Bruce channel, https://youtu.be/hA5G4KvVmnk?list=PLd3QdcBlEm9-b9B3sAnGd86s79M8ib_P3.

...

Why Real Estate is a Unique Asset Class

Real estate has some attributes that I believe are unique to this asset class. Here are ten of them:

1. You can rent real estate to third parties. (Try that with gold or stocks assuming you are not using exotic financial instruments.)

2. By renting to a third party you are benefiting from a wealth effect; every year a renter is paying off part of your mortgage for you—when you sell that property or refinance it, the decrease in principal owing goes into your pocket (assuming that the price you sell for (or appraised value if you are doing a refi) is more than what you paid for the property plus transaction costs).

3. You receive unearned (and untaxed) rent on self-occupied property after your mortgage is retired.

4. When your city builds infrastructure around you, when your neighbors improve their properties, when the density, intensity and overall area of the city increases, demand for your property increases (and presumably its price too) without you having done a thing—as a result your property value benefits from positive externalities.

5. In many countries, you are allowed to deduct a non-cash capital cost allowance (depreciation) against income—a significant tax advantage from holding real estate assets.

6. Real estate generally doesn't go out of fashion.

7. Land, unlike, say, ideas, is in fixed supply. (Many cities are further restricting supply by limiting urban expansion. Great if you are a sitting owner. Not so great if you are a first time homebuyer or newly minted entrepreneur.)

8. The amount of real estate consumed per capita has been steadily increasing almost everywhere for a long time as average dwelling occupancy rates and family size go down.

9. In-migration to urban areas from rural areas is continuing everywhere as cities benefit from network effects[66] so overall demand for urban real estate is increasing secularly, and, at the same time, city after city are restricting boundary expansion making their land and buildings more expensive.

10. Lastly, real estate offers you a unique opportunity to develop a sustainable business model even if you aren't a genius. Real estate develops a concession or franchise for its owners because once you own a particular location, axiomatically, no one else can own at that location.

Everyone knows that real estate is all about LOCATION, LOCATION, LOCATION but perhaps people don't realize why that is so crucial. For you to have a business that will nurture you and your family for a long period of time, you need to have some type of sustainable competitive advantage.

Imagine how difficult it is to run a company like Apple or Alphabet or Amazon or how difficult it is to paint like Rembrandt. Not everyone can be Steve Jobs, Larry Page or Jeff Bezos or create artworks like Rembrandt Harmenszoon van Rijn. Real estate held in fee simple (the highest form of title an owner can have) gives you a franchise forever that tough competitors like Microsoft or Google can't take away from you—IT'S A BUSINESS MODEL FOR DUMMIES, like moi.

A friend of mine owns a great site at the intersection of Woodroffe and Carling avenues in Ottawa. He comes from a tech background but his chosen personal investment vehicle is… real estate. He and his

---

[66] Effect that a single person using a good or a service has on the total perceived value of that product or service for others. The more who use the product or service, the higher it's value becomes to the entire group—examples would include the internet and social networks as well as, of course, the telephone and fax machine. The larger the group of people with access to the internet, social networks, telephones or facsimile machines, the more valuable these systems are to the people who already use them. Source: http://www.businessdictionary.com/definition/network-effects.html with edits by the author. In an urban setting, once a road or bridge or transit system is built, its cost becomes a sunk cost so when more people use it (up to a point) more value is created for society as a whole. These are known as public goods. Indeed, a city (as a rule) becomes more productive as more people and more diverse uses crowd into the same space thereby increasing collisionable hours, creativity and productivity via widespread skill sharing, specialization, and knowledge transfer.

partner built a new, high concept strip mall (not intended as an oxymoron) on top of the old foundation of a previous building and, because of its high traffic location, great visibility, and good design features; they get rents that are about 1/3 higher than other nearby properties. I mean how difficult can it be to own a great location and then have people come up to you, one after the other, to offer you top dollar for your space, year after year?

...

Warren Buffett Methodology Applied to Real Estate Investing

The real estate investment coaching I do is based on an adaptation of some of the strategies that Warren Buffett brought to stock market investing. Here's the formula:

1. Buy targeted, smart, well-located properties in a town or city with a buoyant and sustainable economy and in land use sectors where large, low cost-of-funds players (banks, REITs, insurance companies, pension funds, publicly traded companies) are largely absent; the places where you invest should possess local economies that have diverse and stable engines of growth (eg, government, education, health, real estate and construction, tech, tourism, general industry (catering to a local market), advanced services, plus healthy maker, retail and entertainment sectors)

"Don't wait to buy real estate. Buy real estate and wait," Will Rogers, actor

2. Buy and hold... longterm; ignore market cycles; do not flip or you will flip 'til you flop
3. Only buy when your heart, gut instincts and head are all in alignment (ie, you are passionate about it, you have a good "feeling" about it, and your analysis shows it's a good investment)

"Every person who invests in well-selected real estate in a growing section of a prosperous community adopts the surest and safest method of becoming independent, for real estate is the basis of wealth," Theodore Roosevelt, US president

4. Once you have decided on a sector you know and understand, and a business model that works, do three things—FOCUS, FOCUS, FOCUS on it—the most successful entrepreneurs (not just in real estate but this is true in every field) are those who do ONE thing really, really well and treat everything else they'd like to do as a hobby
5. Real estate is a local business, so local knowledge is essential—stick to at most one or two geographies and try to cluster your investments in close geographical proximity to each other
6. KISS—keep your ownership structure as simple as possible (but no simpler) using personal names where indicated—I've found that interleaved, complex corporate structures are only good for accountants and lawyers and tax preparers not so much for investors
7. In the beginning, use maximum OPM, other people's money, leverage and other financing
8. Avoid partners, use debt instead or, on occasion, investors
9. Distinguish between good debt (mortgage debt, secured debt) and bad debt (unsecured, personal debt, credit card debt)
10. Raise bootstrap capital (government grants, scrip, strategic investment, supplier credit, sponsorship, self-directed RRSP mortgages, signage, SBL, government-guaranteed, small business loans...) to leverage your investment

"Buying real estate is not only the best way, the quickest way, the safest way, but the only way to become wealthy," Marshall Field, department store owner

11. Determine the HABU (highest and best use) for each property and develop/renovate/add to that level as well as analyze each property using a spreadsheet to determine its IRR (internal rate of return) and cap rate
12. Treat even your principal residence as a rental so it becomes an asset not a liability
13. Add value and differentiation—animate your portfolio to increase cap rates through design/renovation/addition including things such as in-home suites, coach houses, tech packages, home

automation, workshops, storage sheds, proper leasing, micro suites, direct access to the outside, severances and much more... boost returns

14. Manage your properties well—ie, no deferred maintenance!

15. Before you refinance, get a CMA (comparative market analysis) done professionally[67] to support a decent appraisal then share it with your appraiser beforehand—if he or she refuses to look at your CMA, fire them and get someone else because if you get a low appraisal, it can quickly become a cashflow problem for you

16. Refinance and pull out funds *tax free*

17. Rinse and repeat—it's the only real perpetual motion machine in the known universe

"If you're not going to put money in real estate, where else?" Tamir Sapir, Manhattan real estate investor

18. At some point stop buying and use your cashflow to increase principal paydown (by shrinking your amortization period) so you can pay off all your debt faster

19. Once your mortgages are paid off, *never* pledge your portfolio for anything else—it's your "iron reserve," a PB4L[68], treat it as such

20. Pass on your portfolio efficiently and effectively to your heirs using joint titles.

"Now, one thing I tell everyone is learn about real estate. Repeat after me: real estate provides the highest returns, the greatest values and the least risk," Armstrong Williams, political talk show host

So answer a few questions for me:

-Do you want to learn how to build a PB4L, one with a business model that ensures the harder you work, the more money you will make?

"No one who can rise before dawn three hundred sixty days a year fails to make his family rich," Malcolm Gladwell

-Do you want to learn how to build an above average real estate portfolio that'll provide for you and your family in perpetuity?

"Money isn't everything, you know, but you can buy freedom with it and freedom is everything," Arian Foster

- Do you want to learn from someone who has actually been a successful developer, investor and real estate broker as well as Ottawa Senators founder plus has a PhD in urban economics?

- Are you tired of the low returns you've been getting on your mutual funds, stocks, bonds, insurance, 401(k)s, GICs, T-bills, LIRAs, IRAs, IPPs, TFSAs, RRSPs, precious metals, gold, and bank savings account?

"Real estate investment coaching with Bruce Firestone has been a great experience. When I first came to Bruce, I explained to him our current situation and that I was looking to expand my real estate portfolio. At that time, I was basically out of ideas—my wife and I had purchased triplex in Little Italy and it was

---

[67] In most jurisdictions, realtors are permitted to do CMAs. CMAs tend to value property at current levels. Appraisals (which have to be done by accredited appraisers) tend to be lower for two main reasons—appraisers look backward, at the past, and also they take direction from lenders not investors so they are usually much more conservative than realtor assessments.

[68] Personal business for life.

doing ok, but I thought we could be doing better. I thought it was probably time to move on to a new investment but Prof Bruce opened my eyes to a new concept—one he calls "animation." Instead of immediately moving on to a new property, we examined my current rental property. How could we animate it? We looked at various options. In the end we ended up converting two of the three units into Airbnb suites. We've now increased our cash low from that property by a factor of 10!" Dave B, technology worker, real estate investor

- Do you want to learn how to get deals properly financed and closed?

- Do you want to know how to find investors and cash to help you fund your dreams?

- Do you want to know the secrets to getting higher returns via real estate investing?

"I realize now that it was my fear holding me back and I'm glad that Prof Bruce helped me push through all that fear, because it has been a great learning experience. I can't imagine my life without having bought my first investment property... I would probably still be hoping and dreaming to do what I'm doing now. It was a very important lesson to me, that you've just got to push through, no matter what could be on the other side," Paul C, former public servant, engineer and novice real estate investor

- Do you want to find a great piece of real estate for your enterprise, one you can own not rent, animate and profit from?

- Do you want to find a great location for your tech company, your service business, your organization/not-for-profit/charity and not get taken advantage of by your landlord?

- Do you want to learn how to buy smart, hold and grow rich using Warren Buffett's philosophy of tax-free refinancing?

"Wow, I was just able to explain everything about a complex multi-residential deal I'm working on to an overseas buyer. Prof Bruce, I can't believe how much I've grown thanks to you!" Roman Monaenkov, Keller Williams – Lifestyle Realty Team

If you have 12 minutes, you can watch this Prof Bruce video capture on youtube that sums up what I do,

How to really provide for yourself and your family,
https://youtu.be/0yXycpt6axo

If you'd like to know more about the above, please reach out to:

Bruce M Firestone, B Eng (civil), M Eng-Sci, PhD
Century 21 Explorer Realty Inc broker
Ottawa Senators founder
Real Estate Investment and Business coach
1-613-762-8884
bruce.firestone@century21.ca
www.twitter.com/ProfBruce
www.profbruce.tumblr.com/archive
www.brucemfirestone.com
MAKING IMPOSSIBLE POSSIBLE

...

Flipping versus buy and hold

Why is it that people flip real estate 'til they flop?
Here's why:

-they underestimate the cost of renos
-they underestimate the time it will take to do the renos
-they underestimate the cost of financing and holding property while renos are underway and when they are trying to flip the property
-they don't factor in the cost of their own time
-they don't factor in the risk that they will not find a buyer at a price that makes it even semi worthwhile to do this
-they don't factor in market risks—interest rates going up, political unrest, economic crashes, market bubble bursting...
-people are like gamblers—they only report (and sometimes even remember) their winners
-the "setup" cost for each project is big—the cost of completion (things like land transfer tax (welcome tax in Quebec), legal fees, due diligence costs such as building inspection, plumbing inspection, foundation inspection, structural report, lease review, environmental assessment etc), the value of your time spent searching and negotiating for a suitable property to purchase as well as the time spent financing it plus organizing your team of contractors to renovate the place, the cost of marketing including realtor fees, more legal fees, staging costs, brochures, photography, website support, advertising...
-there is a hidden cost too just to get mindshare—you only have limited bandwidth and a project like this will suck up a lot of your creativity as well as time meaning there are other (possibly more profitable) projects you don't get to do
-it's not that easy to buy undervalued property since the internet has done a good job of providing more democratic information... even the most motivated seller these days can learn approximately what his or her property is worth in a few keystrokes[69]
-lastly, there is this: say you renovate a property for $100,000, which produces a great cap rate for you with a nice positive cashflow. However, your appraiser only values the renos you did at $75,000. The reason? The comparables he or she is using won't support a higher value. Well, if you are flipping it, maybe the market agrees with your appraiser, and you take a hit on your flip; ie, you lose money. But if you are holding it for the next 7, 10, 20 years, whatever, and then passing it on to your heirs, the only thing that matters to you and your family is positive cashflow (and a great cap rate).

The only caveat is this—you have to find ways to convince, cajole, cadge a better appraisal from your appraiser if you are trying to refinance to pay for your reno costs or to take money out of this project to do another one. Low appraisals are a big problem in that event.

It's why, before we even allow a lender's appraiser to set foot on a property, we do, as I said earlier, our own realtor-provided CMA (comparative market analysis) using not only comparables to establish FMV, fair market value, but also cost to complete less depreciation as well as arrive at a value using an income approach.

I mean how is an appraiser going to know that you added in-floor heating, extra insulation, cured drainage or structural issues or even replaced your roof unless they look at your CMA and the list of work done (and its cost) that you provide?

If your appraiser refuses to look at your CMA, do your best Donald Trump impression, and say two words before they even get into the building, "You're fired!"

---

[69] Many futurists are predicting that appraisers will go extinct—replaced by AI using data provided by buy-sell platforms used by masses of sellers and buyers. This is, in my view, an all too likely fate for residential appraisers. Commercial work is less likely to be automated in the near future due to its innate complexity as well as much smaller and more isolated/walled-off data sets.

By the way, you can download a sample spreadsheet, which shows how we do CMAs based on three approaches—comps, cost to complete, and income from:
https://www.dropbox.com/s/3zolbucldtms51o/QQ-abbeyhill-analysis-16-sept-2016-cap-rate-appraiser.xls?dl=0.

...

What info you should have on each property you buy

What info should you have on hand (which today means digitized with good quality names that you can find on your backed-up computer) for each of your properties? Below is my list.

I'm sure there is more you can and should add.

By the way, most of this info you'll also need before/during/after you make a serious offer on a new property…

1. geo warehouse report (land titles showing ownership history, property assessment, perimeter, area, frontage, depth, plot plan, PIN[70] #, roll # etc)
2. enhanced report (CMA—comparative market analysis, what other properties in the area sold for)
3. MPAC (Municipal Property Assessment Corporation) assessments (last two years)
4. property taxes (last two years)
5. survey by a registered land surveyor
6. building plans including as-built floor plans
7. environmental report (mainly for commercial property, phase 1 report[71] at a minimum)
8. well potability test (rural property)
9. well record (rural property)
10. septic permit and septic inspection report (rural property)
11. copies of leases
12. copies of equipment rental contracts (eg hot water tank rental agreement)
13. property management agreements (manager, snow, lawn care etc)
14. mortgage statements
15. copies of all warranties (eg, roof, HVAC[72] etc)
16. copy of agreement of purchase and sale
17. lawyer's report on closing
18. pro pictures of the property (taken after renovations are complete but before tenant move-in)
19. copy of condo declaration (if condominium)
20. copy of appraisal
21. copy of building inspection report
22. spreadsheet for financials
23. occupancy certificate
24. copies of all utility payments
25. copy of soil test (commercial)
26. copy of hydro geo report (rural property)
27. copy of MLS listing for sale (or for rent)

Believe it or not, I have most of this on most of the properties I've bought and sold on my computer, backed up in two other places plus also in the cloud.

---

[70] Property identification number.
[71] A phase 1 environmental site assessment is done by an environmental consulting company. They look at chain of title (to identify earlier owners such as dry cleaners, utility companies, automotive repair garages, industrial firms, etc who may have occupied the lands and who are potential sources/indicators of possible pollution), and aerial photographs (often going back a century or more). They also walk the lands to inspect them. If conditions warrant, they can recommend a phase 2 assessment where drilling is used to provide soil and groundwater samples for testing. Phase 3 is supervised cleanup of any contamination and obtaining a record of site condition from the relevant environmental authority indicating the site has been cleaned up or the pollution contained to the point where (prescribed types of) development can take place.
[72] Heating, ventilation and air conditioning.

I am a demi-god of information, and look ever so smart when I produce deliveries for amazed clients/lenders/lawyers/suppliers in a matter of seconds… by searching my database, since, you see, my computer is the other ½ of my brain…

…

Every Real Estate Project Requires These Steps

For each real estate project you undertake, you should have the discipline to take these steps:

1. Highest and best use analysis
2. Functional program
3. Concept plan
4. Differentiation and animation strategy
5. Marketing and leasing plan
6. Business model
7. Budget
8. Financial analysis (IRR and cap rate)
9. Finance plan
10. Cost control plan/quality assurance plan
11. CPM, critical path schedule
12. Launch clients
13. Sponsors
14. Operational plan

Remember, every project you undertake, you do so because your head, your heart and your gut are all in alignment. That is, you've done the analysis, you are passionate about your project and your instinct tells you this is a good idea. If one of those is saying, "no," abandon ship.

…

How to value property

There are many ways to value your real property—

1. by completing a CMA, comparative market analysis, yourself or asking a realtor to do one for you, comparing what other similar properties have recently sold for in the same general area within the recent past (aka "comps")

2. by using a cost approach—that is, determine the cost to replace/reconstruct an identical structure so that it is comparable to your existing building less accumulated depreciation
3. by using an income approach—dividing expected NOI (net operating income) by the cap rate for this type of property in that location
4. by spreadsheet analysis using IRR, Internal Rate of Return and comparing it to IRRs for other investment opportunities
5. by obtaining an appraisal from an accredited appraiser
6. by what a willing buyer and willing seller agree to, both being knowledgeable and having adequate access to reasonably complete information over a reasonable period of time without any undue stress
7. by looking at assessed value or by dividing realty taxes by the applicable mill rate
8. by using a residual approach (usually to determine land value) by subtracting the cost/yield of development from net sales to ascertain a price you would be willing/able to pay for a site
9. by experience.

...

How to Buy Low

Remember what I've said before: you make money in real estate when you buy not when you sell or refinance so buy low.

Here're a few pointers that'll help you with that—

-look at property with high DOM values (days on market)
-only buy from *motivated* sellers
-never get involved in multiple offer situations/competitive bidding
-buy handicapped property, the ones no one else wants/buy what no one else will buy (eg, a building owned by a hoarder or a partly finished home where the owner has gone bankrupt and you have the knowledge and expertise to complete the structure/renovation)
-buy *when* no one else is buying (eg, in mid-winter)
-only buy property that cashflows
-buy property with good income potential (which, at least in residential markets, is not usually valued properly because realtors and appraisers use comps (comparables) not cap rates to value property)
-buy in close proximity to where you live (within 60 mins driving distance)
-buy in at most two markets
-buy only property that won't take up too much of your time (microsuites versus rooming houses or airbnb?)
-buy near major employment generators (colleges, universities, government offices, tech parks, hospitals)
-buy places that have decent walk scores—close to transit, shopping, transit, restaurants, learning, parks...
-buy properties that have upside via animation, population growth, close to new development and new infrastructure
-buy where public safety is a priority—safe neighborhoods and good schools
-determine a building's faults then ask for a price abatement
-know your city or town's geography and where markets are hot and where they're not—buy where all boats are rising or close to those areas where all boats are rising/take advantage of new development—if someone builds a huge condo tower, office block, shopping mall... your property nearby is likely to go up in value because demand in the area for EVERYTHING will increase
-buy a lower end property in an already gentrifying neighborhood where you can add differentiation and value amongst other properties that are more expensive than yours giving you plenty of room for value appreciation
-buy property in cities that have sustainable economies—look especially for growing government, education, healthcare, real estate, technology and tourism sectors
-try to buy 20% below market so after you renovate, animate and rent it, you get decent appraisal[73] and refinance—taking your 20% deposit back out and rinse and repeat process—a perpetual motion machine!

...

What Not to Buy?

-in places where zoning and ordinance enforcement is especially strict, which will curtail your ability to animate and improve your revenue streams

---

[73] Do a CMA (comparative market analysis) and provide it to your appraiser before s/he does the appraisal to support a higher valuation. Your realtor can help you with a CMA.

-in already fully priced or overpriced neighborhoods where folks have over-invested in their real estate
-towns or cities with poorly performing economies, high crime rates, low cap rates, low or negative real estate inflation and poor prospects

What to Buy?

I often get asked: what're the best properties to buy?
For most folks, it won't be:
-office buildings
-major shopping plazas
-land
Why?
Well, I expect demand for office buildings to grow slowly, if at all, because of competition from home offices and co-working spaces, based as they are on a booming gig economy.

The competition to acquire assets like major regional shopping centers is fierce with large predators roaming the countryside equipped with ultra low cost (and sometimes negative cost) financing that entrepreneurs just can't match.

And land just takes too damn long to develop in a municipal environment that is rabidly anti-development, and bogged down by a seemingly infinite series of studies and insatiable appetite for public benefits paid for by private developers.

The lowest risk portfolio and one that is within the reach of most people is: a series of residential rental holdings, often single family homes with an in-home suite or coach house in back.

I wrote to a client of mine recently, a woman in her 30s that I coach. Here are some of the things I suggested she should look for:

-what price are you paying/remember you make money in real estate when you buy not when you sell so buy smart
-what will it cost to animate/add an in-home suite with separate entrance, add a tech package, add backyard storage shed(s) or workshops...
-how close is it to existing transit
-how close is it to major employment nodes (colleges/hospitals/tech/gov't)
-how walkable is it (again how close to jobs/shopping/learning/mass transit/health care/recreation ...)
-how rentable is it
-check out neighborhood demographics (who is your target renter)
-neighborhood safety and desirability
-presence (or absence) of gentrification/folks renovating/adding to their homes/tearing down existing ones and replacing them with bigger homes or doubles
-proportion of renters (smaller proportion of neighborhood renting is better)
-ability to add coach house
-locate closer to downtown/not seen as suburban
-does the area support mixed use (ie, are services available nearby, eg, c-store, walk-in clinic...)
-is the area densifying (eg, doubles replacing singles) and intensifying (eg, more work from home)

What to look for in a bungalow or split-level:

-location
-price
-DOM
-faults/price abatement

-min lot size for larger coach house
-separate entry for basement
-frontyard parking capability
-garage office/garage micro suite
-at least 2 baths on main level (including ensuite) and 1 more on lower level

...

Canadian investment options

What are some investment alternatives for Canadians? In no particular order, here are a few. Knowing what is right for you is non-trivial and requires work by you and a *trusted* adviser.

RRSP
LIRA
RESP
TFSA
GIC
Term Deposit
Savings Account
Term Life Insurance
Life Insurance
IPP, Independent Pension Plan
Corporate or government Pension Plan
Own business
Own home or condo
Rental property
Land
Gold/precious metals
Art
Coins
Collectibles
Stocks/bonds/derivatives
Mutual Fund
Stock index

None of the above has worked for me except real estate (land, my own home and some rental property) and owning my own businesses. Maybe I am a terrible stock picker (true), I have had poor advisers choosing mutual funds for me (true), collectibles are too hard or too costly to trade (true) or I don't have a government or corporate pension plan (also sadly true).

-40% of Canadians counting on inheritance for their retirement
-34% hope for lottery win
-28% expect financial assistance from children
Bank of Montreal survey November 2013

I'm on my own like about 80% of other Canadians and 82% of Americans who don't have a defined benefit pension plan... and expecting to win a lottery is not a viable retirement plan, I am sorry to say.

...

How to become an equity lord[74]

The number of mega wealthy people on this planet (a class that includes billionaires and millionaires, the latter, however, must have a net worth greater than $30 million USD to be included) is a tiny percentage of overall population—just 0.004% of adults qualify according to Wealth-X.

This group controls 12% of the world's wealth, and it keeps growing.

How did they get to be so wealthy, and, once, there, how do they stay that way?

A few years ago, I did some research on the 100 wealthiest families in Canada. It might surprise you (then again, it might not) that 61 out of 100, almost two thirds, had all or substantially all of their wealth in real estate. It seems that real estate is foundational—one way to both preserve and enhance multi-generational wealth.

Just to give you some idea how large this real estate investment opportunity is, which I am sure many equity lords (and their advisers) already know, let me quote from Sarah Williams Goldhagen's book, *Welcome to Your World—how the built environment shapes our lives* (HarperCollins, New York, 2017):

Today 428 cities around the globe each house populations of between one and five million people. In the next fifteen years, that figure will increase to about 550 cities. There are currently 44 cities with a population of between five and ten million people; in fifteen years, there will be 63. And the number of megalopolises, the gargantuan cities of more than ten million people, are expected to increase from 29 today to 41…

This is happening not just because of a growing human population, but also because there is a continuing worldwide movement from rural to urban areas and from smaller towns and villages to cities and from cities to megalopolises. This should point out to you, as it does to equity lords, that you ought to be investing your sweat equity, cash, time, and ingenuity in places where *all boats are rising*. Then even business dummies like me can make money through real estate.

In Canada's Capital city, the engines of growth are—government employment, universities and colleges, healthcare sector, real estate and construction, events, festivals and entertainment, technology, and tourism. These are excellent, somewhat recession-proof pillars of growth and change, and, as a result, house prices in Ottawa have gone from an average of $13,351 early in the post war era (1956) to $435,676 in 2017.

This represents a compound annual growth rate of 5.9%.

To put this in perspective, let's say in 1956 you had put your $13,351 into a GIC or t-bill paying 2% over the next 61 years. You would have ended up with a tidy sum—$44,681 to be exact, always assuming that you weren't tempted along the way to spend your savings like most people would have done. But if you'd put it in your own home instead, you would have ended up with nearly 10 times more, and that doesn't take into account that you might have had some rental income from the place (possibly a basement apartment ☺) to help you pay your bills…

Ottawa and its sister city in Quebec (Gatineau) have reached a population of 1.3 million; when a city gets to that size (over 1 million), it starts to be more self-sustaining. That is, there is a large enough population base to begin to see local manufacturing and assembly and other indigenous sectors emerge adding to its growth and stability. In fact, this is happening in my hometown as we speak—house price growth is accelerating from its longterm average to 7.9% pa.

16-Aug-17 **House prices in Ottawa**

1956	$13,351
2017	$435,900

---

[74] "Equity lord" is novelist Neal Stephenson's term for wealthy capitalists; he uses it in his work, *The Diamond Age: Or, A Young Lady's Illustrated Primer*, Bantam Dell, February 1995.

		5.88%
61	$	435,676.05

Alternative GIC Investment

1956		$13,351
2017	$	44,681.14
		2%

multiple?	9.8

E&OE

Sources:
1956   http://www.homesinottawa.com/site/Pages/history-of-average-house-prices.html
2017   http://ottawacitizen.com/business/local-business/ottawa-house-prices-up-7-9-in-april-number-of-units-sold-near-record

...

The 6th Duke of Westminster passed away fairly recently (August 9th, 2016) at the relatively young age of 64, but not from a lack of resources—he had to make do with/get by on a net profit from his real estate holdings (Grosvenor Group) of $14,600 USD per hour or about $128 million per year as of 2012.

The 7th Duke is now 25-year old, sole heir Hugh Richard Louis Grosvenor, deemed the United Kingdom's most eligible bachelor not only because he's a super nice looking young man, but because his pocketbook also makes him attractive.

Hughie is worth about £9.35 billion (~$13 billion USD).

He's in a class of *rentiers*, an old fashioned word meaning: "a person living on income from property". Sounds like a good gig. So how do we sign up?

Well, first of all, how did Hughie get to be where he is today, other than the obvious answer: he chose the right parents?

You have to go back to 1740, the year when the great frost nearly froze everyone in Great Britain. It was to be the coldest year for which reliable records are available. The tune, *Rule Britannia, Britannia Rules the Waves* was sung for the first time, and Sir Robert Grosvenor, 3rd Baronet, age 20, married heiress Mary Davies, age 12[75]. He had the title; she'd inherited 500 acres north of the Thames in London where ultra chic Belgravia and Mayfair are today.

Pretty soon thereafter, Sir Robert began development of mixed use Grosvenor Estate, made up of flats, shops, offices and a beautiful public square.

Sir Robert also hired Warren Buffett as his financial adviser. Mr Buffett's advice was to build and *hold*, much as Warren did centuries later with Berkshire Hathaway.

OK, OK, Warren isn't that old, so maybe he wasn't around in 1740 to give the Grosvenors any advice. In fact, it might have been the other way round.

It wouldn't surprise me to find out that Mr Buffett studied what old European families did to become so wealthy.

In any event, Warren is worth an estimated $65.3 billion USD so his methodology is working.

How would you apply his methodology to real estate? Well, we already know this—

1. buy or build smart
2. in great locations
3. hold onto your property

---

[75] An entirely unsuitable idea in a modern society.

4. add value/differentiate it
5. manage it properly
6. be patient
7. refinance it every once in a while and pull out cash, tax free
8. repeat
9. pass it on to your heirs in a tax efficient and cost effective manner[76].

I'd add a few other things like: keep your costs down, live within your means, focus on one or two types of real estate in one or two places, only buy or build property that cashflows from day one, and have as few partners as possible, the optimal number probably being zero.

The other thing would be this: want to know the fastest way to get poor? Get a divorce. So stay married if at all possible.

Lastly, there is a big hurdle for ordinary folks like you and me to get over, and, frankly, I'm not 100% sure how to do that.

Rich folks have access to very low cost debt, very. Some of the largest investors on the planet are issuing bonds that have *negative* interest rates. Investors can be people like successive Dukes of Westminster or large pension funds, REITs, publicly traded firms, insurance companies and investment banks.

In July 2016, Bloomberg reported that Blackstone Group LP had amassed a rental portfolio in the US of more than 50,000 homes. That's *fifty thousand*. How long did that take them? Four years. I repeat: *four* years.

How long would that take you and me if we were able to buy one, say, every 2nd year? The answer is easy—*twenty-five thousand* years, and, frankly, even Warren Buffett isn't going to live that long.

What does Blackstone have that you and I don't have? Access to low cost, and possibly negative cost debt.

CBC news reported that Canucks are also getting into the game—CIBC sold 1.25 billion Euros worth of debt with a negative yield in July 2016. Amazing.

So as a real estate investor, how quickly could you amass a top performing real estate portfolio if I lent you 1.25 billion Euros at a negative interest rate with loan to value ratios of 100% (or possibly more than 100%)?

Mighty fast I'd be willing to guess.

What's slowing us down is the fact that lenders in Canada won't lend you more than 80% loan to value on most property. They limit you to just four or five rental properties. They certainly aren't giving you negative interest rates.

So basically, the top 0.004% of the world's population and their friends on Wall Street, Bay Street, in the City of London, Shanghai, Mumbai, Frankfurt and other major financial centers have crossed over to become equity lords, and drawn up the drawbridge behind them. They've posted signs saying: KEEP OUT or NO TRESPASSING.

So what should ordinary real estate investors do?

Give up, right?

No way!

You have to be nimbler and cleverer, move faster and invest in sectors where the big guys don't play.

Here's what entrepreneurs do: they do for one dollar what any other fool could do for two. They also know how to make two dollars for every dollar any fool could make.

...

---

[76] Avoid what Ari Wallach in his May 2017 TED talk, *3 ways to plan for the (very) long term*, calls "short-term'ism," https://www.youtube.com/watch?v=tjkrKA1cVdU, embracing instead trans-generational thinking (something many Chinese seem especially aware of) and ethics.

Speaking of equity lords, look at the following list of the top seven wealthiest US presidents. You will note that their wealth had one thing in common—real estate ownership.

Wealth of US Presidents

Rank Name
Party Position
Date Estimated wealth[77]

1 Donald Trump
Republican President
2017–present $4.5 billion

2 George Washington
Independent President
1789–1797 $525 million

3 Thomas Jefferson
Democratic-Republican President
1801–1809 $212 million (died bankrupt)

4 John F. Kennedy
Democratic President
1961–1963 $124 million

5 Theodore Roosevelt
Republican President
1901–1909 $125 million

6 Andrew Jackson
Democratic President
1829–1837 $119 million

7 James Madison
Democratic-Republican President
1809–1817 $101 million

Wealth of US Presidents

Name	Party	Position	Date(s)	Estimated wealth*	Notes
Donald Trump	Republican	President	2017–present	$4.5 billion[1]	Real estate, business, stock market, inheritance.
George Washington	Independent	President	1789–1797	$525 million[2]	Real estate, farmland, inheritance, business, and marriage.
Thomas Jefferson	Democratic-Republican	President	1801–1809	$212 million (died bankrupt)[2]	Land, farming, real estate, inheritance, business, slaves.
John F. Kennedy	Democratic	President	1961–1963	$124 million[3]	Real estate, inheritance.
Theodore Roosevelt	Republican	President	1901–1909	$125 million[2]	Manhattan real estate, inheritance.
Andrew Jackson	Democratic	President	1829–1837	$119 million[2]	Marriage, business, law, slaves and real estate.
James Madison	Democratic-Republican	President	1809–1817	$101 million[2]	Real estate (plantation owner), inheritance, business.

* adjusted for inflation

...

---

[77] adjusted for inflation, source: https://en.wikipedia.org/wiki/List_of_richest_American_politicians

Lastly, if you want to know what some equity lords really think of the rest of humanity, read this exchange between New York City mega landlord Steve Croman's son, Jake, and an Uber driver as reported by Bloomberg Businessweek, Oct 17-Oct 23, 2016:

In March 2016 came broader notoriety, when Croman's eldest son, Jake, a University of Michigan student whose LinkedIn profile lists him as an "associate" at his father's firm, was filmed <u>verbally abusing</u> an Uber driver in Ann Arbor.

"There's 50 of you and there's one of me here who spends the most money here, you little f—," Jake says, flanked by fellow Tau Kappa Epsilons. "Minimum-wage faggot. Go f— yourself. See you later. Go pick up another f—. You working all day? Guess what? I'm gonna go sit on my ass and watch TV."

The lesson here is that if you ever get to join the equity lord class yourself (by reading about and implementing Prof Bruce-approved strategies naturally), show some, umm, class.

...

Passing on your property to your heirs

So how do equity lords pass on their property to their heirs efficiently and effectively? Well, I am sure there are as many different strategies as there are accountants[78] and tax attorneys on this planet.

My advice to many of my clients is to keep things as simple as possible but no simpler.

For most people, this means holding properties in their personal names. Now most bankers, lawyers, and accountants hate it when I say this because it means fewer fees for them crafting complex corporate structures, filing company income taxes, and preparing annual financial statements as well as ensuring that they comply with all sorts of endless corporate statutes.

In Ontario and most places where a form of British common law applies, you can hold personal title in two ways—a) as tenants-in-common (t-i-c) or b) as joint tenants.

Tenants-in-common own property together where a defined percentage belongs to each of them. So if John, Mary and Abdullah own 1234 Any street as t-i-c, they can specify who owns what. Maybe John owns 50% with Mary and Abe splitting the balance.

If John passes away, his defined interest passes to his heirs, assigns or estate, et voilà, Mary and Abdullah have a new partner.

But if they are joint tenants, when John passes, he is simply deleted from land titles (in the land registry office), and now Mary and Abe own the property. No fuss, no muss. No probate tax, no probate, no accountants, no lawyers, no bankers, no thieving executors or heirs, and no busybody tax authority (like CRA in Canada or the IRS in the US) can come around and steal the property[79].

Obviously, this makes more sense if all three owners are family members and represent multiple generations.

Since I have five kids, my plan is to add at least one child (who must be 18 or older) to each property my wife and I own as a joint tenant so when I pass and my spouse does too, presto, the youngster owns the place. Some properties have seven joint tenants, some just three. When my grandchildren reach the age of majority (and if I'm still around), I'll start adding them too.

---

[78] The Institute of Chartered Accountants in England and Wales alone has 147,000 members in 150 different countries. The total planetary supply of accountants would be many, many multiples of this. Source: http://charteredaccountantsworldwide.com/membership/.

[79] Please remember that I am an engineer, an economist, a broker, and a coach, not a lawyer or accountant so I am not giving you any legal or accounting or tax advice. Please seek your own counsel. I am simply reporting my personal experiences here.

The fastest growing form of abuse is elder abuse. I sold a property for an elderly client of mine who was not well. He and his wife lived on a rural property of 72 acres, far from the hospital, medical offices, drugstore, and other needed services. They had to sell.

Still I wanted them to get the most out of their land so we severed off 10-acres, which included their log home and sold that to a nice young couple for $400,000. The balance of their lands (62 acres), I sold to a developer. So they got about $1.4 million.

If I'd just sold the land and the house together, they'd would probably have gotten either $1 million from the developer (who placed zero value on their home—he just wanted their land for industrial/commercial development) or $400,000 from the young couple (because they placed zero value on any land area beyond around 2-acres).

So $1.4 million sounded better to my clients than $1 million and way better than $400k.

When we were about to close the sale to the developer, my client came to see me. He asked me, "Bruce, do you think I can get the $1 million in cash?"

"Why do you need it in cash?"

"Well, you can't tell my wife," he said in a whisper, "but there's this technician at the hospital who told me there's a new treatment for my cancer that is *guaranteed* to work. But the cost is exactly $1 million in cash."

Really?

He wasn't thinking clearly so I called his wife, his son and his lawyer, and we changed the signature on his bank account (it now requires two signatures) so he wouldn't be ripped off.

Elder abuse. It's everywhere.

You need people around you that you can trust, and not just when you are an old dude. It's the BIGGEST, MOST IMPORTANT word in my vocabulary these days.

But if he'd had his wife and son as joint tenants on the property (he didn't, he was the sole owner), there would be no way for that technician to steal his money since you can't sell the place or remortgage it without approval of all joint owners... comprehendo?

...

DBA, doing business as

Ontario is one of the friendliest jurisdictions in which to start a business. You can search and register a business name online (for about $61, and that's in Canadian pesos, err, dollars not USD).

When you register a business name like "My Great Consulting Group" or "Stupendous Student Window Washing" or "Coaching Collective" or "Best Home Builder Ever", you can operate under that name, accept payments, open a bank account, get a credit card, register for HST/GST, get supplier credit (eg, with Home Depot or Rona) and much more.

You don't have to incorporate a company at a cost of $1,000 or more or file a separate (and complicated) corporate income tax (you take all income and expenses into your personal name and personal return) or pay an accountant to create financial statements every year. If I were doing my career over again, I would have kept things much simpler. This is one way to do that.

Your Ontario registration is valid for five years, after which you have to renew. If you have a partner(s), no problemo, you just register using both (all) names.

When you register, you'll receive a Master Business Licence (MBL).

Here's more info about registration,

https://www.ontario.ca/page/business-name-registration

and when you are ready, you can register here,

https://www.ibsa.serviceontario.ca/ibsa/servlet/com.visionmax.servlet.CommandServlet?command=screenflownoscript&screenid=26&_ga=1.39632547.1856046185.1445255535.

I get asked about personal liability if you take this route.

In Canada, I tell my students, "It's business first and legals second, but in the US, it's the reverse. The US has 3% of the world's population but 66% of planetary supply of attorneys so you have to be very careful in America—where you can be sued for almost anything."

Corporations provide you with some liability protection, but even there, the corporate veil can be pierced if you are not duly diligent or you countenance or commit fraud. There are also some liabilities that can attach to you personally as an officer or director of a company; things like employee source deductions, environmental contamination (new or even pre-existing), income taxes or excise, amusement or VAT taxes (like GST/HST in Canada) owing.

So on balance, maybe a simple business registration makes most sense[80].

I think these days if you have a name for your business, a tagline[81], a master business license, a domain name with .ca, .com and .org TLDs (top level domains), a basic website, a Facebook page and group, a blog, a twitter and Instagram account, a YouTube channel and maybe a Pinterest account plus some Kijiji, google, Facebook, craigslist ads, you are set to go. Total cost? Mostly free, or not very much.

Google My Business

Oh, one more thing.

You will definitely want a Google+ account so you can register your business with Google maps, which uses a different search algorithm than the main Google engine. Alternatively, Google has made it even easier to register for both using "Google my business."

Whether you have a home-based business or an office or store or an industrial plant or whatever, register your organization/enterprise/not-for-profit/charity's workplace(s) using,

http://www.google.com/business/.

It'll update both Google maps and search from a single url.

It's free and *highly* effective.

Google will send you a postcard via snail mail to the address you put into their platform; it contains a one-time code you re-enter, which, of course, affirms you are who you say you are and where you are…

Here's what they sent me:

---

[80] More about registering your business in Ontario: http://profbruce.tumblr.com/post/122074364799/registering-a-business-in-ontario-registering-a.

[81] How do you create great taglines? See: http://profbruce.tumblr.com/post/103861541279/some-taglines-i-like-wheres-the-beef-wendys

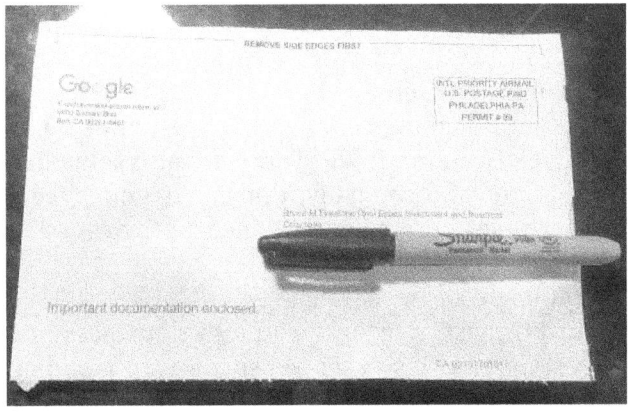

So when you put, "Bruce M Firestone" into Google maps, here's what comes up[82]:

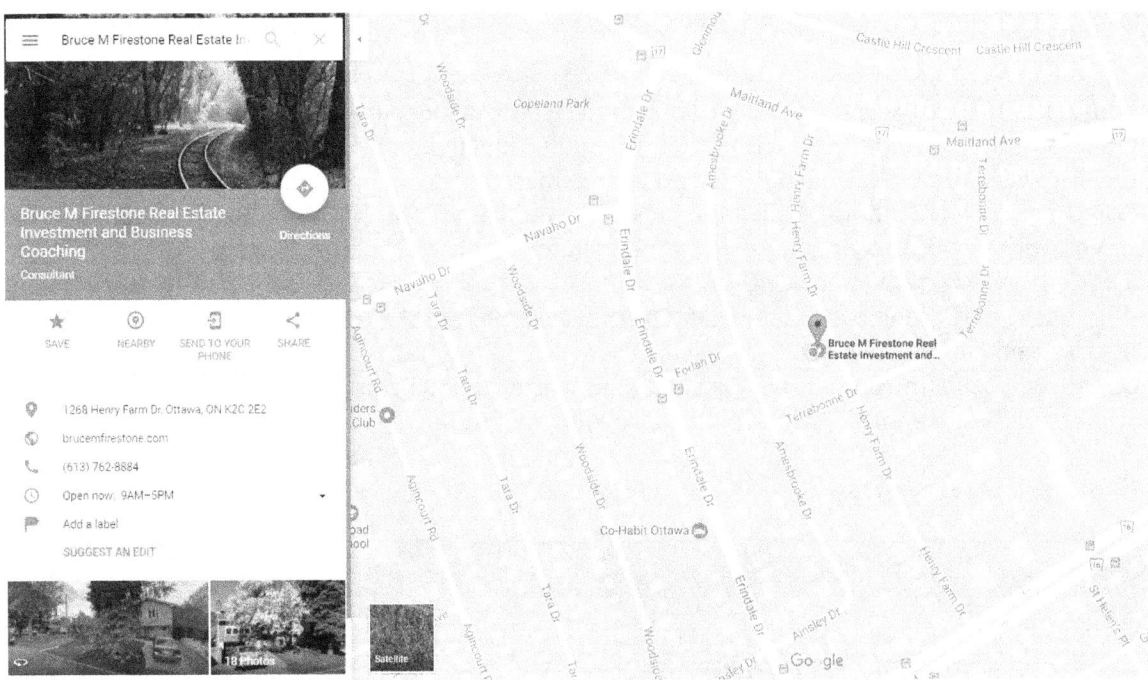

Most small towns have dozens even hundreds of small and medium sized businesses, tons of little not-for-profits, charities, festivals and events–some they don't even know about but do a whopping great volume out of their homes or backyard workshops or basements.

If everyone registers, you'll boost your community's profile, their enterprises, employment, and both sustainability and longterm success…

…

---

[82] Here's my Century 21 Explorer Realty Inc site, http://www.century21.ca/bruce.firestone/.

Donald Trump and late capitalism

Here's an excerpt from a learning outcome novel[83] I wrote (*Jenna's Story*), which has not yet been released.

Set in the future (beginning in 2172), you meet a young woman (Jenna Rose McConnell, 19 when first introduced to readers, soon to be 20), who belongs to a group of *abolitionists*—people who want to reduce or eliminate the intrusive nature of technology, especially personal field generators because of their unknown longterm health impacts, and the fact that a life lived inside a protective bubble is one lacking in creativity, ambition and real experiences. As a result, she's a nascent revolutionary as well.

Abolitionists are in open rebellion against equity lords—those few who control most of the levers of power, and practically all of their nation's wealth and real estate.

Here's that novel's cover:

[cover art by Muse Mariah]

These field generators are implanted at the base of the neck at the top of the spine at a young age. They're unobtrusive and smart, embedded pretty much everywhere, without any moving parts and largely invisible. They *spin up* the world around you… housing, furnishings, vehicles, weapons even clothes are generated by fields so they change shape, color, content, in just a few seconds or micro seconds as different apps are deployed from the universal platform (the UP), which is embedded in the planet's geomagnetic field and run by the Aye (which is what everyone calls "AI", artificial intelligence).

You'll also read about a communications device called an "A." They look like Star Trek communicators (usually they are pinned to your chest), and are used by abolitionists to maintain contact with each other and many other things besides.

---

[83] I began experimenting with learning outcome novels in 2010 as a way to both tell a story *and* teach readers something about subjects in which I was interested, and, hopefully, they would be too. The impetus came from my experience as a professor, first at Carleton University's Azrieli School of Architecture and Design, and Sprott School of Business, as well as later at University of Ottawa's Telfer School of Management and Faculty of Engineering. A learning outcome novel sets out to tell an engaging story into which is interleaved a set of knowledge that, by the time a reader/student has completed the book, s/he has internalized it to the point where they not only understand the information provided, but can act on it independently as well in the real world. It is a new genre of novels I believe.

Jenna is at an after party with a group of friends in a small (fictitious) village named Aanii (in Montana, set on the eastern slope of the Rockies, northwest of Great Falls) at which time, Ms McConnell is talking about equity lords, remittance men and the Donald…

Jenna sometimes speaks like a redneck from her home state of South Carolina, and occasionally she uses what she calls her "Vassar" voice (ie, proper English).

In this excerpt, they talk about the difference between being rich and being wealthy, and a few other topics, most of which are relevant to understanding how fundamental real estate is to the creation of sustainable, long-lasting wealth. There is some adult language and some situations that are NSFO. My apologies.

…

Dancing is over. They are having a group discussion about why the global economy is so sh*tty. So far, they've blamed local and state governments, successive failed presidencies, equity lords and now banks.

"What other sector pays 30-year olds an average salary of $2.9 million a year?" Nathaniel asks.

"That and $825 real jeans sold to women with fake mud on them by high end providers are just symptoms of late capitalism[84]," Paco says, looking somewhat accusingly at Jenna, who is the only person present who (mostly) buys authentic stuff.

She ignores him as she does anything she wants to, and says instead, directing her comment at Nate and using her neutral accent once more, "Remittance men and women make way more than that."

"They do?" someone else adds.

"They shorly does," she answers.

"Can you give us an example?" the guy follows up.

"You bet. Ah read a recent article in Bloomberg Businessweek that broke out land rent for Donald Trump's[85] building at 40 Wall street. They reported that Massa Trumpster 'currently pays $4.65 million a year to the group that owns the land underneath his building, which includes heirs to a German shipping fortune.'"

When she uses the term "Massa," a large part of her audience turn to each other with surprised looks. There is an audible sucking-in of collective breath.

Like many folks outside the Deep South, they assume she's just used a racist term. She has not. It's her way of putting down the overlord class, but no one, other than Tom, gives her the benefit of the doubt.

Nevertheless, Jenna plows onward.

She reaches behind Tom, who is sitting close to her on one of his parentals' vast and comfy coaches, turns on his field, and shows them the building she is referring to:

The Trump Building
40 Wall street, NYC
[Copyright Chris Ruvolo]

"The Aye measured the area of the site; it's around 32,291 square feet. And one of my friends at the Darla

---

[84] *Why the Phrase 'Late Capitalism' Is Suddenly Everywhere: An investigation into a term that seems to perfectly capture the indignities and absurdities of the modern economy*, Annie Lowrey, The Atlantic, May 1, 2017.

[85] She is referring to Donald Trump the seventh or, as she would write it, "The Donald VII."

Moore School of Business[86] helped us figure out what the land is worth."

Tom is wondering who "us" might be. It's without a doubt more of her abolitionist friends. He shudders with worry. Jenna, thinking he's shivering because it's cold, absentmindedly puts her arm around him again and pulls him even closer.

"Anyway, here's what we found."

Jenna shows them this:

To determine the value of this property, you need to determine an appropriate cap rate, r, like this:
r = NOI/value.
Once you have that, value is determined like this:
value = NOI/r,
where NOI is net operating income.

The Bloomberg article also happily gives us the NOI for the building (which simply equals the net net net rent or triple net rents for the building[87]) divided by the building's value (excluding land).

We have those two numbers:

$42,350,000/year triple net rents (ie, rents net of operating costs, property taxes and utilities—in commercial leasing, tenants pay pretty much *all* an equity landlord's costs).

The building's current fair market value is estimated to be $1,050,000,000.

So the *building's* cap rate is thus determined as follows: $42,350,000/$1,050,000,000 or 4.0% pa.

Applying that to the NOI for the *land*, gives a land value of: $4,650,000/4.0% = $115,289,256 or $3,570.24 USD per square foot.

After this, the group sees a slide of a spreadsheet Jenna and the researchers at the Darla Moore School of Business put together:

	A	B	C	D	E	F
1		The Trump Building 40 Wall street			August 2167	
2						
3	frontage		50 meters	approx	Wall street	Pine street
4	depth		60 meters	approx		
5	area of land		3000 sq m	approx		
6			32291.73 sq ft	approx		
7						
8	land rent*	$	4,650,000.00	pa	USD	remittance family/equity lord
9						
10	net net rents	$	42,350,000.00	2008	office rents	
11	value of building	$ 1,050,000,000.00				
12	cap rate		4.0%	pa		
13						
14	value of land	$	115,289,256.20			
15		$	3,570.24	per sf		
16		$	38,429.75	per sq m	USD	

"So you're saying the Trump family is rich? Everyone knows that," the same guy states.

"No, what ah am saying is that the German fambly who owns the land under 40 Wall street is *wealthy*—they get land rent forever and ever—it's a *stipend*, a gift that keeps on giving, generation after generation. It's an asset and an income stream that they own and control; it shelters them from everythin'. The rest of us... we is just wage *slaves*."

"Is there a difference between being wealthy and being rich?" Tom asks Jenna, already knowing that there is.

"Chris Rock once said—"

"Who's that, Jenna?" Nate interrupts.

"An *ancient* comedian and social commentator," she continues in her Vassar voice, "by the name of Chris Rock once said, 'Shaq is *rich*[88] but the white man who signs his paycheck is *wealthy*. Oprah is rich, but Bill Gates is wealthy. If Bill Gates suddenly woke up with Oprah's money, he'd slit his throat.' What he meant was that if you control the underlying assets and real estate that produce income, you are wealthy, which is a sustainable state of being. If you happened to pick the right parents and make it to the NBA, you are rich... for a time."

---

[86] The Darla Moore School of Business, founded in 1919, is the business school of University of South Carolina in Columbia; it has a concentration in real estate, and is ranked 2nd nationally in terms of research productivity in that field.
[87] Triple net rent means base rent or minimum rent paid by tenants to which they must also add property taxes, operating costs and utilities, plus Aye access fees, landlord administration and property management fees, insurance and other equity lord costs. Sometimes, a percentage rent (a proportion of tenant revenues) is also charged.
[88] Here Mr Rock is referring to Los Angeles Lakers former NBA superstar Shaquille O'Neal.

"Makes eminent sense—I'll have to look that *philosopher* up, Jenny," Rebich says nicely.

"Your odds of making the NBA," Tom says checking his facts on the UP, "in Chris Rock's era were 1 in 16,737,826.6."

"Right," says Jenna. "Yo' kinít count on it o' plan fo' it, but yo' kin eff'n, say, yo' own th' lan' beneath 40 Wall street!"

"The odds of making the NBA today are significantly better," Tom adds, undercutting Jenna's argument without meaning to.

"About one in seven million since they expanded to Europe, Asia, and Africa...," he ends lamely.

He was looking at this data produced by the Aye—

21-May-17	How many NBA players are there? And what are your odds of playing in the NBA?				
	opening-day roster list	teams	players/team	world population	odds of becoming a NBA player, 1 in:
1986-1987	301	23	13	5,000,000,000	16,611,295.7
2016-2017	449 opening-day roster list	30	15	7,515,284,153	16,737,826.6
2170-2172	1224 opening-day roster list	72	17	9,000,000,000	7,352,941.2

source: http://rpiratings.com/NBA.php
source: http://www.worldometers.info/world-population/

"In fact," the first guy says, not having paid any attention to what Jenna, Tom or Nate have just been saying, "wasn't Mr Trump the wealthiest president ever?"

...

Then Jenna, because she's somewhat annoyed, calls up this controversial image:

"Holy sh*t, what does it mean?" someone asks alarmed at the potential for violence captured in this painting of a shirtless worker putting his fist through a dance floor from below.

"It's called 'From the Depths[89]'. It's by Canadian artist William Balfour Ker," Nate says smiling appreciatively at Jenna, while supporting her too.

"It's meant to capture the fear that upper classes had of revolution from below," Rebich adds. "It was painted in 1905, I think."

"Man, it sure does that," the guy says.

"Ju know, Mr Rebich, thet his maw was Lily Flo'ence Bell, fust cousin of Alexan'er Graham Bell?"

"Cool. Did not know that, Jenny," Nate replies.

Tom looks at his former teacher wonderingly; not pleased that he's just used his private pet name for Jenna.

Then Jenna gets up and in sort of a pantomimed personal protest removes her pumps and next her tights (careful this time not to take off her panties at the same moment).

This partial striptease silences everyone immediately. You can actually hear some of the men stop breathing.

Next she shows off one of her bare chick legs to the group; she lifts the right side of her mini skirt higher while holding the center down with her other hand to cover her private parts; finally, they can all see that on the inside of her outturned right thigh is a brand new tattoo she has of a fist breaking through a barrier—it's an

---

[89] Source: From the depths / Wm Balfour-Ker. United States, ca. 1906. Photograph. Retrieved from the Library of Congress, https://www.loc.gov/item/2004666561/. (Accessed March 17, 2017.)

obvious riff on and taken from or derived from *From the Depths*.

"Look hyar, y'all granny-slapping, whistle-dicks, this is th' noo symbol of th' revolushun," she says defiantly looking directly at Tom, daring him to say anything to contradict her.

All Tommy notices is that there is a redness around her tattoo it's so recent, and that he'd like to kiss her there.

Some of the guys might be thinking exactly the same thing at this instant.

Finally, she lowers her mini skirt, and normal respiration is restored, whereupon Tom wonders how and when she got her tattoo since she has almost never been out of his presence in recent memory. It's a mystery[90].

"Well, look, since they didn't arn it," Tom blithely replies, returning to a safer topic, mimicking her while putting an affectionate smile on his face to partially offset their differences but still loving her southern expressions and even insults more and more as she pulls an endless stream of them out of her subconscious, "in the first place, those remittance men and women won't have their wealth very long. They'll get greedy. They'll borrow against the capital value of their property, thinking they'll pay it back somehow only they won't. They'll spend it on useless stuff like vanity sports franchises, bigger yachts, fancier homes, younger women or men. Pretty soon, their lenders will come a'callin'."

Jenna shrugs slightly mollified by Tom's astute comeback. He's partially redeemed himself in her eyes.

"Right, which brings us back to the banks," Mr Rebich says. "The property will trade from one useless remittance family to an equity lord who manages his or her estates better. No one else has access to financial products that have negative interest rates, which allows them to buy more and more—it's accretive, a perpetual motion machine... for real. Do you have access to negative interest rates, Tom?"

"Nope."

"So you can never become an equity lord. Never. Nor can anyone else in this room."

"Is that why," Paco asks, disappointed that Jenna didn't decide to come sit between him and Mikom, awesome dancers that they are and all, and picking up clear signals that Mr Rebich has gone sweet on her, which makes him want his second best friend's girlfriend all the more, "no one can afford to move to any of our major cities?"

"Exactly," Nathaniel answers. "It's an oligopolistic system, where equity lords control most of the levers of the economy, and all the political power—so rents—including Aye access and usage fees just keep going up. Did you know that in South Korea, just nine clans control over 92% of their GDP, through their chaebol, their conglomerates[91]?"

Mr Rebich added that last bit as a tribute to Jenna's argument.

He continues, "In Africa, parts of Asia and South America, it used to be called an 'extractive economy', and it was the primary reason why nations there failed in the post-colonial period[92]."

"What was the process involved—I mean how did it work or... fail to work?" Tom asks.

"Anywhere extractive institutions—ones that are geared solely to unfairly expropriating value for the ruling class—exist, economic development is blocked, innovation is stifled, and initiative snuffed out. They concentrate power and wealth in the mitts of those who control the state, and do nothing to earn it, opening the way for civic unrest," Rebich says.

"Is that what you reckon is happening in America today, Mr Rebich?" Paco asks.

"For sure. You folks ever heard the story of the Zimbank national lottery?"

No one will admit to knowing this obscure tale.

Rebich goes on: "It was January 2000. The bank's master of ceremonies, a man by the name of Fallot Chawawa, well, it was his honor to draw the winning ticket. The lottery was open to every bank customer who kept a minimum of 5,000 Zimbabwe dollars[93] in their account the previous December. The prize—Z$100,000—

---

[90] Jenna tattooed herself whilst she was in a private Menlo Park studio with Sophinie. Well, not exactly. She had her avatar learn the trade whereupon it used a Royal College of Art personal tattoo machine to create this symbol on her body. Sophinie got one too—in the same place, her inner right thigh.

[91] Conglomerates have absorbed most of the available capital in that nation. Singapore-based Oxford Economics economist Oliver Salmon says, "The chaebol have really strangled investment" in entrepreneurial businesses in South Korea for the last 40 years. Combined revenue of the top nine chaebol accounted for 75% of GDP and 60% of the Kospi 200 stock market index. Source: Bloomberg Businessweek, March 12th 2017.

[92] *Why Nations Fail, The Origins of Power, Prosperity, and Poverty*, Saron Acemoglu, James A Robinson, Crown Business, New York, 2012.

[93] The Z$ was trading at about 100 to the USD in 2000 so Z$5,000 was equivalent to around 50 bucks (US). By July 2008, the Z$ had fallen to 758,530,000,000 to the USD. That is not a misprint—it was 758.53 *billion* to a US dollar. Source: Wikipedia.

went to none other than president-for-life, his Excellency Robert Mugabe[94]. Now did Mr Mugabe need an extra Z$100,000, a tiny sum really in a practically worthless currency? No. But if you worked for Zimbank, a partly state-owned bank, and you wanted to keep your job, and maybe your life, you made sure that every single thing of value ended up in the hands of your overlords."

"How much was 100,000 Zimbabwe dollars worth at the time?" Mikom asks.

"About 1,000 US dollars, Mike."

"His worshipfulness fixed the national lottery for a grand?" Paco marvels.

"That's about the size of it," Nate responds.

"Can you give us an example of an extractive institution today, Nate?" Tom asks already knowing what he's going to say.

"Sure. The international banking system, allied as it is with national and local institutions, exists solely to take economic value from three sectors of society—the working and middle classes, and small business owners—and siphon it away to benefit equity lords, and their pet politicians, their domesticated attorneys and themselves, of course. Everyone outside the privileged few are essentially vassals; it's déjà vu all over again. We're no different really from peasants who were tenant farmers[95] in medieval times. Everything, except a pittance, gets extracted today—our savings, our homes and businesses, most of our incomes, any chance at wealth—"

"Ain't nothin' no one kin does about it anyway," Jenna interrupts, "unless…"

"Unless what, honey?" Tom asks.

"Unless, we occupy public lan's an' private open space."

"What would you put there, Miss McConnell?" Rebich asks, smiling broadly at Tom's pretty companion.

"We reckon thar's room fo' 180,000 tiny houses—them new fangled pods[96]—jest in San Fran right proper," she answers.

"Whoa, Jenna, there's no way they'd ever let you get away with that," Mikom says. "Those scary new police, the SS, would arrest you guys in hours if you trespass on any equity lord property."

Jenna gets that secret smile on her face again and says, "Mebbe not, Mike. Then agin', mebbe we c'd."

Tom wants to shake her when she says this, knowing, as he does, her secret plan is to blackmail them. It is such a dumb plan; he can't fathom how she even thinks her abolitionist revolution has any chance to succeed. Dumb, dumb, dumb, dumb!

What he says instead is: "There are other reasons why cities might not want those pods, babe."

"Like whut?"

"Well, for one, they already have rules on the books making it illegal to live in your field generated RV year-round."

"That's a circular argument, Tom. I've heard it before," Nate says supporting Jenna's idea. "Tiny houses are regarded and plated as homemade recreational vehicles, so they are a subclass of RVs, and zoning ordinances already ban permanent habitation of same. QED."

Nate continues: "The real reason tiny houses are banned is that anything on wheels cannot be assessed for property taxes so cities, towns and villages are afraid that their realty tax bases are going to shrivel up and die."

"Righty right, Mister Rebich—" Jenna says in agreement.

"Call me Nate, please."

"Alright. So Nate, whut are th' two thin's polish*tans like best?" she asks.

"I'm sure you're going to tell me, Miss Jenna."

"Money an' power, an' them two is related.

'In fac', th' only thin' enny politician stan's fo' these days is re-eleckshun[97], which, of course, nets them the ducats an' control they's af'er anywho," Jenna adds.

Nate laughs. He adores people with strong views, especially when they are well argued, and he particularly likes the way this girl expresses her views in her own strange but spellbindingly colloquial way. Jenna isn't afraid to go after the high hanging fruit, Nate thinks despite not really knowing half of what the young woman is actually

---

[94] Why Nations Fail, p 368.
[95] Known as sharecroppers in America.
[96] Jenna knows something about these "new fangled pods" that no one else present that night knows—the abolitionist underground is secretly manufacturing (using quantum tunnels) more of them than all the tanks featured in World of Tanks, the Belarusian-Cypriot created game that is still being played today; only now gamers are able to climb into actual field generated early to mid-20th century tanks, and go to war for real. The saving grace? When they die, it only takes a few seconds for them to respawn.
[97] Jenna borrowed this line from Samuel L Jackson's character, Richmond Valentine, who said it in the film, *Kingsman: The Secret Service*, 2014.

up to.

"What are the nine scariest words in the English language, Miss Jenna?" he asks to test her.

"Ah's fum th' goobermint an' ah's hyar t'he'p," she replies readily.

"That's eight words," a guy notes—he's the one who is furthest from the fire so he has a blanket wrapped around his shoulders to ward off cold night air creeping into the old building at every crack, window and door.

"I'm from the government and I'm here to help," Jenna interprets.

"Nine eff'n yo' please," she adds with a self-satisfied look.

"Alright, but who said it?" blanket man asks.

"Ronald Reagan," answer Nate, Tom and Jenna at the same time although Tom says, "Ronald Wilson Reagan," and Jenna says "Ronnie Raygun."

"Then there is the NIMBY problem," Rebich adds to the political mix and this abolitionist rant.

"NIMBYs?" someone (not blanket guy) asks Nate.

"Yeah, NIMBYs—not in my backyard equity lords—who fear that tiny houses, literally in their backyards, will attract immigrants, poor people, the homeless, criminals, and other 'undesirables', and their property values will drop.

"They've already produced endless engineering reports that talk about overloading sewers, water mains, and other utilities. They also say that they'll produce too much traffic for our streets to handle. Plus they've rustled up architects who'll say tiny houses are ugly, a form of visual blight. They sometimes use the term 'visual pollution' whatever the hell that means.

"It's my view that all these concerns are unwarranted. I'm sure politicians could find a way to tax tiny houses so they'll pay their fair share of municipal services.

"And demand from a tiny house in terms of municipal services is certainly going to be a lot less than what we've already seen with coach houses, which many cities already permit or soon will in backyards. Of course, coach houses have permanent foundations and, thus, can be added to the tax base, which makes them more acceptable than tiny houses.

"In terms of design, your generation," Nathaniel says pointing at Jenna who is the youngest member of the group, "are redesigning pretty much everything to be better not only in terms of performance but look, feel and brand as well. There's no reason tiny houses (or for that matter RVs) have to be ugly.

"Furthermore, equity landlords really have nothing to fear except fear itself. In almost every case where a city densifies and intensifies[98], property values go up not down, all else being equal, meaning as long as public order is maintained, an essential component for any civilization. In fact, it's the sine qua non for development of any economic value."

"I agree with everything you said Mr Rebich, except what's the one thing equity lords hate above all else?" Tom asks his former teacher.

"Anything that threatens their position?" Nate answers.

"In a way… it's competition. They've lived lives that are so easy, so bereft of any striving, their every need catered to, for so long, they're incapable of real work and, if, *if* someone found way for the people to access cheap credit, the masses would stomp them into the ground by outcompeting them."

"Yo' all is soun'in' like an abolishunist now, Tommah," Jenna says proudly.

*F*ck, so I am*, Tom thinks.

"I didn't mean literally *stomping* them, Jenna."

When you talk to a teenager, you have to be careful what you say lest they take your message too seriously, ie, at face value. Especially Jenna.

"How do you know, Mr Rebich, that equity lord property values will go up not down if there is a pod invasion?" Paco asks.

"Well, I can prove it to you."

He boots up another field.

"In the table below, we calculated the cap rate on a theoretical tiny house at 10.9% pa, which is quite a bit higher than your "normal" residential rental (around 6.4% pa).

---

[98] "Densify" implies fabricating more built form on a given property, but with more of the same type of single use, ie, more housing or more office space or more retail space. Intensify implies both more density (ie, more built form) plus more diversity of use allowing multiple activities to occur on a single property—live, work, learn, make, create, entertain, shop, play…

	A	B	C	D	E	F	G	H
1		Tiny House calculation	E&OE					
2								
3	bungalow	$400,000						
4	rent	$1,650	per mth	3-bed	1.5 bath	upstairs		
5	rent	$1,230	per mth	2-bed	1 bath	basement with separate entrance		
6	total	$2,880	per mth					
7	vacancy	($144)	5%					
8	total	$2,736	per mth					
9	operating costs	($601.92)	22%					
10	NOI	$2,134	per mth					
11		$25,608.96	pa					
12	cap rate	6.4%	pa					
13								
14	tiny house	$100,000						
15	rent	$1,230	per mth					
16	vacancy	($62)	5%					
17	rent	$1,169						
18	operating costs	($257.07)	22%	assumes "property taxes" on tiny house				
19	NOI	$911	per mth					
20		$10,937.16	pa					
21	cap rate	10.9%	pa					
22								
23	overall	$500,000						
24	NOI	$36,546.12	pa					
25	cap rate	7.3%	pa					
26								
27	appy residential cap rate	6.4%						
28	NOI	$36,546.12	pa					
29	fair market value	$570,833.33						
30	tiny house added value	$170,833.33						
31								

"If you apply a "normal" cap rate to the total annual net operating income for both the bungalow and tiny house, you get an increase in property value of $170,833. But the tiny house only cost $100,000 in this example to build and install (or buy and install or field generate[99]), which means this proud equity lord made a capital "profit" of $70,833 on her/his investment.

"In other words, her/his property's fair market value went up an extra $70,833 over and above their costs, as long as public order is maintained…

"They will also, in my view, make our cities and towns more interesting and animated.

"Some people are banding together to try to change these anti-tiny house views and regulations," here Nate looks directly at Jenna, who already knows that he has an Ꭺ on him because hers vibrated noiselessly when he first came in the room, and flashed at her as did hers at him.

"It still won't work, Mr Rebich," Tom says to Nate who has to look away from Jenna to concentrate on Hatch.

"How come?" Paco intervenes. He's excited about this plan—he'd like to transfer out of this one goat town except he can't afford to move anywhere else.

"There's another aspect to finance—not just access to negative interest rates as a borrower. You also need the cooperation of appraisers."

"Appraizzer? Whut thet gotta does wif ennythin', sunshine?" Jenna asks Tom.

The only appraiser she's ever heard of is someone who tells you what your diamonds are worth, which her maw needed to know before she pawned her wedding ring.

"Good question, babe. Bankers hire appraisers to do property valuations for them. They want to make sure they don't lend more than a certain percentage of a property's value. It's to protect them from any loan losses in case property values drop or the owner falls on hard financial times, and can't pay their mortgage. Those guys—the appraisers—will have trouble coming to grips with the increase in value, from not only tiny houses but coach houses as well. There aren't many comps (comparables) around, and most of them are not familiar with valuing

---

[99] Real buildings have the advantage over field generated ones that, once they're erected, landlords or owners only have to worry about paying repair and maintenance costs as well as expensing depreciation and amortization (if they have a mortgage on the property) on their accounting statements. Field generated buildings must pay monthly platform access fees; failure to do so results in revocation—your building simply disappears. Before vanishing, the Aye will cause your structure to ring scarily; it actually sounds a lot like the bells of the Cathedral of Saint Tryphon in Kotor, Montenegro, which have been in continuous use since being consecrated on June 19th, 1166. If you don't leave immediately, you'll simply fall out of an empty sky. If you are hearing impaired, no worries… the Aye also pulses then strobes the structure before zeroing it out so you should have plenty of warning that now would be a good time to evacuate. Lastly, equity landlords have no trouble evicting tenants who don't pay their rent these days since the Aye can also selectively dematerialize individual apartments. Lastly, the capital cost of a field generated building is simply the present value of an infinite series of monthly platform access fees, which can be found by dividing annual Aye payments by an appropriate cap rate. Equity lords take the same approach when estimating the value of a human life to them—they straightforwardly take the expected value of a person's annual earnings and divide it by the relevant cap rate. Currently, those values are 3,000,000 Euros and 2.75 million USD, in Europe and America, respectively, and dropping as both national and global economies falter.

property any other way.

"The three main ways to value property are: comps, replacement value less depreciation and on an income basis. The industry mainly uses the first methodology so any homeowner will be shortchanged in terms of getting fair valuations for mortgage purposes."

Tom's very familiar with these concepts thanks to Denton Holman.

"Don't thet effeck equity lo'ds too?" Jenna asks.

"No, because they access financial markets directly. There are no interveners—no appraisals, no banks. So they load up on finance to 100% of the value of their properties plus people—all of us—are paying *them* to take our money. That's what negative bank interest rates really mean."

"Actually, Tom," Mr Rebich intervenes, "equity lords can load up on more, maybe much more than 100% loan to value financings."

"They can?" a surprised Hatch remarks.

"They can. It's called negative pledging. They simply pledge *not* to use their properties as collateral for *any* borrowings. That way they can obtain non-recourse loans equal to many times the value of any individual building from any number of gullible and impressionable bankers."

"That's legal?" Mikom exclaims.

"Apparently so," Nate adds.

"They's shuttin' th' dore on most entrepreneurs these days too, right Mr Rebich, umm, Nate?" Jenna asks.

"Correct, Miss Jenna, they are. It's one of the reasons why our national economy tanked. In a previous era, if an entrepreneur went to see a moneylender, the banker might refuse a loan because the entrepreneur's credit rating or track record was poor. However, if the manager approved the loan, ze might say, 'I know you wanted a loan for $150,000 to get your new business off the ground, but I'm not going to approve that. Instead, I'm going to authorize $185,000,' at which point the entrepreneur does her or his happy dance. Do you know why, Miss Jenna, the manager approved more than the amount asked?"

Jenna is aware of the answer to this question, but, like many women, she understands that men, even educated ones like Mr Rebich, want to proudly expound before an audience. It's a male ego thing so she says instead: "Kin yo' tell us, Nate?"

She restrains herself though—she does not bat her long eyelashes at him—there's a limit to what she's willing to do to support male self esteem.

Suitably impressed with himself, Nate says: "It's because they realized that the worst outcome with any startup is to end up with a ½ done project. What's the value in, say, a half done code project, a platform app that doesn't work? It probably has a negative value—it'll take longer and cost more just to unwind it. No, they used to give entrepreneurs in *all* sectors more than they requested to make sure it was completed. Now they just say, 'No,' or short change them to the point where they're bound to fail."

"What's the point of that? Why loan money to a project you know is going to fail?" someone else in the audience asks.

"It's so they can publicly plug what they're doing, saying: 'See, we're giving ordinary folks a chance but, heck, look what they've done with it! They've mucked it up *again*.' It's so, without any pushback from our citizenry or a co-opted media, they can make fewer and fewer loans to entrepreneurs, who are potential future competitors to their equity lord friends who also, by the way, own those self same banks," a bitter Rebich says as he nearly completes the narrative.

"So thar's no way out? 'Cept fo' a revolushun?" Jenna asks.

Tom knows she's baiting them/manipulating them to try to get folks to say what she wants to hear.

"There's one, hun," Tom intervenes.

"Whut thet be?" she obliges him.

"Start our own fund—I call it the 'red circle group'. It'll lend up to 100% of the value of property at competitive rates, but it'll also get a piece of the equity so it'll have legs—that is, the fund'll be sustainable."

"Why call it 'red circle', what's that mean?" a friend of Paco's asks, speaking up for the first time.

"It's what lenders call an informal commitment to fund—you know, they've 'red circled', set aside, the funds you'll need for your project..." Tom answers.

"How will that change anything?" Paco's friend asks.

"Say you are an entrepreneur and you need $100,000 in equity to start a new project," Tom continues. "But you only have $10,000. The Red Circle Group will chip in the other $90k. But if they put all that in as equity, the entrepreneur would only end up owning 10% of her or his new venture and the Red Circle fund would own the rest... 90%. It's not only bad for the entrepreneur to end up with so little of her or his own startup, it's bad for the enterprise too because she or he won't be very motivated to build a great company in which they only own 10%. So instead, the Red Circle Group would *lend* the project, say, $85,000 and invest just $5,000 as equity. The result?

The entrepreneur owns two thirds of the company while the Red Circle Group owns the remaining third. You can play with the numbers so the equity is divided up any way you want—it's all a matter of negotiation. If the entrepreneur is a good negotiator, maybe she or he can get the Red Circle people to structure their investment as, umm...," Tom pauses for a moment to calculate something on his field then he adds, "as $88,888.89 in debt and $1,111.11 in equity, which would leave the entrepreneur with a 90% ownership, and the fund with 10%."

"Thet there is symphonic, Tommah," Jenna says, proud of him. "Is itcher idear?"

"Yeah, I think so," he answers.

"No it isn't," Nate says maybe a little too quickly... as if he wants to impress someone and depress someone else.

"It ain't?" Jenna asks.

"Nope. A form of this type of financing was used in the medieval Islamic world. It was called a 'qirad.' And I think the Romans used it before that—their term for it was a 'societas.' These were the likely predecessors of the Venetian *commenda*, where basically a trader, an entrepreneur, one with guts but little or no money would ship out with a cargo paid for (mostly) by a stay-at-home merchant. The latter would get 75% of the profits of the venture, the entrepreneur, the balance. But if the trader had any skin in the game, he'd get more, maybe as much as 50% of the profits of the voyage when trading was completed. It was the single biggest factor in making Venice an incredibly wealthy city-state in the period from AD 960 to 1314."

"What happened after 1314, Nate?" Tom asks not in the least bothered to find out that his great idea is not, in fact, original. Entrepreneurs borrow best practices all the time, needing only seconds or, at most, minutes to adopt something that works better than what they are doing on their own, which is why they can run circles around governments, their agencies, most NGOs, large companies and public institutions who need to study things for years before (if ever) making any changes.

"In 1314, the Venetian government was taken over by a corrupt nobility whose unassailable hereditary positions in their 'Great Council' meant that they could, with impunity, nationalize international trade; that is, they could squeeze out their entrepreneur class without fear of reprisal. By doing so, they thought they'd end up with all the spoils but equity lords," Nate says with a nod to Jenna, "are horrible at production. Pretty soon, there were little or no spoils to appropriate. Basically, they cratered their local economy for the next, oh, 860 years. Venice's economic output and population began a long-term decline that is still ongoing. It's just a mausoleum for the occasional tourist now."

"So," Jenna says switching over to her other voice, "if I understand it correctly, equity lords are not only using their political cronies and police to keep their privileged positions secure, they're using cheap capital as a barrier to entry. Right? So to get our sh*tty economy going again, we're going to need to unleash our entrepreneurs. We all know that. To do it though, they'll need access to abundant and cheap capital to put them on a more level playing field vis-à-vis equity lords, after which they'll whack those suckers because they can outthink, outwit, outwork, outhustle, and outmaneuver them like nucking futs."

"Exactly, Miss Jenna," says Rebich with another smile at the girl.

"Then Tom is right, give o' take a rabbit's foot," Jenna says reaching across to squeeze Mr Hatch's hand. "We don't turn the moneylenders out of the temple. We set up our own instead—this Red Circle Group thingy. We break their monopoly on inexpensive funding, and then napalm the heck out of them. We'll beat them at their own game."

"It'll operate like Svenska Handelsbanken, Jenny," Tom says.

"Seven what?" someone asks for them all.

"Svenska Handelsbanken AB... it's a Swedish universal bank."

"Oh."

"It's an ur-bank," Tom adds.

"An err bank?" the blanket guy queries.

"Ur, as in 'U-R.' It just means ancient or original. It's what banks were supposed to be—a method of fairly and efficiently deploying pooled capital to deserving entrepreneurs to create growth and opportunity for all," Tom answers.

"In th' golden days," Jenna says, her eyes shining and twinkling at Tommy—she is, of course, referring to the days before shields and fields.

"Yep, those golden, olden days. Anywho," he continues with an affirming nod in Jenna's direction, "Svenska's return on equity surpassed all its European peers from 1971 until a few years ago. It had 73,000 associates, but with only three levels. Decision-making was entirely decentralized with each associate making his or her own loan decisions, and setting their own prices for both loans and deposits."

"They must have taken a beating when it came to loan losses, Tom?" Nate asks.

"Nope. They posted industry-beating loan-loss ratios, and their costs were also a lot lower. They also issued scrip—every loan came with a bonus, something that one day could be redeemed in return for equity in a property of their own."

"I heard they went bust," one of the gathered says.

"That's not what happened! They got taken over by Gold In Sacks in 2168 and shut down!" Tom says testily, using a nickname for a predatory New York-based investment bank. "They also imposed an expiry date on the scrip that had been issued to that point in time so most of it became worthless, the motherf*ckers!"

Jenna reaches once more for Tom's hand... to comfort and support him. They can see (if they're close enough to him like Jenna is) these thumbnail images floating about on Tom's activated field:

-equity needed: $240,000
-investor: $230,000 (2ⁿᵈ mortgage)
-investor: $5,000 (50%) equity
-entrepreneur: $5,000 (50%) equity

OR

-investor: $233,333.33 (2ⁿᵈ mortgage)
-investor: $1,666.67 (25%) equity
-entrepreneur: $5,000 (75%) equity

RED CIRCLE GROUP

Jenna looks at his notes—one of them handwritten; he's already got some type of business model worked out to launch the thing on any scale—from tiny to humongous.

"We've got to restart Handelsbanken, only this time, we've got to give it staying power so it won't get squashed again," Tom finishes.

Jenna says with an approving look, "Good idear, Mister Hatch, ah's liking it already," certain now that one way or t'uther, she'll find a way to get Tommy onboard the abolitionist train with her.

"It won't work, Tom," Paco says.

"Why not?" Tom asks.

"Look poor people are poor for a reason," he replies.

"Like whut reasons?" Jenna responds belligerently.

"You give them scrip; you know what they'll do with it? They'll sell it for short term cash. There's no way they'll save up for a property of their own."

"And whose fault is that? If you can't feed your family, and if you're hungry yourself, there's no telling what you'll do, what lengths you'd go to," Tom says.

"You don't know what you're talking about, Tom," Paco says. "When a poor person shows up late for work, he blames the snowstorm instead of allotting extra time to get there in the first place. If he can't understand something he's supposed to master, it's cuz the sh*tty video tutorial is defective. Then when someone reports him for not doing something he was asked to do, well, the guy who ratted him out is a f*cking liar. When he's fired, he says to his wife and kids, 'See I told you the deck was stacked against me,' and he goes back to drinking his life away. It's always someone else's fault. The difference between successful people and unsuccessful ones is not how they act, it's how they react. The successful guy, when something bad happens in his life, looks in the mirror first to ask himself what he did wrong, what he could do next time so as not to make the same mistake a second time, and then says to himself, 'What can I do to fix this problemo today?'"

"It's a psychological condition known as 'fear of success,' Paco," Nate says.

"Is that the same as fear of failure, Mr Rebich?" another member of the group asks.

"No, not at all. It's a more pernicious effect, and it's very widespread. It's counter intuitive and seemingly illogical. Here's how it works—

A guy says to himself, "I won't really work too hard on this project just in case it fails."
Then the project fails.
Next he says, "The real reason I wasn't successful was because I actually didn't work that hard at it."
Finally, he adds, "But if I had worked hard at it, I would have been successful."

Ergo, his ego is protected.

"This approach guarantees that: a) his ego is insulated from harm and b) his project *will* fail. Since it must result in failure, it must be that, logically, he sought failure not success. Therefore, he must have been more afraid of success than failure. QED.

"It's not logical for people to behave in this way, it just happens to be true in many instances. Markets and people aren't necessarily logical. Understanding this about yourself—acquiring some self-knowledge as well as a greater understanding of others are very important in trying to become more successful and a wiser person.

"Bottom line? Just make sure this fear of success thing doesn't infect your thinking."

Jenna is no help to Tom or anyone else at this point in the argument because Paco and now Nate have accidentally lanced her heart through and through—especially Paco's comment about going "back to drinking his life away," it fits her paw to a fare thee well. She looks away and up to her left, suddenly feeling very sad.

Tom presses on tone deaf to her feelings: "We've got to get to their kids so by the time they reach middle school, they're ready to listen to a different message, right Jenna, Mr Rebich? Education is the key. If children feel hopeful and they're armed with knowledge that all things are possible, well, then they will be. Jenna?"

She turns her head and refocuses once more on her friend: "Yessuh Tommah, hoomin bein's kin't live wifout hope."

"Bravo, Miss Jenna. Here's to *hope*!" says Nate.

They all raise a glass, even Paco, "To *hope*!" they toast as one.

...

How to really finance real estate

Over the years, I've been involved in a lot of real estate financings. If you can do 80% to 100% loan to value financings, it means less money down and more properties… but these days, you have to get creative.

Here're some of the things I've tried:

-strive for decent appraisals
-ask for high ltv, loan to value
-do a good quality CMA, comparative market analysis—see if you can figure out a property's value three different ways—income basis/cost less deprecation/comps
-aim for high cap rates, drive up value (tech packages, other animations like walkout basements, coach houses, in home suites, backyard workshops, home offices, garage offices, micro retail, backyard storage, converting residential homes to commercial on main streets, and make your residential leases more like commercial net net net ones placing more of the costs of running your buildings on tenants)
-do some severances including corner lot severances or subdivide and sell off part of the lands
-decide whether to have partners or no partners[100]

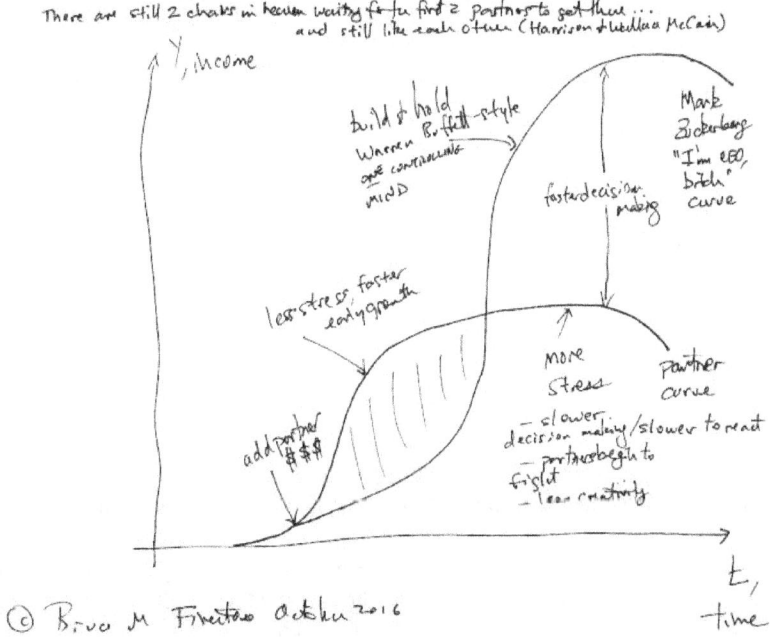

Go a Bit Faster at First with a Partner, Then Much Slower and Plateau Out Sooner

-invite investors via structured equity and planned exit, eg, Mad River/red circle structure
-acquire strategic partners[101]

---

[100] In my drawing here, I show that when a partner gets involved, one with complementary skills and some cash, projects initially seem to move a bit faster but eventually decision making seems to bog down, partners begin to quarrel about who does what/who is working harder… and things slow down or even start to decline. So if you can start a business or building your real estate portfolio without a partner that often bodes well for the longterm.

[101] A strategic partner is someone or some organization that has a *strategic* interest in your success. For example, a general contractor or a subtrade, an architect or a structural engineer will have a strategic interest in your success since, if they help you become successful, they will have created a lasting relationship with a person from whom they can expect future work. As a result, you can often ask them for an investment, a loan guarantee or a sponsorship, and they may very well not ask for much in return, ie, possibly zero equity but, say, a promise that they'll acquire a right to bid on your next job along with a right to match if they're not the low bidder…

-use second or even third mortgages
-use self directed RRSP mortgages or RRSP mortgage "swaps"
-turn up amortization "heat" and pay off your principal faster then refinance
-ask for supplier financing (eg, contractor, trade, sub-trade, financing or Leon's don't-pay-a-cent-event [see my above comment on strategic partners/investors])
-get sponsorship using storytelling and storyliving—where potential donors get to actually *participate* in something (clients, clients' clients, suppliers, trades, sub-trades, contractors, marketing partners, co-branding...)
-sell your building's naming rights[102]
-host an event
-do a fundraiser/get donations and endowments/sell tickets
-pre-sell signage and product placement/get license fees
-approach BDC[103] for 100% ltv (based, partly, on property value and partly on the strength of your balance sheet)
-set up a HELOC, home equity line of credit (don't use CHIP reverse mortgages)
-use scrip[104]

-sell negative interest rate bonds
-use seller take back mortgages
-get land mortgages
-use mortgage brokers

---

[102] I like naming things—Robertson House (a retirement residence), the Palladium (now called the Canadian Tire Centre, where the NHL's Ottawa Senators play) and so forth. Even residential buildings can be named. What's classier? To say that you live in "Henderson House" or at 1234 Any street? So name your buildings/put a plaque on each one. I like names that are easy to say and spell as well as ones that have some connection to the site being developed. Often, I'll look at the history of ownership to see if I can come up with something inspirational. It might even be that as a landlord, you can charge more simply for a project that has a fancy name. Heck, it worked for Donald Trump (for a while).

[103] Business Development Bank of Canada.

[104] Scrip is an old form of financing. It was used to build the original Maple Leaf Gardens in Toronto in the 1930s and even earlier by the Reynolds Bros to build a new sawmill in the 19th century. More recently, Bridgehead Coffee did it in Ottawa—they sold about $3 million in scrip—basically, Bridgehead customers could buy scrip in denominations of $150, $250, $500 and $1,000, which entitled them to purchase Bridgehead products at (if I remember correctly) 10% off. If you're a regular customer, it doesn't take many visits to use up this scrip so if you purchased, say, $300 and you made three visits a week and spent $5 on each visit, why in just 20 weeks, you've used up your credit. Now 20% off over a 20 week period kind of implies an interest on your dough of more than 50% pa, just slightly better than what most banks are offering today (around 1 to 1.7% pa). So it's a good deal for Bridgehead customers. But is it a good deal for Tracey Clark (Bridgehead's owner)? Darn right it is. Coffee margins are huge so her actual cost to drum up $3 million in "equity" (the amount she needed to have on hand to unlock a $15 million capital investment in a new roastery and outlet including $12 million in debt financing) is negative. Tracey is in equity lord territory with her scrip. Now think about how much equity Tracey had to give up... what percentage of her company did she have to part with to raise that $3,000,000? The answer is zero. So I want you to think about your customers, clients, suppliers and employees as strategic partners or strategic investors—they have a stake in your success and will often be prepared to help you in ways that you might not have thought of yet... [Please note I breakdown the exact costs of Tracey's scrip issuance in an addendum to this mini book.]

-partner with Penfunds, eg, Foundry Capital—deployment of pension fund money (80% LTV+), insurance companies, REITs, Pub Cos

-approach venture funds

(Canada, http://www.canadianinvestmentnetwork.com/page/canadian-venture-capital, US and elsewhere, http://www.boogar.com/resources/venturecapital/realestate_funds.htm)

-do some PPSA[105] financing (eg, desjardins.com or Meridian Credit Union does PPSA financing for coach houses)

-ask for a GMP, gross maximum price, from your general contractor

-talk to credit unions re financing

-approach other CMHC[106] approved lenders similar to Foundry

-apply for government grants for NFP[107], green investments, affordable housing...

-finance over 6 units, over $1 million with People's, First National...

-start a family savings plan

-start a business, a PB4L (personal business for life) to earn extra income

-get a 2nd job

-ask for a raise at your day JOB

-move in with your folks or into a less expensive rental to save more

-make your own lunches

-cut back on vacations, presents, restaurants etc

-retire your pet (!)

-sell stuff you've collected but don't need anymore

-get rid of your cable and landline

-sell your car and take public transit, walk more or buy an electric scooter, which typically costs about 50 cents to charge and goes 40 klicks, like Prof Bruce does...

"Hi," says Prof Bruce on his e-bike

-apply for a SBL, small business loan[108]

-consolidate your debt/pay off your credit cards/freeze your credit cards in a bowl so that if you want to use them, you have to wait 24 hours for the water to unfreeze during which time you may have cooled off and decided you don't really need a new Roomba after all

-improve your credit score

-ask your landlord for an inducement and a rent free period

-get a construction loan

---

[105] Personal property security act registration whereby a lender registers their financial interest in something—like a car loan or furniture bought on credit...
[106] Canada Mortgage and Housing Corporation.
[107] Not for profit.
[108] Up to $500,000 in Canada, which can be used to finance building improvements, equipment, etc. The GOC (Government of Canada) guarantees 75% of these loans leaving you, the entrepreneur, personally responsible for just 25% if the business tanks. This program is funded by the GOC but run by Canada's chartered banks. The US has a similar program, their SBA.

-use your credit cards (this contradicts paying off your credit cards but still many people use this approach as long as it is a bridge to something—a takeout mortgage or a flip)

-use hard money loans (http://www.investopedia.com/articles/investing/012617/how-get-loan-flip-house.asp) as a bridge to takeout financing or a flip

-get an unsecured bank loan based on personal creditworthiness

-get "cash back" from a mortgage closing

-put in costs for construction management/project management to get paid by mortgage financing/put a fee in for all your time and effort

-choose closing date just after the 1st so that seller who has just collected rents from tenants will have to credit you the buyer with 29 days of rent plus the damage deposits/last month's rents already collected upon completion

-ask seller to pay your closing costs

-use negative asset pledging [see the excerpt from Jenna's Story above]

-get a co-signor

-do some paid consulting

-collect early/pay late to boost your cashflow

-ask a competitor (a coopetitor[109]) to cooperate and shoulder some project costs

-consider franchising/branchising

-issue debentures

-receivables factoring

-trading/flipping

-start an ESOP (Employee Stock Ownership Plan)

-sell pre-sold services

-sell merchandise

-start an investor syndicate

-obtain retainers

-ask for higher down payments from tenants/buyers

-ask for progress payments/draws

-become a reseller

-buy under option agreement

-ask your partners to loan you your share of startup costs [a riff on my Mad River financing idea]

-enter/start competitions

-ask for larger deposits from tenants (six months in advance instead of one or two)

-find a lender willing to add rental income to your income

-use a crowdfunding real estate site, eg, http://www.openavenue.com/

-pre-sell rights fees (eg, parking rights, F&B (food and beverage), security etc)

-use financial leasing for equipment and tech

-obtain mezzanine financing

-put in a lot of sweat equity

And, of course, animate your properties/projects by increasing their revenue potential/income streams… more on that in a subsequent section ☺

…

---

[109] For example, if you are a homebuilder, invite other homebuilders to set up their sales centers right next to yours and ask them to contribute to the overall cost of the project and its marketing. The idea is that not every possible buyer will like any one particular home style/type. So if three or four homebuilders team up, they *all* actually do better than if only one kind of home is available…

Executive Travel Apartments—reducing your capital requirements, a form of bootstrapping

A decade ago a student of mine introduced me a new form of bootstrap capital (BC), or at least, one I hadn't considered before. It seems obvious to me now but I think it takes some creativity to apply it to any business model.

In fact, of all the things I've taught, self-capitalization is the hardest subject for my students to comprehend. I can give a three hour lecture on this topic, and immediately afterwards, students will come up to me and say, "Yeah, sure, that's all well and good for all the cases you showed in class but what I really need is for a VC fund to simply write me a BIG check," disregarding the fact that most of them (especially if they're interested in anything other than tech) have as much a chance of this as I do of regaining the ability to have a 30-inch vertical jump[110].

Anyway, my student was in the executive travel apartment (ETA) business—those are extended stay suites that executives use and many prefer to a long stay in a hotel room. Today, it's dominated by Airbnb but when she started, each ETA biz was essentially on its own... to develop relationships with future potential clients, whether it was execs themselves or their companies.

It is a very capital-intensive business; she needs equity to buy her units, renovate them, and furnish them. She can reduce her capital needs by mortgaging the units using high LTV (loan to value) ratios and leasing (or leasing to own) the furniture she needs for each unit. Still her equity requirements are non-trivial.

She came up with a very inventive method of expanding her budding empire without having to bring in a partner or sell her soul to finance companies.

Bootstrapping is simply a way to lower the level of capital you require in the first place.

She charges about $3,500 to $4,500 per month for her ETAs, which works out to about $120 to $150 per night for a one, two or three bedroom unit which is fully furnished, the internet and TV work, VOiP phones are on and there is a starter kit (soap, salt and pepper, bread, milk, cheese etc) on hand. Just let yourself in using a lockbox combination, and relax, you're home.

Because these are ETAs, she comes under the Innkeepers Act[111] and not the RTA (Residential Tenancy Act) so she is much less likely to have trouble with her tenants than a typical residential tenancy where delinquency is high, collections are tough and getting rid of them (evicting them) is even harder to do.

A typical unit can cost her $200,000 or more to buy (with anywhere from 5% to 25% equity required), $20,000 to renovate and another $10k or so to furnish. So each unit can easily consume $70 or $80k of her available equity. Other ETA operators solve this problem by selling units to investors and keeping management in their hands plus a share of ownership.

She came up with another way—what if she went to existing residential landlords and told them, "Hey, guys, I will rebrand some (or all) of your units, umm, I mean repackage them as executive travel apartments. And, by the way, make you more dough at the same time with less hassle and less bad debt. What do you think?"

---

[110] About average for a NCAA division 1 football player; source: https://www.bodybuilding.com/fun/henkin6jjjj.htm.

[111] Many hosts in the Airbnb model reject any form of regulation, a constant irritant to the established hotel industry as well as to permanent residents in a neighborhood where Airbnb is active or in a tower where units are being offered for stays as short as one night. Airbnb also attracts the wrath of so-called affordable housing advocates who, at least in my view, target Airbnb hosts (especially if they own multiple locations) of taking affordable rental units out of the marketplace. I think potential regulators are looking through the wrong end of the telescope. Many of my clients, many of them not especially well off, depend on these revenues for their livelihood or, in some cases, just to pay their own rent or mortgage. I will have more to say on this subject in a subsequent mini book, no doubt.

From a Landlord's POV[112], that takes him or her out of the purview of the RTA and he or she now only has to manage one tenant (the ETA operator) who worries about furnishing the units, renting them out, managing, and maintaining them, etc.

In the buy scenario described above, she will need $80,000 in equity per door. If she rents each unit out for $4,000 per month and has a mortgage at 6% with a 20-year amortization period, she will be left with a NOI (Net Operating Income) after deducting a vacancy allowance, marketing costs, admin, property taxes, insurance, and contingencies of about $1,077 per unit per month.

If she sublets some of her units from a cooperative landlord at $1,400 monthly, she is left with less—just $766.49 per month per unit. This is because she is paying less on her mortgage than she is in rent to the property owner.

But in the first case, she needs $80k of equity; in the second case, she only needs $30k.

Now her simple ROE (Return on Equity) is 16.2% pa when she buys her own units versus a whopping 30.7% when she rents them instead. (See my spreadsheet below.)

Now this model ignores the wealth effect of owning your own units (the annual paydown of your mortgage principal, in effect, by your tenants) and real estate inflation (that goes solely to the equity holder).

If I considered those factors, the ROEs would probably be a lot closer. However, that doesn't matter if she can't afford to expand her business because the equity demands of the first model are too high for her to handle.

So the obvious choice is to do both—own some units and sublet some. As her cashflow improves, she should probably be buying relatively more of her units.

But at least initially, from her POV, her capital requirements have dropped from the $70 to $80k per door range to $10 to $30k per door and her ability to grow the business faster has just taken a quantum leap upwards.

Today, this model has been integrated into Airbnb's platform. Now they ask hosts if they would consider managing other nearby properties for other hosts, many of whom given up because they find running an Airbnb is too much work or they find the platform too hard to use or they aren't very good at marketing their units or engaging in dynamic pricing—driving prices down during slow months and up during busy times.

To give you some idea of the power of dynamic pricing, look at this screenshot (below) that one of my clients sent me from his iPhone.

He owns a brand new double (side-by-side units) near the University of Ottawa, a downtown location.

From a standing start in February 2017, he makes about $3,414.88 per month per door, a total of $6,829.76 monthly in rent revenues from Airbnb. But July 2017, marked Canada's 150th birthday so, by the middle of that month, they'd been paid $13,748 (almost $6,900 per door).

How come? Because they raised their pricing as the world descended on Canada's Capital City for a BIG partay and vacancies for every (hotel and Airbnb) room available within 100 kilometers approached zero.

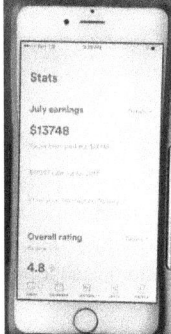

---

[112] Point of view.

The fact that they even own these buildings is a story in itself.

He and his partner loaned the original builder $225,000 (as a second mortgage, postponed to a first construction mortgage provided by a local MIC, mortgage investment corporation) to complete his buildings. But instead of the guy using those funds to finish construction, he used them on other projects after which he filed for bankruptcy. What the heck!

Now what are buildings that are only ¾ done worth? Not very much, I can tell you. In fact, they often have a negative value because, in the worst case, you have to take them down (which costs money[113]) and start over.

Firstly, you will probably never be able to sell them to the public because, at least in Ontario, you'd have to register them with Tarion (the industry's regulator). A Tarion registration and warranty is required for all new homes sold to the public; it's so consumers don't (hopefully) lose their deposit(s) and they have some protection for deficiencies/shoddy workmanship, some of which almost all new homes will (unfortunately) have.

Secondly, when you buy something that is not finished, you don't really know what you are getting no matter how many and types of inspections you do. Therefore, there's a big risk.

When the "boys" (both in their early 30s) came to see me, there was some good news. Their mortgage had foreclosure provisions in it, which meant they had the ability to cure the first mortgagee's default and take over *ownership*, ie, put the project in their own names.

Mind you, you don't do this without having a plan on how to—a) complete construction, b) animate/differentiate it, and c) make some money.

A couple of other factors you need to know. They already owned about 80 towns of their own and know construction so they are way ahead of most investors. If you've never built anything before, you might just accept the write-off of your investment rather than doing what they did—basically, doubling down.

Anywho, they got that MIC to take a haircut of $100,000 per door and also to provide them with enough funding (curiously, an amount exactly equal to $225,000) to finish the project.

Their aim? To furnish the units and then put them on Airbnb.

So they managed to turn a frog into a prince.

This:

Into this:

---

[113] You have to disconnect all services, apply for, pay for and obtain a demolition permit, bring in a high hoe excavator to knock the building(s) down, then load all the crap and truck it away to a landfill site, where you pay a disposal fee, then you go back to your site and prepare it for a new build or otherwise make it safe so that kids don't end up hurting themselves in a giant hole with sharp metal things laying about everywhere. It's expensive. And if it's a taller building (more than three stories), forget about it. It gets *really* costly.

Thus, they found a way to turn an almost certain $225,000 *total* loss of their second mortgage into a $455,000 equity position plus now they own two excellent units in a hot market with a great longterm outlook. See my spreadsheet below.

Their plan is to hold onto these units until they are old guys, and then pass them onto their kids. Good plan.

They also don't intend on giving any more construction loans to contractors, at least without first talking to their real estate investment coach (moi).

MIC total initial construction financing (1st mortgage)	$550,000	per door	2	doors	$1,100,000
the "boys" 2nd mortgage with both POS & foreclosure rights					$225,000
total financing					$1,325,000
MIC "haircut"	$100,000	per door	2	doors	($200,000)
the "boys" haircut					($225,000)
MIC	$450,000	per door	2	doors	$900,000
MIC					$225,000
MIC new 1st mortgage	$562,500	per door	2	doors	$1,125,000
appraised value after completion	$790,000	per door	2	doors	$1,580,000
Equity position	$227,500	per door	2	doors	$455,000

E&OE

...

If we take into account the wealth effect and the impact of real estate inflation, the two rates of return (this time measured using the IRR instead of a simple ROE ratio) are, in fact, closer. In the "buy" scenario, the return increases from 16.2% pa to 22.8% while for the "sublet" scenario, the return remains that same at 30.7%.

The latter doesn't change because, in this model, I have assumed that when she sells the business (or revalues it) at the end of year 7 (an arbitrary timeline, I might add), she realizes exactly what she put in initially for renovations and furnishings. Of course, in reality what she gets for the business would depend on what she and a buyer agree to which could be greater or less than this amount. Nevertheless, in order not to bias the comparative analysis, it seemed reasonable to make this assumption.

ETA Case Study—Buy the Units

Cost per Unit $200,000
Equity ($50,000) 25%
Mortgage $150,000 75%
Interest 6% pa
Amortization 20 years
Monthly Payment ($1,089.81) to Lender
Renovations ($20,000)
Furniture ($10,000)
($30,000)
Interest 10% pa
Amortization 7 years
Monthly Payment ($513.51)
Total Cost ($1,603.32)
Monthly Rent $4,000
Marketing ($320) 8%
Vacancy ($480) 12%
Other ($240) 6%
Contingencies ($280) 7%
NOI $1,077 per month
Equity ($80,000)
ROE 16.2% per annum
Year
0 ($80,000.00)
1 $ 12,920.15
2 $ 12,920.15
3 $ 12,920.15
4 $ 12,920.15
5 $ 12,920.15
6 $ 12,920.15
7 $ 167,186.31 $ 12,920.15 $ 124,266.15 $30,000
IRR 22.8% pa Assumes the business is sold or "revalued"
and the sale price of the biz
Real Estate Inflation 2.75% equals the investment in
Selling Price $ 241,825.90 furniture and renovations.
Agency Fees ($12,091.29) 5%
Legal Fees/Closing Costs ($1,105.00)
Net $ 228,629.60
Principal Repaid
1 ($5,436.91)
2 ($5,763.13)
3 ($6,108.91)
4 ($6,475.45)
5 ($6,863.98)
6 ($7,275.81)
7 ($7,712.36)
Total Principal Repaid ($45,636.55)
Mortgage Balance Due $104,363.45
Net to Seller $ 124,266.15 on completion

ETA Case Study—Sublet the Units

Cost per Unit 0
Equity 0
Mortgage 0
Monthly Payment ($1,400) to Landlord
Renovations ($20,000)
Furniture ($10,000)
($30,000)
Interest 10% pa
Amortization 7 years
Monthly Payment ($513.51)
Total Cost ($1,913.51)
Monthly Rent $4,000
Marketing ($320) 8%
Vacancy ($480) 12%
Other ($240) 6%
Contingencies ($280) 7%
NOI $766.49 per month
Equity ($30,000)
ROE 30.7% per annum
Year
0 ($30,000)
1 $9,197.84
2 $9,197.84
3 $9,197.84
4 $9,197.84
5 $9,197.84
6 $9,197.84
7 $39,197.84 $9,197.84 $30,000
IRR 30.7% per annum Assumes the business is sold (or valued)
and the sale price (value) of the biz
equals the investment in furniture and renovations.
E&OE

Another client recently showed me how he could acquire inventory for his retail store at a negative cost to him—other retailers are paying him to feature their products and services in his outlet store. They pay him a monthly fee for this plus they give him a percentage of each of their products or services that he sells for them on consignment.

We are now busy applying this philosophy to other types of businesses with great effect.

...

Why use mortgage brokers

Why use mortgage brokers? Why not just go to your bank?

Here's why—

1. they can source mortgages from 8, 10 or more lenders from just one credit report (up to 42 I'm told by one mortgage broker not counting private lenders)
2. they can get more competitive interest rates and terms than you probably can
3. they are paid by lenders at least for most residential mortgages (commercial borrowers usually pay their fees directly; note some residential clients may pay a fee to B or C lenders and mortgage brokers too)
4. they save you (a lot of) time
5. they protect your beacon/credit score from multiple hits
6. they can often get you higher LTV, loan to value ratios
7. they can get you a second mortgage if you need it
8. they can help you structure financings
9. they can make investor/partner introductions
10. they can advise you on ways to retire debt faster (eg, paying your mortgage 2 x a month)
11. they work for *you* not lenders
12. they keep you away from banks that use tied selling to push their own (often) more expensive products like mortgage insurance or (often) poorly performing mutual funds
13. mortgage brokers are licensed by FSCO
14. they are not selling you a limited number of bank products—they pull from the entire spectrum
15. lenders pay mortgage broker fees whether it's to an independent or someone from within their own institution

...

The More Leverage You Take On Early in Your Career, the Less You will Have Later On

Huh?

Yes, you heard me right. Taking on more debt early in your career, can help you retire your overall debt faster later on.

Real estate in my experience is the only known perpetual motion machine in existence anywhere in the universe.

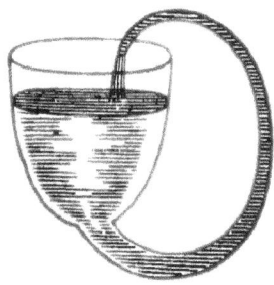

Say you buy a single $300,000 property with 25% (ie, $75,000) down. It's a nice one—well located, and it earns a decent rent.

You sell it (or better yet, you refinance it) after five years.

After you take into account cashflow, paydown of mortgage and a bit of property inflation on the +ve side, and some realtor and attorney fees on the -ve side, you end up with $159,146 in cash[114]. Cool.

This represents an IRR (internal rate of return) of 18.5% pa. Sure beats your bank savings account, which has been paying you a measly 1.5% pa.

But what if you'd been able to buy five properties with 5% down (instead of just one with 25% down)?

Well, because you have higher mortgage payments, you make *less* on each property than you did before: only $80,718 after five years.

But remember, you own five of the suckers so your *total* cash on hand after five years is $403,591! Way better than the $159,146 with just one property.

Now I realize that 5% down is tougher to do in 2017 than it was before the modern economy nearly crumbled in the Great Reset (recession of 2008/09). But even if you can only do 2 and ½ buildings (at 10% down) instead of one at 25%, the same set of facts will apply.

There are some other caveats such as you must: a) buy good performing properties that appreciate in value and are in demand, b) be able to add value by animating them, c) write smart leases and d) manage them properly (no deferred maintenance please).

Of course by now you know, you can goose your returns even higher if you subscribe to the Warren Buffett method of investing. Instead of selling them after five years, you re-evaluate them, re-appraise them and refinance them. This allows you to avoid transaction fees (realtor, legal and opportunity costs) as well as income or capital taxes on your gains.

Then you repeat the process. Pretty soon (in 12-15 years) you have an amazing real estate investment portfolio of surprising size.

I haven't found anything else that works reliably like this does. Everything else I've tried (mutual funds, pen funds, hockey team (the Ottawa Senators), newspaper (Ottawa Business News now Ottawa Business Journal), taxi sign company, stock market... you name it, I've done it) has flopped.

And as you will recall, the money you take out via refinancing is tax-free.

---

[114] Of course, if you refinance it, you don't pay any realtor fees or legal fees and you don't pay any taxes on your profits either so that's why I implore you over and over again to buy and hold not buy and sell.

Worked for Warren.

Here's a spreadsheet I did for a client of mine who buys industrial property. But if you change "industrial condo" to "residential rental" the principles are identical…

https://www.dropbox.com/s/oglyh5ud032bhuu/Sample-IRR-2-commercial-5%25-v-25%25.xls?dl=0

Sample IRR 2   Commercial

Sample IRR for an Industrial Condo-- 5% down payment   WEALTH EFFECT

Your new industrial condo costs:	$300,000
Your downpayment must be:	5%
Your equity (downpayment) is:	$15,000
Your First Mortgage is:	$285,000
Your interest rate is:	6.5%
Your amortization period is:	20 years
Your imputed rent is:	$2,300 per month
Your mortgage cost is:	($25,865.57) per year
Your net rent or net imputed rent is:	$1,734.43 per year CASH ON CASH RETURN
The annual inflation rate in commercial real estate is:	2.20% INFLATION
You sell your industrial condo after five years for:	$ 334,484.30
Realtor fees	$ (16,724.21) 5%
Legal and Closing Costs	$ (2,508.63) 0.75%
Net Selling Price	$ 315,251.45

Principal paid on your mortgage is:

	Year 1	($7,340.57)
	Year 2	($7,817.71)
	Year 3	($8,325.86)
	Year 4	($8,867.04)
	Year 5	($9,443.40)
	Total	($41,794.59) FORCED SAVINGS

Principal remaining after five years $243,205.41

Your cashflow profile is:

	Year 0	-15000 1
	Year 1	$1,734.43 1.4387
	Year 2	$1,734.43 2.06989849
	Year 3	$1,734.43 2.9779923
	Year 4	$1,734.43 4.28447974
	Year 5	$73,780.46 6.16414174
	Net cash gain	$ 65,718.17
	Total cash returned	$ 80,718.17

Your equity IRR is: 43.9% $0.00 check

Five projects like this, your cash returned in 5 years is: $ 403,590.86 $80,718.17 per property

Project IRR is

	Year 0	-300000

Year 1		$27,600.00
Year 2		$27,600.00
Year 3		$27,600.00
Year 4		$27,600.00
Year 5	$	362,084.30
Net cash gain	$	172,484.30
Total cash returned	$	**472,484.30**

Your project IRR is: 11.0%

The IRR on the project is made up of the 'weighted average' IRR on your equity: 43.9%

plus the IRR on your debt: 6.5%

...

Accretive Finance

I have a client who runs a mini storage business whose biggest profit center is not actually renting 10'x10' or 10'x20' lockers either heated or unheated, but leasing parking spaces on his graveled lot.

Trucks, RVs, trailers, loaders, pickups, backhoes, semis... all find a resting place in his yard, and the more local ordinances the municipality passes (like no RVs permitted in your driveway), the more demand he sees for his parking lot.

There is more good news—his site is big, over 13 acres so he has lots of room for expansion.

The bad news is that no lender will back him with cash to expand his parking business—they don't like the fact that there are no long term (say 5-year) leases (I mean who would sign a 5-year parking lease, really?) plus there are no additional structures built to secure their loans—only a bigger graveled yard.

How much does it cost to gravel a yard?

Well, an acre is 43,560 sq ft, and if you strip the topsoil off and add 12 inches of compacted engineered fill (granular B topped by granular A, ie, gravel), you need 43,560 cu ft or 1,613.3 cu yds of fill.

Note that he has a sandy soil under his overburden (topsoil) so it has a decent bearing capacity. Thus, he can get away with 12 inches of fill instead of the 18 inches he'd need if he had a clay base instead, so in a way he's lucky.

If he orders loads that deliver 15 cu yds at a time, he'll need 108 truckloads. In a place like Ottawa, that'll cost him around $300 a load or $32,400 total.

He'll rent a dozer, loader, grader and roller, and operate them himself (he's licensed to operate machinery of this size and complexity), so he'll save some more money.

But for you and me, we are more likely to order the equipment together with skilled operators so it'll cost us more. We'll also need a water truck to spray H_2O on our fill to get a nice tight compacted fill and excellent parking surface.

My client can probably gravel an acre for $38,000, which might cost you and me $45,000. If you need 18 inches of fill or more, you'll have to adjust these numbers upwards. You'll also need to adjust the numbers up or down for the price of fill in your neighborhood, to the extent it's higher than $300 a load or lower.

So how is he going to pay for it?

Easy.

He'll find a supplier[115] who'll finance it for him this way:

1. cost is $38,000 for an acre of parking lot
2. he can fit 48 semis on each acre (with double-loaded parking aisles)
3. he charges by the linear foot so short RVs pay less than longer ones, which pay less than semis
4. making things simple, let's assume he rents to 48 semis/acre at $100 per month per semi
5. that's $4,800 each month in income
6. if he pays his supplier by pledging half of his increase in income, he'll retire his obligation in 38,000/2,400 or 15.8 months

He might offer his supplier an extra month to compensate them for the fact that they have to wait for full payment, but he can entice them by saying, "I've got another 12 acres to fill, so when we get this done and mostly rented, let's do it again. So look at this not as a $38,000 sale but more like a ($38,000 + $2,400) x 13 or $525,200 sale."

"Deal!" his supplier exclaims.

---

[115] Ah ha, a strategic partner—someone who has a strategic interest in his success like a friendly quarry operator who wants to make him more successful so they can sell him more gravel...

In a way, you've just created a (for-real) perpetual motion (money) machine (as long as demand is buoyant).

This is not a new concept. Accretive finance has been around for a very long time. You know those "Don't pay a cent events" that furniture and appliance stores run? A form of accretive finance in a way.

Say you offer your 1-bedroom flat for rent at $930 a month + utilities ($145) + a tech package ($115 for high speed Internet, wi-fi, basic cable, Netflix and wall-mounted, large screen TV) or a total of $1,190 per month. However, you just found out if you furnish it; you can get $75 a night on airbnb. That works out to $2,250 with a 70% occupancy rate or $1,575 per month, an extra $385 for you.

But whoa there cowboy or cowgirl, now you gotta buy some furniture. It costs you just $1,750 to do that because you are one smart person—you put $750 cash in your jeans and take your pickup for a tour of your city whereupon you find out that people in an aging population like Canada's are dying like flies. So you are able to get a fabulous dining set plus living room and bedroom furnishings from lazy heirs for almost nothing because they want to empty out grandma's house as fast as possible so they can sell it and use the proceeds to pay down their stupidly high personal debt.

Where do you get the other $1,000? Well, you got it from the furniture store who tells you that you won't have to pay a cent til next year—January and it's just March now so you've got 9 months to save up. In 9 months, you'll have an extra $385 x 9 or $3,465; plenty to pay off the store.

What's your cap rate on the cost of furnishing your 1-bedroom flat?

It's $385 x 12/$1,750 or an incredible 264% pa; ie, this is worth doing brothers and sisters since cap rates on residential rentals in Ottawa are anywhere from 4% to 8%; in Toronto, 2-3%, in Van city even less. So if you can get a marginal cap rate of a few hundred percent, that's pretty decent.

You should also know that due to traffic theory, he will never actually get to 100% parking lot occupancy. I've told him that when he gets to 75%, 85% or 95% occupancy on each acre, it's time to gravel the next acre. Don't wait for 100%.

The reason?

Occupancy rates are asymptotic so it's like crossing a room by going halfway across then half of that half then half of that quarter etc. You'll never actually make it to the other side of the room so don't try this at home.

In practical terms, even for very busy mini storage buildings/parking lots/co-working spaces/mini offices and so forth, they experience vacancy even when they are full.

Say you decide to terminate your parking agreement mid-month, and I need to park my RV at the end of the month, there is a vacancy even though the lot is "fully" leased.

Even residential subdivisions that have been around for years and years almost always have a few lots not built on.

So if there is a neighborhood that you absolutely want to live in, but you are told there are no building lots, walk or drive around—you'll see a home somewhere on a double lot, maybe hidden behind a hedge, which you may be able to pry from the hands of the existing owner… the extra lot that is.

…

15 Reasons Why Most Partnerships Fail

Why do most partnerships fail? In my experience, it's because—

1. no one is really in charge
2. partners battle over unequal contributions either in terms of sweat equity (workload) or money
3. the decision making process is ill-defined and takes too long
4. one partner thinks the other one will take care of problems/seize opportunities when really no one is
5. they argue over their partnership agreement, which is like a prenuptial agreement—agreeing to the terms of a divorce before you get married
6. differences of opinion on who to hire
7. differences of opinion on who to finance with and how
8. no one is really controlling costs
9. no one is really taking responsibility for sales
10. the new enterprise eventually becomes an orphan while the principals and erstwhile partners look for better opportunities where they can deploy their creativity more freely and put in "100% of the effort to reap 100% of the rewards"
11. the partners don't really share the same values, vision, goals, and plan for the business
12. one partner has significantly more financial resources so, when there is a call for capital, they end up owning more and more of the enterprise
13. they argue over how to divvy up income from the business, and how much to reinvest in the business
14. they fight over succession planning especially as and when their families get involved
15. there is a breakdown of trust, especially during trying times

So consider this: if you can, whether you are starting a real estate investment business, a service business, buying a franchise or possibly even launching a tech firm, go it alone. If you can't afford it or don't yet have all the skills, wait a bit until you've found a way finance your launch on your own (ie, sans partner(s)) or hire the skills you need paying them with anything other than equity.

Sometimes the slower you go, the faster you'll grow.

...

Trade-off between Property Management and ROI

As I get more experience with other forms of rental such as Airbnb and rooming houses, furnished apartments, rooming houses, old-style bed and breakfasts, and travel apartments versus unfurnished yearly rentals, I've come to realize there is a tradeoff between the intense property management that arises when you have functional programs involving, say, roommates or executive travel apartments versus when you are simply renting out unfurnished rentals on a yearly basis, which are the simplest form of landlord property management other than possibly old fashioned mini storage buildings. You know the types of places that are basically unheated garages where folks even have to provide their own locks.

The trade-off probably goes something like this:

Tradeoff between time invested and ROI in property management

type of rental	Typical time invested (hours per month)	Typical cap rate (pa)
single family home	1.5	4.5%
duplex	3	6%
triplex	3.5	6.5%
airbnb	7	7.5%
rooming house	8	8%
microsuites	4.5	9%
industrial condo	1.5	10%

Note: notional data based on author's experience

E&OE

The data when graphed looks like this:

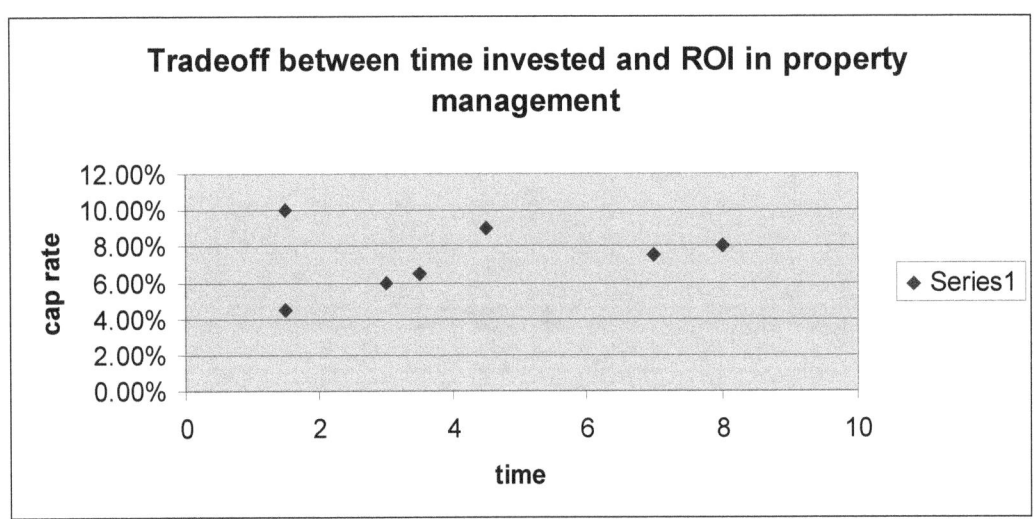

And then there are micro-suites, possibly the hottest trend in real estate in NA, North America. These are small self-contained units—bachelor or 1-bedroom with (preferably) their own ingress/egress from the street.

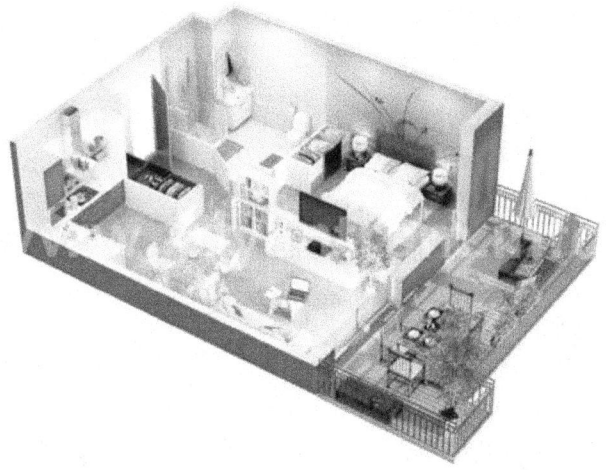

Micro-suites appear to come with a high ROI but a low investment at least in terms of property management time[116].

Tenants in micro-suites likely stay longer (than, say, roommates), lowering your churn rate, decreasing damage to your building, reducing your marketing costs as well as your costs to prep a place for your next tenant once it becomes vacant…

Why do folks prefer micro-suites to being a roommate?

It avoids arguments like:

"Who ate my (leftover) pizza?"

"Who drank my beer?"

"It's your turn to clean the bathroom!" "No it isn't. I did it last week."

"Could you please not leave your dirty dishes in the sink!"

Etc

Basement micro-suites can be full of light with their own private or semi-private outdoor space if you "manufacture" a condition that looks like this—

dug basement

---

[116] Micro-suites appear to be an outlier as are industrial condos, which in my experience are relatively easy to manage for a number of reasons including—longer term leases (typically five years), plus industrial tenants tend to pay their rent on time, and they're generally a low maintenance breed of people. If something breaks, they're just as likely (or more likely) to fix it themselves than call their landlord. The main downside of industrial leasing is that it can take a long time to fill a vacancy.

So micro-suites could be a way to get off the property management time versus ROI tradeoff curve; in fact, it's a new condition where you have relatively low management intensity combined with a relatively high return on investment.

And every time you add independent ingress/egress, what I like to call a WOW (window on the world) effect, you add yet more value. A client of mine did exactly that with two of his suites as shown in the series of photos below.

If you look carefully, you can see two fire exit doors have been added on either side of the main access to this converted 6-plex. Before it was renovated, it was a women's shelter.

My client bought it in a competitive situation where, interestingly, they were *not* the high bidder. The reason they got the place (which is in a desirable, inner city location in Ottawa) was because their offer came with a personal letter from the designer (the wife in a husband-wife investor duo) describing their plans for the building, promising to make something special out of it.

It required a near total gut job as well as structural repairs. They did an outstanding job but missed the opportunity to use the two new fire exit doors as, in effect, front doors for two of their six units. As soon as I pointed out that they could replace their steel doors with fire-resistant glass ones, they implemented this idea.

So instead of all six units using the same main entrance, they now had two with independent ingress/egress. Guess which ones rented first and for more dough?

…

Staging your home and even your commercial space

Your Home Staging Checklist

Staging is about building your brand and there has never been a generation more conscious about branding than this one. Branding builds trust and trust creates the opportunity to make a sale.

Here are my 16 tips on staging a home. Note that we have also staged office space, even industrial warehouse space (using a similar yet different set of rules) to great effect.

1. De-clutter (remove excess furniture/create attractive furniture groupings)
2. De-personalize
3. Patch, repair and paint walls (neutral shades that match especially in adjacent rooms) as required
4. Clean everything (including under sinks)/wash windows and doors
5. Tidy cupboards
6. Air out home
7. Make sure everything works
8. Cut grass, tidy yard
9. Beds made, fresh linens and towels set out
10. If you have children, one designated play zone
11. If you store surplus things in the home, one designated storage area only (neat)
12. Add one memorable design element such as—elegant-looking (but inexpensive) chandelier, simulated antique bench with fold up seat for additional storage, hotel-chic towel bars, outside art-deco awning over entrance or street-facing window, decorative shutters bordering street facing windows, California shutters instead of curtains or drapes...
13. Increase wattage in your lamps to 100 watts per 50 or 60 square feet using LED bulbs
14. Hang compatible art in rooms
15. Accessorize in groups of three
16. Don't spend a lot of money but do spend enough time on staging

...

Home Staging in a Commercial Setting

I am a fairly recent convert to the value of staging.

Imagine if you went to your favourite men's store to buy a new suit and you found all the suits strewn about the shop floor. To find one, you had to walk over others, pick it up, dust it off and try it on. The store probably wouldn't sell many suits.

In commercial real estate, I have long known that you need to merchandise your products. If you own an old industrial building, it will lease (or sell) a lot faster if: a) it is super clean, b) the paint is fresh, c) all the ceiling tiles (in the office portion) are in place and none are water stained, d) the grass is cut, e) the gardens tended to, f) broken windows and signage are fixed. If you own a piece of land with an old building that is at the end of its economic life, take it down, run a dozer over the land and let people see the lot and imagine the possibilities—trust me, land with nothing on it is worth more than land with a near-derelict building on it.

This is similar to when you buy a new car—you spec the color, whether it is automatic or not, tint the windows, add fog lights, sunroof and rear deck spoiler, etc. You drive it off the lot to work where you are promptly let go so you drive it back to the car lot the same day you bought it and they offer to take it off your hands for 30% less than you paid for it a few hours ago. You freak out.

But believe it or not, from the dealers POV, this is rational.

Why? Because now that you have spec'd all this stuff, they have to find a buyer who wants exactly what you want plus s/he wants what is now a secondhand car.

So they have to restock it, re-warranty it, re-plate it and prep it for a new buyer when one is found. Plus they have to finance it while it is on the lot.

Thus, if you have an old building that has to come down, spend the extra money to take it down—it's a "merchandising" cost. If you put up a building, realize that the moment you do, you have locked in all the options (size of building, materiality, function, and form) which reduces the value of the land underneath... it's weird but true.

The Broken Windows Syndrome[117] was first discovered in the 1980s and is now widely applied in the field of urban planning. For example, if you leave a middle-of-the-road car which is clean and in decent shape in a difficult part of town, it will experience little vandalism even if left for quite some time. But throw a brick through one window then stand back and watch—within minutes the car will be stripped to its hubcaps.

When he was Mayor of NYC, Rudolph Giuliani, a former prosecutor, read about Broken Windows and he knew instinctively that this was the right approach for his city. He brought in a no-tolerance policy for vandalism, graffiti and petty crime. He understood that a neighborhood that looked like it was in decay and that tolerated petty crime (prostitution and other so-called victimless crime like drug taking) would attract major crime and even faster decay would result. In urban planning terms, you cannot create any value from real estate if public safety is at risk. Just look at Detroit practically giving away 100s of vacant homes per year—homes that you can buy for as little as $500 and still there are few takers.

In NYC, if your outside lamp is busted, a window or fence is broken, a door askew, graffiti on your wall, whatever, you will get a notice to fix it and, if you don't, the city will fix it and charge you for it. There is no tolerance for decay in either the public room or the property facing the public room and NYC has become a much safer place as a result.

Home staging for houses has been known to be an effective selling tool for a long time—if you are going to sell your home, do a few simple things that don't cost very much and you will add a lot of value; the basics are: a) clean it up, b) paint what needs to be painted, c) cut the grass, d) tend the gardens, e) patch any holes in the drywall and fix whatever is broken, f) de-clutter the home, garage and any outbuildings, g) stage it.

You notice I don't say spend thousands of dollars updating your kitchen and bathrooms, finishing your basement or adding a swimming pool. The reason for this is simple—almost all major investments like this have a negative ROI—it costs you more to do it than you can get if you sell it.

There is a useful online calculator that the Appraisal Institute of Canada has on its site (http://component.aicanada.ca/e/resourcecenter_renova.cfm#select) that shows a typical investment of $5,000 (say) in a bathroom renovation and another $15,000 in a kitchen update may yield expected returns of between 75% and 100% or $15,100 to $20,000. I learned a long time ago not to make investments that turn four quarters into a dollar and I don't encourage clients to do that either.

I love this one—add a swimming pool for $30,000 and your ROI ranges from 0 to $7,500. In fact, heating, cleaning, repairing, opening and closing a pool are so expensive and the risk of accident and home insurance premium increases that may result from installing the pool in the first place, make me think that AIC is overestimating the value—it may very well be negative.

So there are some smart, cost-effective things you can do to help you merchandise your home or commercial property and one of those things is staging.

A recent experience proved that for me: we had taken over leasing of an office penthouse floor in downtown Ottawa with spectacular views of the Parliamentary Precinct. The floor had been the head office of a major company but they had left behind some office furniture in jumbled heaps, there was garbage everywhere, the place was a mess and the floors were dirty.

---

[117] The Atlantic Monthly, James Wilson and George Kelling, March 1982.

The space was incredibly funky (in a good way) and would make terrific space for a marketing company, an embassy, a tech firm, what have you. Yet the place has been empty for more than a year.

We finally got the OK from the landlord to stage it—clean it, de-clutter it, arrange the furniture, take professional photos and do basic merchandising.

Before they even finished (the cleaners were just completing vacuuming), we had a showing and a day later we had an offer (from a finance company).

The value proposition of the two ladies who run the local staging company was unbelievable. The IRR (Internal Rate of Return) on the $1,600 investment (to clean, take photos and stage it) was a ridiculous 10,683% pa for the landlord.

I calculated their IRR as follows:

Value Proposition: Home Staging in a Commercial Setting

Office Space 5,400 sq ft
Net Rent $15.95 per sq ft per year
Op. Costs $16 per sq ft per year
Total $31.95 per sq ft per year
Total $172,530.00 per year
Cost of Staging $800
Cost of Cleanup $600
Cost of Expert Photos $200
Total Costs $1,600
Time vacant 1 year
Time to offer 15 minutes
IRR
0 ($1,600)
1 $172,530.00
IRR 10683% pa

This is, of course, another example that is ripe for a negative cost selling approach. If you are a stager, when you visit with a property owner you tell him or her that by hiring you and your team for $1,600, they will make $172,530 or, put another way, their cost for hiring you is a *negative* $170,930, well that is a pretty strong value proposition. Or to paraphrase one of my students, "I will pay you $170,930 to hire me to stage your office building!"

...

I use this quote from Sarah Williams Goldhagen[118] elsewhere in this mini book but it's worth repeating, "Our relationship to the built environment differs from that of any other art. It affects us all the time... It affects our moods and emotions... What the new paradigm of embodied or situated cognition reveals is that the built environment and its design matters far, far more than anybody, even architects, ever thought that it did."

This idea—that humans have a situated cognition highly sensitive to built form—together with our current understanding about Broken Windows Syndrome—are why I argue over and over again against deferred maintenance.

My clients think I am a nuisance when I remind them that fixing *everything*, right away is incredibly important.

I'll bore them with a story of how a lender who cheaped out on a power of sale (Canada's kinder, gentler answer to American-style foreclosure) turned a $10,000 roof leak problem in the spring into a $350,000 collapse in the sale price of a small 24-unit apartment building in the fall because they didn't

---

[118] *Welcome to Your World—How the built environment shapes out lives*, HarperCollins, 2017.

fix it until black mold (the worst kind—deadly to human health[119]) got loose in the building. In fact, they never fixed it—the buyer did but not before offsetting his cost for remediation against an accepted purchase price.

So this everyone can understand. But more subtly, if a tenant (commercial or residential, it doesn't matter) walks into a well maintained building, where everything gleams even if it's an old place, they are far more likely not only to rent the place but to take pride in it themselves.

You will see far less damage to your buildings, and get much higher rents as well as attract a better class of tenant if you have no deferred maintenance and not just when you are trying to lease the place.

When a tenant calls, answer your phone.

Fix what needs to be fixed asap.

My wife got a call recently from a tenant of ours—they pay $2,400 a month for a townhouse we own. They had ants and didn't know what to do about it.

So I went to Home Depot and bought $6 worth of ant traps and took it over to them the next day.

My wife asked, "Geez, why couldn't they do it themselves?"

I answered, "Miss Dawn, that's the first call we've gotten in two years from someone who has given our family nearly $50,000. For $50k, I'll gladly go to the hardware store and purchase six dollars worth of any traps and personally deliver them," which I did.

The tenants are super nice people who treat that place as if it were theirs and I appreciate the fact that they help support an old dude like me (I'm 65 as I write this ☺) and his family. I'm grateful, truly.

Brian Dagenais (I also talk about Brian elsewhere in this work) told me, "Prof Bruce, if you owned a $400,000 Lamborghini would you take good care of it?"

"You bet I would, Brian."

"Well, I can't understand then why people who own a $400,000 home or townhouse let their buildings go to sh*t?"

Well said, Mr Dagenais.

...

---

[119] Brittany Murphy, the fabulous 32-year old, *8 Mile* film actress, died in December 2009 from pneumonia and anemia caused by exposure to mold in her ultra-luxury LA home. Her partner, British screenwriter Simon Monjack, died five months later (May 2010) apparently from the same cause. He was 40. Her Hollywood Hills house was put back on the market in 2016 for a mere $18.4 million USD, a drop of $1 million from its previous list price. I haven't heard if there were any takers…

Every Dollar You Save is Two You Don't Have to Earn

Property management may not be a very sexy business, but it's a core competency. It's about attention to detail, cost reduction and savings, revenue enhancement, supplier and project management, product and service knowledge and, above all, client satisfaction—which means keeping both landlords and tenants happy. It may also require significant marketing and sales skills as well as knowledge of regulations affecting tenant relations and building codes…

Former Ottawa Senators head coach Jacques Martin used to say, "Every goal you prevent is like two you don't have to score."

The same is true in the property management business I believe.

Here's an example from one of my property manager clients that highlights the level of attention to detail that can make a big difference in yearly results…

Fred[120] manages a triplex in Ottawa that had four gas meters: 1 meter does the furnace; the others do each of 3 hot water tanks.

Fred currently pays all four gas bills on behalf of the building's owner and tenants[121].

Enbridge (the gas supply company) has a monthly fixed charge of $20+HST(harmonized sales tax) per account so Fred had a gas technician disconnect 3 of those meters and run all the gas through just 1 meter instead; then Fred cancelled the other 3 accounts.

It cost $800 to do it, but saves the building $815/yr in service fees; now that's a 100% pa ROI.

Not bad, huh?

Not bad at all…
Go Fred!
☺

…

---

[120] Not his real name.

[121] In Ottawa, in the past, most landlords preferred to put utilities in their tenants' names until they discovered that certain utility companies have ultimate recourse to *them* if a tenant fails to pay, for example, his or her electricity bill in the last few months of their lease term. The utility will say, "Sorry, either you pay up or we cut off your power." Then you reply, "But the account's not even in my name! How can you collect from me?" To which they add, "So sad, too bad. We are allowed *by law* to assess a property owner if a renter is in arrears. So if your property needs power, he-he-he, you gotta pay up. But hey, here's some good news—you can always pursue your claim against your tenant. Where did you say they'd moved to? Kinakuta? Well you can sue them there…" In Ontario, power is expensive—around 24.5 cents per kilowatt-hour including all sorts of extra charges for peak power and connection fees (versus about 6.5 cents in Quebec and anywhere from 10 to 16.5 cents in states that are close to Ontario and with which Ontario competes). So the amount of arrears a tenant can ring up can be mighty impressive (in the thousands of dollars) especially if they have a few computers or servers on premises. So what we recommend now is that landlords pay utilities but chargeback their tenants one month in arrears with an administration fee of 15% tacked on for the time, trouble, hassle and risk property owners are assuming.

Highest and Best Use, HABU—What do Planners Mean When They Refer to Highest and Best Use?

For decades the principle of highest and best use has guided town/city/township/county officials and their municipal planners and economic development officers. To paraphrase Sir Winston Churchill, "It is the worst possible system except for all the others." It can be defined this way—

"Highest and best use for a property is achieved when the value created by its development for a specific set of physically possible, permitted uses (its functional program) and a particular form of structure combine to produce the highest present value of rents less costs (excluding mortgage payments, depreciation and amortization) over the economic life of a project," Bruce M Firestone

Since the beginning of civilization, many models have evolved as organizing principles for villages, towns, cities and regions. The first villages were founded by a handful of families joining together for mutual protection. Serendipitously, they discovered that a division of labor could increase the wellbeing of their village. Those who were more skilled at, say, farming did more of that while those who were better hunters, gatherers, flint knife carvers or textile producers specialized in those tasks. The result was a marked improvement in the wealth of the village from intra and later inter-village trading. Over time, a surplus may have developed in one village leading to trade with other nearby villages, which had their own specializations. Regional trading blocks emerged, prompting faster growth, even more specialization, and eventually the development of city-states, which in turn led to the formation of nation-states.

As cities, towns and villages grew, the problem of how to efficiently organize them became more pronounced. How to rid budding urban area of wastes, where to place dirty industry, how to bring products and services into and out of a town for a growing numbers of artisans and guild members, how to best protect citizens from external attack and internal predators, how to move people and their domesticated animals safely within the city, how to gather people together for religious observances, markets and entertainment, where to put courts, jails and schools, where to locate government officials, judges, kings and queens, emperors, their subjects and nobles—these are some of the tough questions regional governments have wrestled with for millennia.

Spatial organization of cities, towns or villages and their hinterlands has, at various times, been based on: a) religious or other hierarchical systems, b) defense principles, c) royal edict, d) class or race-based systems, e) guild-based separation, f) master planned community consistent with zoning codes or combinations of the above.

Structuring cities based on the principle that each individual parcel should be put to its highest and best use is an idea that has come into prominence over the last century. The highest and best use for a particular piece of land is that use or combination of uses that produces the highest net land rents. This is derived from a comparative analysis of the costs and benefits of alternative projects; the project that produces the highest IRR (internal rate of return) on a cash basis (that is, ignoring a project's capital structure because what a penfund developer would pay in terms of their COF (cost of funds) would be significantly lower than what most private developers would pay) is arguably the right use for a subject property. It presumably also produces the highest land rents too.

This rule can also be thought of as the "DAD rule," Dollars are Democrats rule. The DAD rule suggests that those persons or organizations which have the where-with-all to develop a parcel to its highest and best use will also be those willing to pay the highest price for the lands or the highest land rent. This means that: a) land supply will be rationed using a price mechanism, b) anyone can participate irrespective of race, creed, gender, religion or sexual orientation and c) lands will be used efficiently at the greatest practical intensity and density of use.

That land is a limited resource and should be used efficiently seems self-evident. However, it is remarkable how often neo-urbanists run into NIMBY (not-in-my-back-yard) trouble. Special interest groups often oppose further development of villages, towns, cities and regions, rejecting growth and increased density as well as more intensive uses of lands often associated with that[122].

People may fear that urban growth, development and change increases congestion and lowers property values. However, allowing the highest and best rule to work in a de-regulated environment where a community consensus has been reached as to what constitutes sound, sustainable development will often produce more variegated, interesting, efficient, and sustainable communities. It lowers the decibel count at town hall public meetings and leads to a better understanding of what constitutes excellence in urban design. Application of the highest and best use rule is subject to the constraints of building, health, and fire codes as well as economic limits.

Cities, towns, villages and regional economies are survival machines that produce the greatest good for the greatest number of their citizens; they allow people to exchange goods, services and ideas that best utilize individual skills of their residents to greatest effect. Cities make best use of scarce resources including land and infrastructure as well as human capital, natural capital, social capital, manufactured capital, and financial capital.

If we put our trust in the highest and best use principle subject to public safety codes (instead of an overwhelming reliance on prescriptive zoning ordinances and official plans that are hopelessly out-of-date no matter how often they are revised because the global economy and stakeholder needs are changing far too fast), we can produce better towns, cites and regional economies that are more interesting places to live, provide more options and varying lifestyles at a higher level of efficiency.

James Howard Kunstler's advice to local governments in Home from Nowhere is to, "Burn all your zoning codes." Short of this, local governments that adopt proactive zoning codes (also called performance zoning) where everything is permitted unless expressly forbidden instead of traditional zoning where everything is forbidden unless expressly permitted, will develop an experimental environment where people can allow their creativity to flourish. Public safety codes and public input on things like site plan control will take care of nuisances and correct mistakes as well as improving overall urban design which should be, like any creative pursuit, an iterative process anyway.

---

[122] Intensity as opposed to density measures the degree to which mixed uses are found at any one location or within an individual project. For example, a mixed-use project that combines office, retail, entertainment and housing has a higher level of intensity than one that is solely residential or office-based.

[Comic script by Prof Bruce using online service]

Zoning change, official plan amendment, sub-division application, site plan control and other public processes can either be looked at as confrontations or as opportunity for affirmation of a project amongst stakeholders. A switch to performance zoning, negative property taxes (where neighbors pay for deleterious effects superimposed on adjacent property owners—these are called special assessment zones) and the use of public safety codes to greenlight, amend or stop a development will produce superior results in every way—including faster, more sustainable economic development and higher property tax revenues for local governments as well as more harmonious communities.

...

NIMBYs are Wrong to Oppose Mixed Use and Higher Densities, the annual cost of NIMBYism to the economies of the United States and Canada

NIMBYs fear growth and sprawl; they also oppose densification and intensification.

Highest and best use rules imply an increase in city density and intensity over time as urbanization increases and population grows. Pressure for adjustment also derives from: changes in average dwelling occupancy rate (which has been decreasing in developed nations for a long time as average family sizes decrease, more people choosing to live alone and an aging population), competition from home offices increasing for office buildings, internet commerce continuing to take a big bite out of retail and other industries, transportation options proliferating (Uber and Lyft, for example, have significantly impacted (decreased) the number of parking spaces required for inner city development) and other technical as well as technological advances rapidly altering the types of uses (functions) inside the existing built form of a city as well as in its public room[123].

Rent curves, measured cross-sectionally at a point in time, tend to peak in a city's center and fall towards its urban/rural boundary, all else being equal. As a city expands outward over time, overall demand for all types of land uses and demand on the public room increase. Rent curves tend to secularly increase as demand for land, apartments, commercial and institutional space increases.

To meet such demand, landowners will be inclined to increase the density of their built form. If they own a home, for example, they might add a granny flat in the rear yard or an above-the-garage apartment or an in-home apartment in the basement or attic. In the aggregate, total rents achieved will be greater. They might even add an in-home office, convert to a duplex or triplex or rooming house or add a "corner store" type operation with apartments above. Rents for existing housing stock and commercial property will be secularly increased due to a combination of greater demand and densification. Creeping commercialization of residential areas, the addition of commercial uses to homes and more mixing together of various uses will, prima facie, also contribute to rising rents.

As long as public order and safety are maintained, homeowners should not fear densification or mixed use coming to their neighborhood. Land rents will go up and property values will go *up* not down. If a new office tower is constructed nearby, more would-be potential homeowners or renters have just moved into your community. Demand for housing goes up, so do prices.

Densification and increased mixing together of different land uses make for more interesting communities; that better support public transportation and can be safer too (with more eyes on the street). It makes no sense to construct single purpose suburbs of single family homes where no employment uses are permitted. Every weekday morning, homeowners depart for work leaving behind deserted, expensive suburban homes that easily fall prey to break and enter. How much more sensible to allow people to work from their homes, start businesses there and provide increased daytime and weekday security. It also lowers traffic congestion.

Communities that are wistful that the corner store, neighborhood pub, local hardware store and such have given way to the megamall, the big box store and the burger franchise need to arrive at a new consensus that pedestrian-friendly, live close-to-work, mixed use, denser, more intense, vibrant neighborhoods deserve their support. This will increase local demand to the point where these types of uses become feasible again.

Indeed, an overhaul of urban design thinking as well as the myriad planning rules that govern the built form will have to take place before we can build any places actually worthy of human settlement.

---

[123] For example, I did a lease a few years ago for a tech company, http://www.fuelyouth.com/, who converted an old sewing factory into office space, music studio, and film studio (complete with green screen). This inner-city building was built in the 1970s, a time when no one (other than a Tom Swift-style sci-fi writer that is) could have foreseen such a future use.

...

Here is an excerpt from *The Atlantic* written by noted urbanist James Howard Kunstler[124] on what the underlying cause of urban blight really is. The culprit? Our prized zoning bylaws and ordinances…

ALMOST everywhere in the United States, laws prohibit building the kinds of places that Americans themselves consider authentic and traditional. Laws prevent the building of places that human beings can feel good in and can afford to live in. Laws forbid us to build places that are worth caring about.

Is Main Street your idea of a nice business district? Sorry, your zoning laws won't let you build it, or even extend it where it already exists. Is Elm Street your idea of a nice place to live—you know, houses with front porches on a tree-lined street? Sorry, Elm Street cannot be assembled under the rules of large-lot zoning and modern traffic engineering. All you can build where I live is another version of Los Angeles—the zoning laws say so.

This is not a gag. Our zoning laws are essentially a manual of instructions for creating the stuff of our communities. Most of these laws have been in place only since the Second World War. For the previous 300-odd years of American history we didn't have zoning laws. We had a popular consensus about the right way to assemble a town or a city. Our best Main Streets and Elm Streets were created not by municipal ordinances but by cultural agreement. Everybody agreed that buildings on Main Street ought to be more than one story tall; that corner groceries were good to have in residential neighborhoods; that streets ought to intersect with other streets to facilitate movement; that sidewalks were necessary, and that orderly rows of trees planted along them made the sidewalks much more pleasant; that roofs should be pitched to shed rain and snow; that doors should be conspicuous, so that one could easily find the entrance to a building; that windows should be vertical, to dignify a house. Everybody agreed that communities needed different kinds of housing to meet the needs of different kinds of families and individuals, and the market was allowed to supply them. Our great-grandparents didn't have to argue endlessly over these matters of civic design. Nor did they have to reinvent civic design every fifty years because no one could remember what had been agreed on.

Everybody agreed that both private and public buildings should be ornamented and embellished to honor the public realm of the street, so town halls, firehouses, banks, and homes were built that today are on the National Register of Historic Places. We can't replicate any of that stuff. Our laws actually forbid it. Want to build a bank in Anytown, USA? Fine. Make sure that it's surrounded by at least an acre of parking, and that it's set back from the street at least seventy-five feet. (Of course, it will be one story.) The instructions for a church or a muffler shop are identical. That's exactly what your laws tell you to build. If you deviate from the template, you will not receive a building permit.

Therefore, if you want to make your community better, begin at once by throwing out your zoning laws. Don't revise them—get rid of them. Set them on fire if possible and make a public ceremony of it; public ceremony is a great way to announce the birth of a new consensus. While you're at it, throw out your "master plan" too. It's invariably just as bad. Replace these things with a traditional town-planning ordinance that prescribes a more desirable everyday environment.

The practice of zoning started early in the twentieth century, at a time when industry had reached an enormous scale. The noisy, smelly, dirty operations of gigantic factories came to overshadow and oppress all other aspects of city life, and civic authorities decided that they had to be separated from everything else, especially residential neighborhoods. One could say that single-use zoning, as it came to be called, was a reasonable response to the social and economic experiment called industrialism.

After the Second World War, however, that set of ideas was taken to an absurd extreme. Zoning itself began to overshadow all the historic elements of civic art and civic life. For instance, because the democratic masses of people used their cars to shop, and masses of cars required parking lots, shopping was declared an obnoxious industrial activity around which people shouldn't be allowed to live. This tended to destroy age-old physical relationships between shopping and living, as embodied, say, in Main Street.

What zoning produces is suburban sprawl, which must be understood as the product of a particular set of instructions. Its chief characteristics are the strict separation of human activities, mandatory driving to get from one activity to another, and huge supplies of free parking. After all, the basic idea of zoning is that every activity demands a separate zone of its own. For people to live around shopping would be

---
[124] Home From Nowhere, James Howard Kunstler, *The Atlantic*, September 1996.

harmful and indecent. Better not even to allow them within walking distance of it. They'll need their cars to haul all that stuff home anyway. While we're at it, let's separate the homes by income gradients. Don't let the $75,000-a-year families live near the $200,000-a-year families—they'll bring down property values—and for God's sake don't let a $25,000-a-year recent college graduate or a $19,000-a-year widowed grandmother on Social Security live near any of them. There goes the neighborhood! Now put all the workplaces in separate office "parks" or industrial "parks," and make sure nobody can walk to them either. As for public squares, parks, and the like—forget it. We can't afford them, because we spent all our funds paving the four-lane highways and collector roads and parking lots, and laying sewer and water lines out to the housing subdivisions, and hiring traffic cops to regulate the movement of people in their cars going back and forth among these segregated activities.

The model of the human habitat dictated by zoning is a formless, soulless, centerless, demoralizing mess. It bankrupts families and townships. It disables whole classes of decent, normal citizens. It ruins the air we breathe. It corrupts and deadens our spirit.

The construction industry likes it, because it requires stupendous amounts of cement, asphalt, and steel and a lot of heavy equipment and personnel to push all this stuff into place. Car dealers love it. Politicians used to love it, because it produced big short-term profits and short-term revenue gains, but now they're all mixed up about it, because the voters who live in suburban sprawl don't want more of the same built around them—which implies that at some dark level suburban-sprawl dwellers are quite conscious of sprawl's shortcomings. They have a word for it: "growth." They're now against growth. Their lips curl when they utter the word. They sense that new construction is only going to make the place where they live worse. They're convinced that the future is going to be worse than the past. And they're right, because the future has been getting worse throughout their lifetime. Growth means only more traffic, bigger parking lots, and buildings ever bigger and uglier than the monstrosities of the sixties, seventies, and eighties.

So they become NIMBYs (not in my back yard) and BANANAs (build absolutely nothing anywhere near anything). If they're successful in their NIMBYism, they'll use their town government to torture developers (people who create growth) with layer upon layer of bureaucratic rigmarole, so that only a certified masochist would apply to build something there. Eventually the unwanted growth leapfrogs over them to cheap, vacant rural land farther out, and then all the new commuters in the farther-out suburb choke the NIMBYs' roads anyway, to get to the existing mall in NIMBYville.

Unfortunately, the NIMBYs don't have a better model in mind. They go to better places on holiday weekends—Nantucket, St. Augustine, little New England towns—but they think of these places as special exceptions. It never occurs to NIMBY tourists that their own home places could be that good too. *Make Massapequa like Nantucket? Where would I park?* Exactly.

These special places are modeled on a pre-automobile template[125]. They were designed for a human scale and in some respects maintained that way. Such a thing is unimaginable to us today. We must design for the automobile, because… because all our laws and habits tell us we must. Notice that you can get to all these special places in your car. It's just a nuisance to use the car while you're there—so you stash it someplace for the duration of your visit and get around perfectly happily on foot, by bicycle, in a cab, or on public transit. The same is true, by the way, of London, Paris, and Venice.

...

By the way, I actually tried to estimate the annual cost of anti-democratic and often irrational NIMBYism and bad zoning codes to the economies of the United States and Canada.

First, I asked myself the question: what are some of the factors holding back these economies? Here are some of those factors:

1 low birth rate

---

[125] Sarah Williams Goldhagen in her excellent work, *Welcome to Your World—How the built environment shapes our lives,* HarperCollins, 2017, says, "Our relationship to the built environment differs from that of any other art. It affects us all the time… It affects our moods and emotions… What the new paradigm of embodied or situated cognition reveals is that the built environment and its design matters far, far more than anybody, even architects, ever thought that it did." So getting urban design, the public room, and built form right counts a great deal towards human happiness, productivity, and achievement. [Please note this quote obviously does not form part of the original article written as it was by Ms Williams Goldhagen 21 years after The Atlantic published Kunstler's work. I have added it, Ed.]

2 low productivity growth
3 lower workforce participation
4 lack of lifetime learning
5 underemployment
6 misfit of skills
7 early retirement/force out of over 50s
8 lack of startups and PB4Ls
9 poor urban design, urban planning, zoning and NIMBYism

To estimate the cost of NIMBYism and zoning codes, I looked at just one variable—adding more density to existing residential areas by permitting coach houses (tiny "granny" flats in your backyard)[126]. Here are my sample calculations:

				Gross		NOI	
house value before animation	$380,000 "liability"	no passive income		$ 2,000.00 per mth	$	1,520.00	$18,240.00 pa
in home suite				$ 1,200.00			
coach house				$ 1,800.00			
storage sheds		2		$ 170.00			
tech package		4		$ 460.00			
home office				$ 700.00			
backyard games				$ -			
backyard maker space				$ 800.00			
house value after animation	$680,000 "asset"	produces passive income		$ 7,130.00 per mth	$	5,418.80	
				$85,560.00 pa	$	65,025.60	
increase in NOI after animation						$	46,785.60 pa
increase in GDP per household						$	46,785.60 pa
number of households in Canada and the US		370,000,000 people	dor		1.9		194,736,842 dwellings
percentage that animate					20%		38,947,368 dwellings
increase in GDP						$ 1,822,176,000,000.00 pa	

THIS IS THE COST OF HAVING BAD URBAN DESIGN, BAD PLANNERS, NIMBYS IN US AND CANADA

If 20% of the housing stock in the US and Canada added a coach house, I estimate that the annual increase in GDP is more than $1.8 *trillion*.

Now that's a big number.

I think the unwillingness to experiment with better urban design is holding back both innovation and growth as well as making our cities, towns and villages less interesting and less vibrant than they otherwise could be.

Official plans that purport to dictate the type of growth and uses that will be permitted to locate within a city or town over the next 20 years (or even longer) is a fool's errand in my view—if a town planner thinks s/he can predict what will be needed/in demand over the next generation, it's only because they are time travelers from the future or like Biff Howard Tannen[127], they've met someone from the future who told them who the next 20 Super Bowl winners are.

...

---

[126] This has been permitted in Ottawa since November 2016.
[127] Biff in *Back to the Future Part II* acquired *Grays Sports Almanac* in 2015 and then made one trip back in Doc Brown's (DeLorean) time machine to November 12th 1955 to give it to his younger self, making him incredibly rich because he could reliably predict winners in multi-sports including: football, baseball, hockey, horse racing, boxing, slamball, golf, tennis, track, polo, bowling, surfing, sailing, auto racing, rugby, soccer (aka football in the UK), ping pong, darts, swimming, diving, ice skating, racquetball, rodeo, and more. Source: http://backtothefuture.wikia.com/wiki/Grays_Sports_Almanac

Approval of Coach Houses Opens the Way to Better Urban Design

The city of Ottawa recently changed its bylaws to permit construction of coach houses on many existing residential lots.

This is part of a worldwide effort by neo-urbanists to densify and intensify existing urban areas to make them more interesting, more diverse, and more successful places to live.

I expect coach houses (which used to be called "granny" flats because most of their residents were female elders who tend to survive male partners by eight or so years) to have a profound impact not only on the urban fabric of Ottawa, but also on an individual homeowner's ability to take care of themselves and their families, mostly from a financial point of view.

How so?

Let's assume you own an existing house in Ottawa that is worth a citywide average of $380,000 (2016). You decide to add a 2-bedroom, 1-bath coach house in your backyard covering 40% of the area there. The thought is that it's going to add a bit of income for you when you retire at 55! (Remember the preposterous Freedom 55[128] campaign? I've never known anyone who successfully retired at 55. By successful, I mean could not only afford to do that but also had a plan to continue to be useful to his community. The only person I know who had the means to do that and did it, also died a year later at age 56, having lost, I believe, the joie de vivre because he lived in a Florida exile, isolated from his friends and family back in Ottawa, sitting for most of the day in his condo watching TV...)

Now, let's suppose it costs you $120,000 to build your new coach house and maybe you use a design like the clever one shown below created by architectural technologist Leo Clement and coach house builder Chris Long from Conrad Construction and CoHouse.

The turning circles you see on the main floor are for wheelchair access—having a 0-step entry, wider corridor/doorway widths, and a roll-in or step-in shower are important elements. Why? Because CMHC predicts that by 2032 nearly a quarter of Ottawa's population will be seniors so why build something that excludes as much as 25% of your potential marketplace?

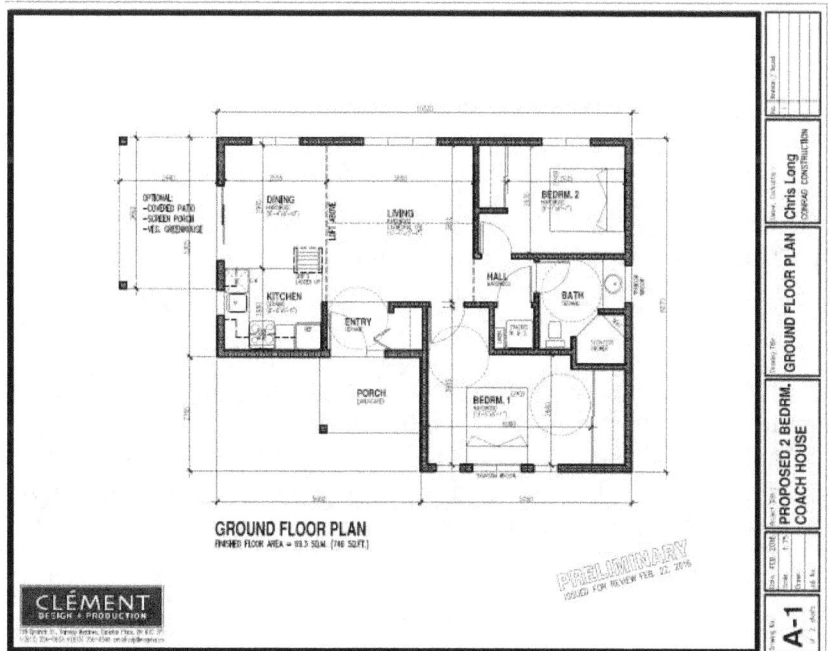

---

[128] © London Life Insurance Company 2001 – 2017.

Two bedrooms are essential too—not just because most couples by the time they are in their 50s, 60s, 70s and 80s are sleeping in separate rooms—but also because then it's set up for roommates (young or old) to occupy.

They also cheated a bit—Mr Clement included a loft-sleeping platform accessed by a ship's ladder—that's for visitors to use, most probably grandkids[129].

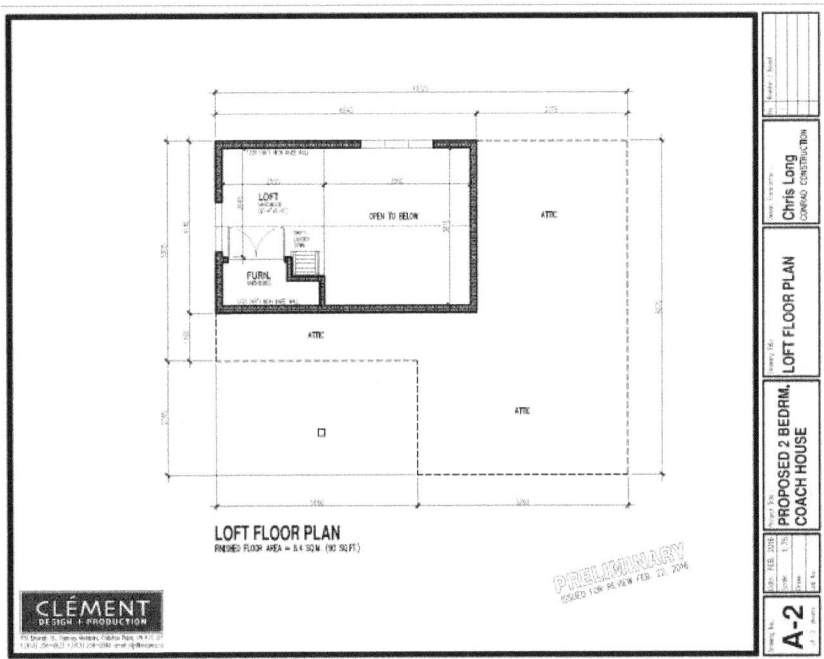

So what is your ROI, return on investment, if you build something like this?

Here're my calculations:

cost of construction: $120,000
rental income: $1,800 per mth including utilities
tech package (Netflix, basic cable, net phone, internet, wi-fi, large screen TV): $115 per mth
total rental income: $1,915.00 per mth
operating costs, utilities, property management, tech package, administration, insurance: ($459.60) per mth based on 24% of total rental income
vacancy allowance: ($95.75) per mth based on 5% vacancy rate
NOI, net operating income: $1,359.65 per mth or $16,315.80 per annum
    cap rate: 13.6% per annum
E&OE

So your cap rate (capitalization rate, a measure of return based on you making this investment as if it was funded in cash, ie, without adding to your mortgage) is 13.6% pa. When you compare this to what you get on your savings at your bank (anywhere from .99% to 1.7% pa today) or what most of your mutual funds are probably doing (mine are horrible—around 2% to 4% and sometimes negative, ugh), it looks quite satisfactory. There is also the hope that your real estate will go up in value over time,

---

[129] One other thing, clients of mine are doing—they're adding a full basement (sometimes with a "manufactured" walkout condition so they can get another bedroom or two or an office in their coach house's lower level… increasing its yield even more.

which compounds your return. As you know by now, cap rate only measures cash returns not inflation or mortgage principal paydown (if you have a mortgage).

Now $16,316 of extra annual income might not sound like a whole heck of a lot but when you compare it to the average CPP (Canada Pension Plan) payout today (2015) of just $550 per month, it can make a big difference, especially to elders living on fixed incomes.

All right, so far so good.

But changing bylaws is not sufficient to see a new industry bloom in Ottawa. We have to be cautious in our early assessment because the coach house idea is not new.

I worked on a Kanata (westend Ottawa) subdivision (called Briarbrook) more than 30 years ago when I was at Terrace Investments Limited, the first parent company of the Ottawa Senators. We put right in the zoning that granny flats would be permitted—on larger pie-shaped lots, you know the ones that are created when a roadway turns a corner.

None was ever built. How come?

Because the city of Kanata (long since absorbed by Ottawa) imposed rules that made their construction impossible—rules like you could only rent them to *related* persons, you could only get a "temporary" building permit of five years (presumably after which you'd have to remove the structure or tear it down!), and you had to pay a full development charge to help fund off-site infrastructure even though none was needed.

The coach house bylaw passed by Ottawa city council in November 2016 includes a significant development charge (around $6k for transit development) and it prohibits having both a coach house and an in-home suite… a big mistake, in my view.

Essentially, you have to choose between, say, a legal basement apartment, and a granny flat in your backyard. As someone who coaches 100s of real estate investors, I already know this is a difficult choice.

So here's what's likely to happen: we are going to go back to the same condition that prevailed before in-home suites were legalized more than a decade ago. Folks will build coach houses and after they get their occupancy permits, they'll build out illegal basement apartments. Bad idea.

We probably had tens of thousands of those, many of them not only illegal but unsafe as well[130]. If the city really wants to intensify and densify, both should be allowed.

So why not allow both?

Well, city planners and local councilors live in perpetual fear of the NIMBY movement, not in my backyard political activists who detest almost any change in their neighborhoods. Their concerns? You'll hear lots of talk about more traffic, more pressure on infrastructure and schools, negative environmental consequences such as tree removal, more policing costs (due to "undesirables" taking up residence in basement suites or coach houses) but in reality it all boils down to one thing—money. They fear that their property values will drop.

However, in almost every instance I have studied, greater densities and intensities resulted in higher property values not lower ones. Take the Glebe, for instance. A desirable Ottawa neighborhood to live in. It has lots of sideyard, backyard and basement apartments plus coach houses, metal bashing

---

[130] I was actually in one. A student of mine rented a flat (in the Glebe, a tony part of Ottawa) not far from Carleton University where I was teaching at the time (in their School of Architecture). He entered it via a twin hatch—basically, two doors mounted at 30 degrees that swung up and out to reveal a ship's ladder to descend into his place, whereupon he would halt on the second or third lowest rung, turn around awkwardly to pull both doors above his head and shut them with a horrible *clang*. He also had to duck really fast so he wouldn't get El Kabonged (a reference to cartoon character Quick Draw McGraw's masked alter ego having a tendency to hit his opponents over their heads with his acoustic guitar screaming, "KABOOOOOONG.") It was his only way in or out and if there was ever a snowstorm *and* a fire, an all too likely combination in a cold northern shelf city like Canada's Capital City, he and his girlfriend were both dead. He wanted to show me a series of scale models he was working on of new kiosks created to animate the public room. Essentially, his plan was to create "products" he could sell to pubs, restaurants, artists, makers, stores that they could park outside their locations to animate the public room, demo their products, and promote themselves. It failed because he was 20 years too early—urban planners and traffic engineers at that time believed in their souls (some still do) that we build towns and cities for cars not people so anything that impeded traffic (now called *traffic calming* and widely accepted by both communities and their political and bureaucrat overlords) was verboten.

shops, garage mechanics, restaurants, offices, arena, stadium, and traffic galore, but trust me; a home in that area is not going down in value. The caveat on this is that order and peace are maintained, the sine qua non of creating value in any society or town. Fortunately, Ottawa-Gatineau is still one of the safest million+ population places in the world to live in.

If we are still afraid of NIMBY attack, maybe we could do worse than borrow a concept from radical English prime minster Theresa May—who found a way to turn NIMBY activists into PIMBYs (please in my backyard) supplicants. She did it by making sure that any so called "undesirable" use pays a royalty, which instead of going into the coffers of municipal, provincial, state or federal governments goes instead directly to neighbors affected by the change.

That might be a bridge too far for councilors but it would probably work.

Out of curiosity, I calculated what would happen if other cities, towns, and villages followed Ottawa's example and started to permit coach houses.

As shown earlier in this mini book, I estimated that there are about 195 million dwellings in the US and Canada, and if 20% of those are suited to adding coach houses, and if all of them did so, then it would add $1.8 *trillion* per year to GDP in those two nations[131]. Wow.

Here's the thing—I love what the tech industry can do for a town like Ottawa. It's also great to have other economic engines running flat out such as the government sector, tourism, education, health, and entertainment. But there is no industry bigger than the real estate industry—everyone needs a place to live, shop, work, learn, make, play, earn… so if we could take the planning shackles off urban designers and real estate investors, they'd be able to create a much more vigorous environment for everyone else to generate wealth in.

Hey, they did it in Rotterdam, a failing industrial port city in the Netherlands, which is now a world-leading hotbed of highly experimental, sustainable urban development and design[132]. Ottawa could do worse than follow their lead—so what about co-opting an entire neighborhood here where creative new solutions to off-grid energy issues, grow local, or live-work-play-shop-learn-make-entertain challenges could be encouraged without the dead hand and expense of planning regulators shooting them down in flames?

All that is needed is political will and political leadership, things that are generally in short supply in a world where, as I've noted before, the only thing that most politicians seem to stand for is reelection.

…

---

[131] You can download my spreadsheet and play around with the numbers yourself, https://www.dropbox.com/s/6ywyf3gab1g8ox8/whats-holding-back-the-economy.xls?dl=0.

[132] It's called Concept House Village, a test bed for neo-urbanist ideas and sustainable built forms. "Concept House Village is an attempt to take things in different directions, experimenting with more radical features, such as a garden that takes up the entire second floor. It's an example of something that's common in Rotterdam: This is a city that loves to play with new ideas… the city also helps push to make those solutions happen. A competition called CityLab010, for example, will give out more than 3 million Euros in 2016 to the best new ideas—in categories like sustainability and education–to improve the city," Adele Peters, staff writer at Fast Company, *Experimental City: How Rotterdam Became A World Leader In Sustainable Urban Design*, Dec 5, 2016.

Negative Property Taxes—a Possible Response to NIMBY'itis

NIMBY behavior is not limited to exclusive residential areas and gated communities. It is surprising, perhaps, that NIMBY behavior can manifest itself shortly after a neighborhood begins to ameliorate/gentrify; people who see their lives improving in urban areas that are experiencing a renaissance can demonstrate the same impulses—to seek to limit the flexibility of land use to prevent the incursion of "undesirable" types of built form. One of the greatest impediments to renewal of derelict urban places is the degree of difficulty in effecting zoning changes and the resistance to change—residents whose lives are improving almost immediately want to "gate" themselves off from change and development.

It has been suggested by planner, Lily Chi, that one way of addressing the impulse to exhibit NIMBY behavior is to give the neighbors an ownership stake in the proposed "undesirable" use like what more recently the UK's Theresa May has suggested; that is, to address the "greed" part of NIMBY motivation by giving the community a financial stake in any new, problematic development. The question she addressed is how to accomplish this efficiently and fairly.

One way to effect this would be to create a special assessment zone (SAZs) in which a *negative* property tax would be levied on immediate neighbors. Most municipalities have experience with the creation of SAZs often to levy *additional* property taxes on benefiting owners—landowners who, for example, benefit from a new piece of municipal infrastructure like a main sewer line or new road. It would be a simple matter to create a SAZ to *credit* property taxes for lands which abut or are adjacent to or proximate to a new development. This could be at no cost to the municipality, as the decrease in property taxes for nearby owners would be offset by a higher assessment on the "non-conforming" or otherwise intrusive use.

In this way, value is permanently transferred to neighbors giving them a financial or *quasi ownership* stake in the outcome of a rezoning. For example, rezoning to allow a change of use from single family residential to permit development of, say, a rooming house, a halfway house, a shelter, a McMansion, a corner store, a coach house, an outdoor amphitheater, an arena or stadium, a restaurant, a big box store, a warehouse, a hospital, a daycare center, a bank with a drive thru, a retirement residence, a new Trump Tower or what have you, would result in an increase in assessed value together with a special assessment. The latter would be redistributed to abutting lands.

This tax credit would continue as long as the new uses and new zoning remain in place. A $15,000 special assessment on, for example, a proposed rooming house would save, say, five neighboring properties $3,000 annually on their property tax bill. Capitalized at 6%, this would result in a whopping $50,000 one-time increase in each neighbor's property value. It is compensation for the "intrusive" nature of the proposed use. It is a way to bring market discipline to the NIMBY problem or as Theresa May would say, "Convert a NIMBY to a PIMBY."

Defining the watershed for the imposition of a negative property tax should be based on some simple formula and probably should be extremely localized. The amount of the special assessment levied against the proposed development would be determined as a function of the increase in rents caused by the proposed change in land use but should be set low enough so that the development does not become infeasible and yet high enough that it is meaningful compensation for neighbors and sufficiently interesting to them to defuse their NIMBY impulses. Let us leave it to some talented econometrician to derive a precise formula for this.

It may be, as argued above, that there will be no negative impacts from the proposed uses. Indeed, as we have already seen, uses that create higher densities can increase property values, all else being equal.

One way to test for this could be to do a cross-sectional regression analysis using MLS (Multiple Listing Service) data of house prices to see if we could measure the impacts of, say, introducing a group home into a micro neighborhood. If we could show no negative impacts, this in itself could serve to diffuse NIMBY opposition without the necessity of introducing negative property taxes.

...

Why Land Prices are Taking Off

Why are land prices (and home prices) accelerating in many North American cities? Simple, because of wrong-headed municipal, county, provincial, and state policies

When I see the price of industrial land in my hometown of Ottawa, it makes me sick. I mean it.

The city of Ottawa believes it has an adequate 50-year supply of vacant industrial land but they don't take into account that: a) a lot of it is owned by the NCC (the National Capital Commission aka the no-commitment-club) and may never come on the market/be available, b) the balance is owned by a very small number of landowners who have a quasi monopoly—they'll do build-to-suits but only to lease them to organizations—if you'd like to own your own premises as many entrepreneurs would prefer to do, you're out of luck, c) it's in the wrong place or d) undevelopable because it has other constraints like perhaps part of it is EP (environmentally protected) land...

How do I know there is a shortage of industrial land? Or for that matter, commercial and residential development land?

Easy. Prices have gone from around $125k an acre to $1 million plus in le$$ than ten years.

ANY economist (without even looking at additional data) could tell you that the city of Ottawa's (and many copycat municipal) policies are wrong—they are causing a land shortage and consequent price spike. They are crippling industrial and commercial development (not to mention making homes much more expensive, especially for first time homebuyers).

Why do you really think Toronto, San Francisco, Portland, Seattle, Vancouver, Boston... home prices are out of control? Greedy landlords? Unscrupulous developers? None of the above!

It's wrong-headed provincial, state, county and municipal policies.

By not making more supply of development land available, they are perpetuating/creating a situation that is highly reminiscent of a medieval society, one in which desirable locations are all owned and controlled by kings and a handful of favored nobles.

What's worse is that they are not only stopping urban development from moving outwards from the city center in what is falsely termed "urban sprawl," they are duplicitously capping the height of buildings (under pressure from neighbors and often contrary to their own policies), putting the kibosh not only on increased density but also greater intensity (the mixing together of different types of uses–like, say, combining commercial and residential).

Then when rents take off, they embrace or tighten rent control laws making shortages worse and driving (rental) prices even higher.

Now Ontario is threatening to neuter or abandon/terminate the OMB (Ontario Municipal Board), the only professional planning body with any common sense it seems to me...

At 2810 Sheffield road in Ottawa, they are not only asking $2.36 million for an awkwardly shaped parcel (narrow and long: 200 feet by 655 feet) that is just 2.78 acres ($848,921/acre!), there is also the added cost for environmental cleanup as well as building demolition... look at this picture below: there are a lot of old buildings that have to come down, so it'll be very expensive.

They should be making much more land available for development, and relaxing many of their development standards too... allowing for higher buildings, smaller setbacks, narrower roads etc.

In addition, they should permit much more mixed use including homes and light industrial, retail/office/residential etc... ie, allow much more intensity as well as density.

The city of Ottawa recently had some Toronto-based consultants do an industrial land review and their findings were just a political cover for relaxing Ottawa's long-held goal of having 0.3 jobs per resident in suburban Ottawa.

It was all a sham in my view—political cover for converting large swaths of Orleans (an eastern suburb) from industrial development to more tract housing.

What should they have done?

Allowed development of commercial property that is really in demand—heavy industrial in places, light industrial mixed with housing and commercial uses in others, ie, mixed use communities.

Instead, what you'll get is more vast, soulless suburbs with endless identical, ugly, unsustainable, uneconomic, every-trip-is-a-car trip, unwalkable, unanimated, nearly identical boxes with 0 jobs, 0 stores, 0 interesting places and spaces on curvilinear roads that are an indecipherable maze.

Of course, you have to also ask, "Who benefits?" from such stupid policy blunders.

Sitting owners do. After all, what's the closest substitute for a new home, office, commercial or industrial space? Why, an existing one of course.

So when any city makes new builds more expensive via more regulation, more curtailing of urban expansion, and more taxes (masquerading as "development charges"), councilors have just voted themselves (as homeowners) and allied, oligopolistic, major landowners a nice, big fat raise.

...

Over-Investment in Real Estate and Why You Should Treat Even Your Principal Residence as if it was a Rental Property

Over-investment

The highest and best use rule constrained by building, health, and fire safety codes should allow for the development of interesting, safe, "organically" grown villages, towns and cities, which achieve a level of density and a mixing together of uses that are decided by the market rather than by fiat. Sound application of the highest and best use rule also requires that potential projects are put through a rigorous financial review.

Too many developers and architects analyze their projects from a cost point of view only; they are constantly cutting costs to meet a budget. This is a one sided approach—project analysis must take into account benefits as well as costs and a time dimension too. The most effective means to do this is probably by using an internal rate of return calculation that can reduce the cost/benefit equation to a single number.

Thus, there is a feedback loop between design and costs and revenues so that the design program can be modified as required.

The objective is not to get as much development as possible on a given site but the right level of development and the right mix too, the one that produces the highest present value of income less costs.

It is interesting to note that many successful people do not apply this type of approach to their own homes; there are plenty of examples in nearly every city of people over-investing in their residences. They may not be able to sell their homes for anything close to their costs. Examples such as Bob Campeau's former home in Toronto, Michael Dell's home in Austin and Bill Gates' home in Redmond come to mind. Indeed, both Dell and Gates have publicly argued that their (property) tax assessments should be lowered for exactly this reason. Clearly, this is *not* an application of the highest and best use rule.

Bloomberg reports[133] that Nile Niami, a Los Angeles speculative residential developer, is building a 100,000 sq ft home in Bel Air with an asking price of $500 million. Here's what Bloomberg has to say about it:

(It's) a 74,000-square-foot (6,900-square-meter) main residence and three smaller homes, according to city records. The project, which will take at least 20 more months to complete, will exceed 100,000 square feet, including a 5,000-square-foot master bedroom, a 30-car garage...," Niami said.
"The house will have almost every amenity available in the world," he wrote in an e-mail.

I even calculated the cap rate for Mr Niami's monstrosity; it turned out to be (according to my calculations) -0.6% pa. Now that's one heck of a bad investment.

I wouldn't want to pay just the property taxes, maintenance and operating costs plus utilities on that place even for an hour let alone a whole year.

Next, I asked myself, "If I (unfortunately) somehow came to own this place (because Nile decided he didn't like me very much so, to damage my current prospects, he *gave* me the home for *free*), what would I do with the darn thing? How would I animate it/make it work for, instead of against, me?"

---

[133] Source: http://www.bloomberg.com/news/articles/2015-05-26/california-dreaming-record-500-million-tag-on-l-a-home

The answer I came up with was: "I know. I'll add a *commercial* casino to it[134]."

[Nile Niami's Ultra Mega McMansion under construction at 944 Airole Way, Los Angeles dwarfing all structures around it; aerial photo from Google maps]

When I did that, I got the cap rate up from -0.6% to 22.8% pa[135].

You realize, of course, I am just trying to make a point here. Your assets should work for you, not the other way round. Even your principal residence should work for you otherwise it'll be what Robert Kiyosaki (Mr Rich Dad, Poor Dad) terms a liability not an asset. To Robert, an asset is something that puts cash in your jeans after you stop working. Everything else is a liability…

…

Why You Should Treat Even Your Principal Residence as if it was a Rental Property

I ask the people I coach on how to be successful real estate investors to treat even their own homes as if they were rental properties.

Why?

Well, first of all, one day, they may move out and rent it[136]. So it could become a rental property especially since I preach buy and hold not buy and flip.

---

[134] Not sure if Bel Air residents would want a high traffic casino in their midst so let's pretend it's for a fewer number of high rollers only and that somehow I managed to get such a license. Alternatively, we could add thrusters to that place and fly it out over the Pacific (into international airspace) where our guests could gamble away their money in mighty splendiferous comfort… legally without needing a license. By the way, Mile Niami did say he was going to add a Monaco-style casino to his place. I've just taken it a step further by running it as a commercial casino.

[135] You can download these super elaborate spreadsheets from my dropbox and see what I did (mostly for fun BTW): https://www.dropbox.com/s/twbfzzlmgyeueq2/nile-niami-500-million-dollar-house.xls?dl=0 and https://www.dropbox.com/s/i0qco39yhjltm1r/nile-niami-500-million-dollar-house-with-casino.xls?dl=0

[136] One of my clients, a successful developer and investor, Brian Dagenais, founder of Dagenais Properties and BlackSheep Developments (a land developer and institutional builder), told me he thought investors should live in every property they buy/own, if only for a short time. "I've done that with more than 20 of the units I own (out of a total of 32). That way, you learn pretty quickly how to improve things for yourself, how to make each place a better experience for yourself and consequently, later on, for your tenants. And guess what? You'll get better tenants and much higher rents as a result because you'll know the story of what it's like to live there because, well, you have," Brian added.

I also believe everything you own should work for you instead of the other way round—you working to buy them.

"Ninety percent of all millionaires become so through owning real estate. More money has been made in real estate than in all industrial investments combined. The wise young man or wage earner of today invests his money in real estate," Andrew Carnegie, billionaire industrialist

It's why I convinced my middle daughter Mimi (I have 5 great kids—3 girls and 2 boys) to buy a semi-detached home with a walkout basement last year. We converted the basement into a nice, *legal* one-bedroom apartment, which rents for $1,230 per month. Miriam lives upstairs in a 3-bedroom, 2 and ½ bath home with a roommate (one of her sisters) who pays her $675 a month.

So today, she lives in her own home for about a net cash cost of $500 a month, a lot less than she was paying in rent before ($1,000/month).

Front and back (with walkout condition)—Mimi's place

New lower level apartment

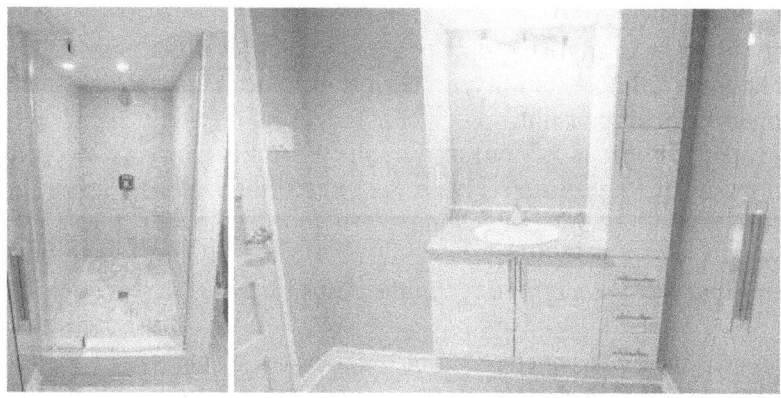

Nice w/c!

So here's the process:

1. determine the HABU (highest and best use) for each property you are going to purchase, even your own home
2. think about how you would animate/differentiate/renovate/increase the value of your property
3. ask what will each part of its functional program (for residences, you are talking about: the main part of the home, an in home suite, a coach house, a workshop, a storage shed, a garage office...) rent for
4. build a spreadsheet valuing the property three ways—a) on a cost to complete basis less depreciation, b) on an income basis based on actual and FMV cap rates, and c) on the basis of comparables
5. figure out what your IRR, internal rate of return, is
6. share this spreadsheet with your appraiser so you can support higher valuations and improve your chances of getting decent financing and refinancing.
7. make sure your head (the analytical part of you), your heart (whether you are passionate about the place) and gut (your instincts) are all in alignment; if so, this is probably a good decision

Real estate cannot be lost or stolen, not can it be taken away. Purchased with common sense, paid for in full, and managed with reasonable care, it's the safest investment in the world, Franklin D Roosevelt

8. then buy the place, and live happily ever after...

Master bedroom in lower level apartment and laundry room

If you have time, please listen to what Rich Dad Poor Dad Robert Kiyosaki says in his video, *60 Minutes to Getting Rich*. While I don't agree with everything Robert says, he'll certainly convince you (I hope) that investors beat savers each and every time, and that there *is* such a thing as good debt (as well as bad).
https://www.youtube.com/watch?v=buK-a70E0bI
I love his definition of an asset: an asset is anything that produces cashflow (via passive income) for you even after you stop working at your JOB[137]. A liability, on the other hand, is something that sucks money out of your jeans, whether you are working or not.

So, according to Robert, your principal home is, of course, a liability... in his world view. Naturally, if you animate it the way I've described what Mimi did, it'll become an asset as well as a storehouse of value (which happens because your are "forced" to save by paying down your home mortgage).

If you liked it then, you should have put ~~a ring~~ an offer on it, LighterSide.

---

[137] One of my former students, Fred Carmosino, a successful entrepreneur and one of two co-founders of http://www.mapleleafcustomhomes.ca/ told me that "JOB" stands for *journey of the broke.*

I encourage people to buy a principal residence that performs double duty. Obviously, this rules out buying homes that are vast suburban ornaments—those clearly are money suckers, not investments. That's also called "over investment". See above.

Don't let that be you.

...

I think people have misunderstood some of Robert's messaging, particularly around "no money down" deal making. I actually think he's referring to self-capitalization of real estate deals via such methods as seller take back mortgages or resorting to credit cards (!) for downpayment.

And he's not talking about flipping properties either. He has a (mostly) build and hold philosophy, which I agree with.

I would also de-emphasize alternative investments like 401(k) plans in the US or RRSPs in Canada or mutual funds and insurance since many of us have experienced significant disappointment with those types of "investments."

The other thing I would add to Robert's teachings is how to manage property properly (a core competency) and how to add value and differentiation to your real estate (via some of the animation techniques I teach, of course!)

"The best investment on Earth is earth," Louis Glickman, real estate investor

One other thing I like from Robert's *Rich Dad, Poor Dad* thing is that he recommends that you should retire on *debt* not savings. This counter intuitive concept actually makes sense I believe.

If you save, say, $100,000 and get 1 or 2 points from your bank, that nets you $1,000 or maybe $2,000 in income per year. If, on the other hand, you borrow $100,000 to buy another income property, and it gets you a cap rate of say 6% plus some inflation protection plus some paydown of your mortgage by your tenants, you probably will see an IRR (internal rate of return) of more than 24% pa.

So skill testing question: what's better—1 or 2% ROI or 24%?

"You can invest your way to wealth a lot faster than you can save your way there," Prof Bruce.

Just to make sure I drive this point home, look at what happens to your $100,000 of cash over 20 years. If you put it in your bank, you'll turn that $100,000 into $134,685.50, 20 years later. But if you buy a rental property and you get a 24% internal rate of return on your equity, you can change that $100,000 into over $7 million at the end of that period.

What the heck. Are you kidding me?

No, I'm not.

For real.

That's a $7,251,729.48 difference.

And, if you are a young person, the difference over a 40 year period (which is not out of the range of possibility for a 35 or even a 45-year old) is mind boggling—I won't even put the number in here, it's simply too big.

Savings versus Rental Property

cash on hand	$100,000		
term	20	years	
savings plan	$ 134,685.50	1.50%	bank interest
rental investment property	$7,386,414.98	24%	IRR, internal rate of return
difference	$7,251,729.48		

E&OE

So repeat after me, "Investors beat savers."
Once more, say it aloud, three times…
INVESTORS BEAT SAVERS
INVESTORS BEAT SAVERS
INVESTORS BEAT SAVERS
Every single freaking time.

…

Conclusion

You will note that in our investment calculations, there are no tax consequences from unearned rents taken into account, so don't look for them. Nor is there any mention of other potential tax liabilities—income taxes, value added taxes and capital gains taxes are ignored because each individual's position tends to be unique and often taxes do not impact ROI calculations, especially when you are comparing one investment possibility with another.

Most of our clients experience significant improvement in their financial positions through real estate investing but they all need three more things... patience, focus, and hard work. There is no business, including the real estate one, that is both work and stress free. Sorry about that.

In one of my examples, our client (with a cash-on-cash annual rate return of 25%) pockets over $300,000 in cash every year from his real estate ownership. The term "cash-on-cash return" refers to the cash portion of his return divided by the cash (AKA cash equity) he invested in his project.

Additionally, general real estate inflation has been adding 3% pa of the building's FMV (not his cash portion or equity portion) to his net worth (now accelerating to 5%) and average principal repayments have been adding another 15% to his ROE.

Ownership in this case had a 25% equity share in the deal so you can multiply by a factor of 4 what real estate inflation is adding (based on equity.) That's an impressive additional 12% to 20% pa...

Obviously, as his mortgage is retired, the percentage of equity in the deal goes up, and the ROE derived from general market inflation goes down but we already qualified this approach as an approximate methodology anyway—the key benefit to being an equity owner is that all increase in value comes to *you*. Of course, if anything goes wrong, you are first to be wiped out—your debt holders have prior claim on your assets.

I have also used an approximate way of calculating the order of magnitude of the wealth effect from annual principal repayment in some of my examples. I simply divided the principal amount of the mortgage by the amortization period—this gives the average amount of principal paid off a year (obviously, less principal is paid off in the early years and more in the latter part of your mortgage period). Then I divided this by the equity invested in the project and got the "wealth effect" part of ROE from simply paying off a mortgage.

Bottom line—pay off your mortgage as soon as you can. Reducing debt (all debt) is one of the fastest ways to securing your financial future and simplifying your life too.

This seems to be some contradictory advice—I showed earlier on that having five homes is better than having one—your cash on cash return is greater (and so is your IRR) but it comes from having more (hopefully low cost) leverage (debt). But actually the two concepts are internally consistent—by using more leverage early on in your real estate investing career, you are producing more cash, which if used to pay down debt (instead of buying more toys, say), actually reduces debt faster, later on. Comprehendo?

Another way of looking at leverage is that by allowing you to buy say five rental homes instead of one, if you have a vacancy in one, your occupancy rate falls from 100% to 80% not from 100% to zero.

As long as you are not upside down on equity (ie, finding that your rate of return on your equity is less than the project's overall rate of return), leverage is a positive thing[138]. In high inflationary periods like the early to mid 1980s, when interest rates were 14% to 22% and inflation was 12%, investors would buy real estate and accept the fact that their returns on equity were less than the overall project's return and, indeed, were often negative.

In simple terms, this meant that they had to pump cash into their project's every month.

Say you purchased a $10 million office complex that was losing $15,000 a month. That means that somehow you have to come up with at least $180,000 per annum to keep from losing your project. However, if this type of real estate is increasing 1.5% above the inflation rate and the inflation rate is 12%, the selling price of the project is going up 13.5% pa or $1.35 million every year.

---

[138] In financial circles, you'll sometimes hear investment pros refer to leverage as "gearing." Same thing.

So investors would gamble that they could keep the property long enough to benefit from inflation.

If our imaginary 1980s investor kept this building for two years and sold it for $10 million x (1.135) x (1.135) or $12,882,250, he or she would have made $2,882,250 less the cash he or she pumped in during that period ($360,000) or $2,522,250! We are, of course, ignoring transaction costs for the moment.

But this is intensely risky—1. you might run out of cash before you can sell it or 2. the chair of the US Federal Reserve might decide to once again raise interest rates to 22% to crush inflation.

So you are playing musical chairs and when the music stops, someone is always left without a chair. Make sure it isn't you by buying smart—ie, buy properties where cap rates are high enough that you don't have to pump in cash every month to stay alive.

In other words, never buy property (or anything else for that matter) simply to create a tax loss or purchase something that doesn't cashflow in year one or year two at the latest...

I've met many financial engineers over a varied career and you know what? Every one of them has gone bankrupt, sometimes many times over. A certain US president comes to mind but I have don't have to look to Washington to find examples. There are plenty much closer to home.

If there is a mistake out there I haven't personally made or known someone who has, I'd be surprised. Most of them have found me over the years. It makes me a better coach, keynote speaker, and broker I suppose.

So, for what it's worth, these mini books are based not only on my academic credentials and research but also on hard experience gained from having developed thousands of homes, and many, many shopping plazas, office complexes, residential subdivisions, industrial buildings, auto dealerships, institutional uses, and entertainment complexes, not to mention a certain hockey team.

As I get older, I talk more, teach more, coach more, and do less, which is, I guess, as it should be. Moreover, I am more patient now than when I was a younger man so I don't have to learn everything by doing it myself[139] and making many mistakes as a result. I am more willing to listen to others, learning from them and adopting their best practices as my own, which I do now in an instant.

If I see you doing something in a way that's better than how I know how to do, I'll change in a flash. There's no NOT INVENTED HERE reluctance on my part.

Anyway, this writing gig is a low paying one and, I know it sounds corny, but it's become a calling too. My mission/life purpose now is to pass on, as best I can, the only thing that has worked for me and my famdamily, which is real estate investing.

If you want to take care of yourself and your family, and not have to depend on someone else to do it for you, whether that is an unreliable government or private sector partner, real estate investing may be the only practical way for you to achieve your financial goals. Hey, it worked out all right for the 7th Duke of Westminster and most every other equity lord on the planet so you might as well make it happen for yourself.

...

Bruce M Firestone, B Eng (civil), M Eng-Sci, PhD
Century 21 Explorer Realty Inc broker
Ottawa Senators founder
Real Estate Investment and Business coach
1-613-762-8884
bruce.firestone@century21.ca
twitter.com/ProfBruce
profbruce.tumblr.com/archive
brucemfirestone.com

MAKING IMPOSSIBLE POSSIBLE

---

[139] Which is why this series of books is published by *Learn By Doing*.

ADDENDUM 1
Vertical Rent Curves

How Developers can make More Money and Urban Design can improve by Exploiting Vertical Rent Curves

It has always amazed me that many developers, those veritable profit maximizers, don't understand that neo-urbanist principles can improve their returns while at the same time making them better city-builders and I suppose better corporate citizens. For example, most of them don't know that there is a vertical rent curve in most towns and cities as well as a horizontal one.

In its simplest terms, as you go out from a city centre, rents drop and as you go up at many points within the urban fabric, rents increase.

Moving outwards from a typical city center, density and intensity drop, opportunity for interaction, called collisionable hours these days (chance meetings, jobs, communication, teamwork, entertainment, education, making, shopping, company/industry/individual synergy…) decreases and transportation links become less available, and rents drop accordingly. Meanwhile, people "downtown," whether in offices or residential condominium towers, prefer to be higher up and will pay more for better views, less noise and pollution and, as my Aussie friends call it, higher poser value[140].

It is the latter rent curve (the vertical one) that is often poorly understood by industry.

I took this photo on my way to work; it's an ugly apartment tower at the corner of Iroquois and Carling avenues in Ottawa. It is across the street from the Carlingwood Mall in an improving part of town. It has become quite the desirable area to live in as more folks in Ottawa have realized that being closer to work has its advantages[141].

Apartment Building with Blank Wall—photo by author

The first three storeys are used for a parking garage and the podium facing the street is, essentially, a blank wall; it quashes street life, denigrates the area, lowers public safety,[142] and is basically a throw away by the developer in terms of its economic value. It defies almost all the principles of neo-urbanism and sound city building.

Here's another look at the whole tower:

---

[140] Donald Trump is famous for "floor inflation." He claims that the first few floors of many of his towers, including the Trump Tower in NYC, are so grandiose and volumetric that he is justified in re-labeling, say, the 12th floor as the 20th. It also allows him to charge higher prices since the "20th" floor is perceived to be more valuable than the 12th even if their actual elevations above grade are the same.

[141] That includes my wife and me. At one time, we sold our 7-bedroom suburban home backing onto a local golf course and bought a small townhouse condo not far away from the Carlingwood Mall; it's close to the Ottawa River and walking distance, for me, to work.

[142] Anything that reduces penetrations of a building (windows/doors) and replaces residential uses with parking garage implies that there will be fewer eyes on the street and pedestrians on sidewalks. And that means less public safety.

Vertical Rent Curve Degenerating at Grade

Now what if the developer had instead used the volume at grade for front facing, two storey towns or perhaps for office condos or retail shops with what I call a window-on-the-world (WOW) effect (which is actually made up of portals overlooking and access to and from street level)? Would public safety improve? Would the walkable nature of the City improve? Would the developer make more dough? Would buyers/renters have more options and greater choice? Would the city be made lovelier? You already know the answer to that—yes to all these questions…

I superimposed (rather clumsily I must admit) some towns on the building:

Towns at Grade

Wouldn't you rather see a version of this instead of a blank wall? Therefore, message to the owners of this apartment tower—there's a renovation in your future.

By the way, there could still be a parking garage hidden behind a ribbon of these street-facing towns. In fact, that would further boost the value of these towns because, in a city like Ottawa, having indoor parking (accessed through your backdoor in this case) out of the cold and snow is highly convenient and pleasant.

I drew rent curves for two conditions (see below). The first (in yellow) shows the notional rent curve for a typical condominium or apartment tower that ignores the potential for street-facing uses at grade. All units are inward facing and rents just drop secularly from penthouse to grade—the closer the buyer or renter gets to grade, the more noise and pollution they have to put up with, the worse their views are and the more perceived security risk there is. Hence, they expect and actually do pay less.

If instead, the developer used street-facing townhomes or other built forms that take advantage of direct access to the public room, they could achieve higher rents plus make better urban spaces. If you have a young family, wouldn't you rather have a street-facing town that you and your kids can get out to through your own front door? Or if you are running your architecture practice from one of these towns, wouldn't you rather have clients come to your own front door? And how nice would it be to have your own street-facing sign for identification and 24/7 promotion…

Here is what that rent curve might look like (in red):

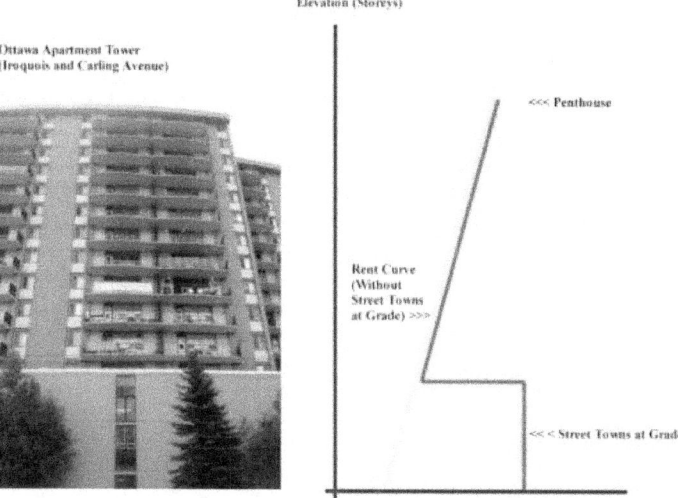

Rent Curves for Two Different Conditions of Built Form

...

ADDENDUM 2
Real Estate Insiders

It is interesting to look at the investing behaviour of SIOR (Society of Industrial and Office Realtors) members when they invest their own money. In Professional Report (Summer 2006), Maura M Cochran and Peter L Holland show that: "Almost 40 percent of the (SIOR) respondents require an initial capitalization rate in excess of 10 percent, a surprising number in this era of cap rates plunging into the range of four to five percent in certain markets for certain classes of assets."

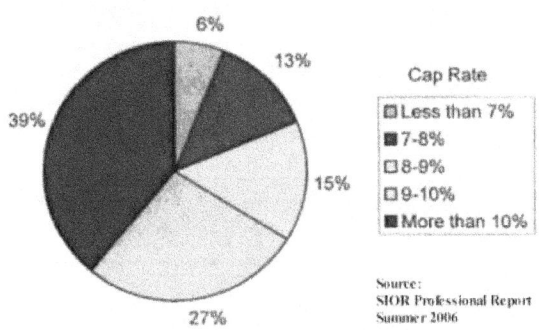

Only 6% of SIOR respondents were willing to invest with a cap rate of less than seven percent and more than a quarter of them in 2003 were looking for IRRs of 26 percent or more!

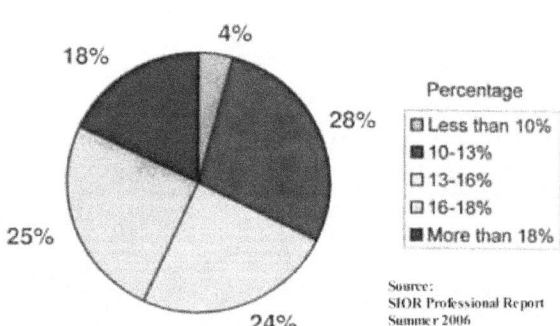

What's good for the goose is good for the gander—if realtors are looking for these types of returns, so should you.

It is interesting to note that this type of behavior does not only apply to commercial realtors—residential realtors tend to keep their own houses on the market a few weeks longer than they do for their clients and get higher prices as a result (typically about 3% more).

Expectations

A person's target IRR rate tends to fall as they get older. My students consistently score in the 20% to 30% range; that is, they won't lend a $1,000 to their poor professor until they get to these types of returns. As they age, they end up lending money to their banks by the time they are 65 or so at less than 2%!

Typical expectations of IRRs on equity are:

    Retiree: under 6%
    Middle age: 8% to 12%
    Student: 20% to 30%
    Major corporation: 20% to 30%
    SME (Small and Medium Sized Enterprise): 20% to 40%

VC (Venture Capital): 30% to 40%
Vulture Capital: 40%+
Real Estate Speculator/Land Speculator: 100%

These are per annum percentages.

Having said all this, there aren't many alternative investments that can produce the types of returns discussed above—year after year, consistently and at a reasonable risk.

In a commercial setting, many of the companies I advise who buy their own premises purchase buildings that are larger than they need for their own use. This serves a dual purpose—firstly, when tenanted in part by others, some of their costs are shared/carried by third parties. Secondly, if their business grows, they have adjacent space to expand into.

Additionally, most sitting owners (ie, owner-occupiers) fill some type of economic niche within an established ecosystem so they are usually able to attract tenants who are tied to them through their supply chain (or on the customer/client or marketing side of things) so they're not likely to bolt on them or not pay their rent...

Of course, nothing is risk free. By having some of their suppliers in their building if there is a downturn in their industry, they are all affected negatively at the same time.

Having said this, I like having third parties in the building with an owner—they might be part of your supply chain and they can help to pay some of the freight; in effect, they are paying off some of the mortgage principal for you. Owner-occupied buildings with some extra third party space can form interesting and synergistic communities of like-minded enterprises—ones that support each other and buy and sell to each other too.

I also like to have real estate held in a separate company with the operating company paying an arms-length, market rate for their space. This is good discipline for the operating company (they will price their products and services at levels that are appropriate to their *true* cost of inputs) and a worthwhile diversification of risks for ownership.

When buying real estate, it is good discipline to calculate your return on equity as well as look at other financial ratios but I have found that no matter how much analysis one does, at the end of the day, every investment is a matter of faith and confidence: faith that things will somehow work out and confidence that if they don't, you can fix them.

…

ADDENDUM 3
Raising Capital by Raising Scrip

Plus Tapping Sponsors/Co-Branders/Strategic Investors and Partners for <u>Free</u> Capital

There's nothing new about raising money by issuing scrip. The Reynolds Brothers ran a sawmill (established in 1870 by Orson L Reynolds) in the Adirondacks that in addition to central logging and operating their mill also ran a company store and developed other sources of income including catering to boarders as well as selling merchandise to loggers in logging camps[143].

When they needed to raise money, they issued their own "currency" called scrip like the $5 promissory note I show below to pay their bills or to fund new ventures or additions to existing ones.

The scrip says it is: "Due to the Bearer…In Trade At…"

What that means is that the bearer of this scrip *cannot* redeem it for cash, ie, exchange it for a sovereign banknote of the nation (the United States of America). The fact that it is redeemable only "In Trade" is key.

Presumably, Reynolds has a margin on each trade so a $5 note with a GPM (Gross Profit Margin of say 40%[144]) only costs them $5/(1 + .4) or $3.57. It's a good deal for Reynolds but is it a good deal for a supplier, equipment maker or laborer who accepts scrip instead of banknotes?

The answer is—it depends.

If you can't get any other work, $5 in credit at a Reynolds Company Store, $5 in cigarettes or candy from a Reynolds vendor (which you could then trade for other stuff) or $5 in Reynolds products (milled lumber) might be better than watching your family starve or having you join them in that unfortunate predicament circa 1876 even if you know in your heart of hearts that it's only really worth $3.57.

Conn Smythe built Maple Leaf Gardens in a six-month period during the Great Depression (1931) at a cost of $1.5 million. He funded it partly with scrip. If the "Carleton Street Cashbox" as it later became known had not lived up to its name, that scrip might have become valueless. Nevertheless, for an out-of-work ironworker back in the day, it beat unemployment. They could always find someone in the grey market to take scrip off their hands (at yet another discount) so they could eat today. It is what it is.

Canadian Tire issues scrip (ie, Canadian Tire money) that can only be redeemed at their stores. Disney issues Disney Dollars at the exchange rate of $1 DD = $1 USD. They can be converted back to US currency but only at Disney Parks. Hardly anyone does that and Disney has several billion dollars of DD on its balance sheet where they sit as *liabilities* lest a horde of grandkids and their grandparents suddenly show up at their theme parks clutching millions of DD they found moldering in their parents' sock drawers.

Don't think that script is relevant to you? Think again. What are gift cards really?

The lesson was not lost on Tracey Clark, owner of fair trade coffee house, Bridgehead, headquartered in Ottawa when she issued several million dollars of scrip to help fund her $15 million expansion. She built a new roastery for her growing coffee empire in a trendy part of Ottawa.

Tracey is a cautious, conservative entrepreneur who bought the assets and name from a bankruptcy trustee years ago and has painstakingly built a successful chain of coffee houses ever since. She has an aversion to debt but not to scrip.

---

[143] Source: Reynoldston, New York, History of a Mill Town.

[144] Gross profit margin is a financial metric used to assess a company's financial health and business model by revealing the proportion of money left over from revenues after accounting for the cost of goods sold (COGS). Gross profit margin, also known as gross margin, is calculated by dividing gross profit by revenues. Source: http://www.investopedia.com/terms/g/gross_profit_margin.asp#ixzz4qrzzP2Jk.

Her customers bought scrip in denominations of $150, $250, $500 and $1,000 to help her get this expansion done. It opened late in 2012. Now why would they do that? Because: 1. they love Bridgehead coffee, 2. they love the ambiance of her stores and free wi-fi, 3. the fact that she is local and able to stack up to and compete with mega chains, 4. she's an underdog, 5. they want to feel like they helped make it all happen, 6. they trust her. But there's another reason—they get a 20% return.

How's that? Tracey gives them $1.20 worth of trade value on every Bridgehead Dollar. That's a lot better than putting a $1,000 into a savings account and getting 0.7% p.a. It's true, on $1,000 in a bank savings account today, you'll get $7 in interest for the year. If you take off bank fees, it'll be obvious that you are paying your bank to take your money from you.

Now what about Tracey? Say her GPM is .6. The cost of $5 in scrip is then 5 x 1.2/(1+.6) or $3.75 so you can see Tracey's cost of capital for expansion acquired this way is a *negative* $1.25 per every $5 raised. Negative perspiration for Ms Clark. Now try getting that kind of deal from your bank where they lend you money at interest rates less than zero. Not going to happen (unless, of course, you are an equity lord and can access international debt markets directly yourself.)

Some time ago, I met with Andrew Craig owner of Major Craig's Chutney who, like the gentleman he is, recently acted in Quantum Entity Short Film, based on book 1 of a trilogy I wrote[145] about AI, artificial intelligence. He's a true volunteer for the acting gig not a voluntold, really.

He told me the backstory on his then three-year-old business. Turns out his great, great grandpappy served with British forces in India circa 1884. While there, Major James Craig experimented with ingredients and cooking methods for all kinds of chutneys and brought those back with him to the British Isles where a subsequent generation somehow found their way to the wilds of northern shelf Canada and brought the knowhow with them and the written recipes waiting to be rediscovered by Andrew in 2009. Thus was Major Craig's Chutney reborn—if you need North India, Cranberry, Jerk, Butternut and Beer (yum) chutneys, well, now you know where to go.

Andrew came to see me and, well, it was a tiny business. He needs capital to expand and he can't take on any debt or partners (it's a PB4L, Personal Business for Life). Why no debt? Cuz he can't yet support any. Why no partners? Cuz if he has a partner (or takes on any debt) it won't be long before either the partner owns his family recipes or the debt holders do (ie, the bank or other lenders).

So what's a progeny of Major James Craig to do nearly 150 years later? Issue scrip and find strategic partners and sponsors, that's what.

His clients, distributors, food prep supplier, his label printer, his ingredient growers, he has a lot of people in his business ecosystem who want him to grow and succeed. If he issues scrip to them in $25, $50, $100, $200 and $500 amounts with a premium of 10 to 20%, that's a pretty good deal for them and even better deal for him—same as for Tracey Clark.

There is some other cool stuff Andrew could do to raise more "free" money. If you look at the image below, you'll see that strategic partners are everywhere, you just have to look. It was there staring Andrew in the face all the time. He was looking but not *seeing*. One of his suppliers is fast-expanding Beau's Brewing. There, right there on the label! How much are they paying Major Craig to be co-branded this way? Nothing.

That should change. What I wanted Andrew to do was to put five strategic partners on his label, his new website (when he raises the "free" cash he needs to build a decent site) and in his nice Xmas gift boxes (see the last image I have included near the end of this addendum) which are perfect vectors to carry his strategic partners' messages to his clients—things like teensy recipe books, coupons, tickets, biz cards, promo items, what have you.

How much of his equity does he give up to get their sponsorship money? Zero.

How much interest are they charging him to give him their dough? Zero.

In fact, he doesn't even have to repay the money since it is a sponsorship/marketing/advertising cost to them, ie, an expense. Truly *free* money for Andrew.

---

[145] The trilogy is Quantum Entity—*We Are All One, American Spring*, and *the Successors*.

Major Craig's Chutney Finds Sponsor and Co-Brand Opportunties
As well as Strategic Investor Possibilities

Please read: How to Get Sponsors for Practically Anything, http://www.eqjournal.org/?p=1649

See also: Strategic Investor, http://www.eqjournal.org/?p=2406

Note the splendid opportunity for Major Craig's Chutney to co-brand/strategic partner w/ folks like Beau's Brewing!

One other note I should add. I suggested to Andrew that he sign up his sponsors for two years. He just isn't going to have time to start over every year at ground zero. He will also give his sponsor partners an option on a third year at the same cost provided they exercise that option at least six months prior to the end of the term of their agreement. After that, if he is as successful as we hope, the price will increase so this is a big benefit to his sponsors.

Lastly, Andrew can use his Xmas packaging as a vector to deliver his sponsor messages. In a way, he could learn something from LooseButton.com: they deliver their monthly Luxe Boxes to subscribers and get paid on three sides of their biz model[146].

Major Craig's Chutney Xmas Gift Box Could Also be a Vector

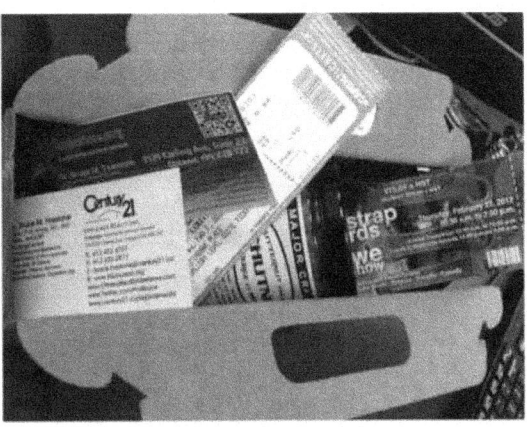

For delivery of coupons, biz cards, recipe books, event tickets and messages from strategic partners, investors and sponsors!

---

[146] First off, clients pay/subscribe to have Luxe boxes delivered to their homes on a regular schedule. Secondly, suppliers donate free samplers (perfumes, lotions, potions, hair care products, food, tickets, premiums, coupons) and pay rights fees to be included with those deliveries and, finally, marketers pay LooseButton.com to be able to offer free Luxe box subscriptions to their clients who renew, for example, their magazine subscriptions.

Or Andrew could do worse than copy the Manpacks.com biz model—they managed to turn products (men's underwear, cologne, razor blades, etc) into a service by delivering their stuff monthly or quarterly or semi annually and developing a nice recurring revenue model for themselves. CMRR (committed monthly recurring revenues) are the holy Grail of not just tech companies but all businesses.

Regular chutney delivery service anyone?

…

ADDENDUM 4
Leisure is the New Infrastructure

CivicArts.com founder and architect Eric Kuhne[147] first told me on a blustery morning in London when we sat down for breakfast at one of his favorite hangouts that, "Leisure is the new infrastructure."

Eric, an American expatriate born in San Antonio Texas, was one of the world's great architects, urban designers, and civic brains; he was responsible for mind-bending projects like the Burj Khalifa sundial in Dubai and Australia's largest mixed-use waterfront development in Sydney (Darling Park).

Titanic Quarter Belfast

So when Eric talked, I listened although, I have to admit, it was sometimes like listening to Marshal McLuhan lecture–you know he is saying something important even if you have no idea what he's getting at.

Getting it

Shown below are a series of pictures of a rehabbed former petrol station in the county of Renfrew Ontario. It's a creative re-use of what otherwise would be a teardown.

The spot is well known in the area for its coffee and sandwiches, and they have cleverly reused the gas station's canopy to offer shelter to their customers who want to picnic outside during fair-weather months[148]. But still there is a lot of asphalt left idle and unused.

Sandy's Deli with Beach Volleyball

---

[147] I am sad to report that Eric passed away July 25th 2016 at age 64. Eric completed the largest mall in Europe (Bluewater Shopping Centre in Kent) in 1999 and was responsible for the fabulous do-over of the Titanic Quarter in Belfast, amongst many other world-class projects.

[148] That part of the world gets 113 days of summer per annum. That's it, that's all. Southern Ontario (Toronto) gets a bit more—about 122 reliably warm days a year.

The Bell Sensplex about an hour to the south is a $27 million P3 (public-private-partnership) project between the NHL's Ottawa Senators and the City of Ottawa—it's become one of Ottawa's highest attended attractions. As a result, it generates over $650,000 per annum in sponsorship and signage revenues (compared to a municipal arena average with less than $10,000 per year) as well as a significant sum in indoor ice rental and field turf revenues. It requires fewer subsidies than any other municipal facility of its size and type and operates at much lower cost than municipally-owned and managed buildings. It is widely praised as one of the most successful arena projects in the world.

Peak ice times are always in demand—the secret to this arena's success, however, lies in their programming. Shoulder hours are rented to recreation leagues, girls' hockey programs, old-timer hockey, tournaments, and other self-created ladders. In other words, the Bell Sensplex is kept busy because it creates its own clients via programming.

So what could be done with the leftover asphalted area of Sandy's Deli?

Well, for example, they could add one or two beach volleyball courts and create their own leagues/ladders to fill the time. One would have to think that twin volleyball courts in use would also create more demand for coffee and sandwiches too.

Eric (shown below) relocated to London, England a couple of decades ago.

Eric's firm was a design research firm, which meant it works like this:

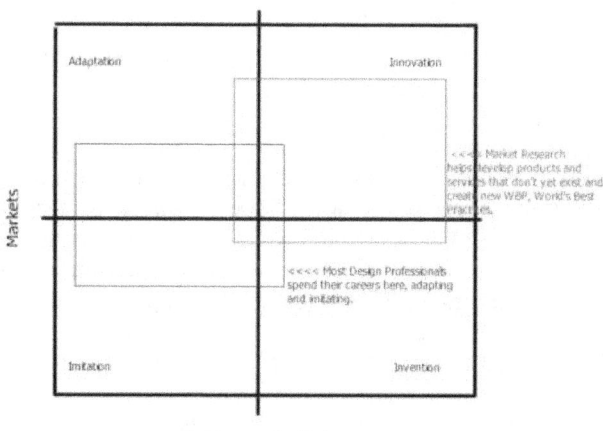

The theory is that scarcity and a desire to wisely use scarce resources power invention and innovation.

For example, using the North Grenville theater as both a place for plays/shows and as a chamber for their local council is an example of adaptation and innovation.

Kuhne said to me that most design and architecture firms spend nearly all their time imitating the work of others or adapting it. His model called from its earliest days for more emphasis on invention and innovation based on market research so they could push best practices to a completely new level.

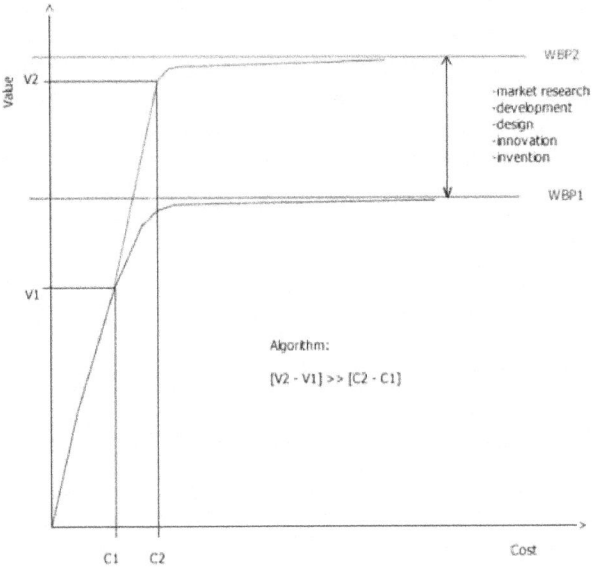

What it all boils down to is that for a small additional investment (C2 – C1) in innovative design and development, you get an amazing increase in value (V2 – V1) and secularly push World Best Practices (WBP) values to a higher level through market research and invention.

The key is to create differentiated value. By adding beach volleyball courts to Sandy's Deli and then developing the programming that keeps them in use, Sandy's Deli differentiates itself from its competitors, becomes a valued destination, creates a new point of interest for the county of Renfrew, improves fitness levels in the community, creates or sustains existing jobs by improving the profitability of the business, makes more intense use of the property, and generates a complex economic ripple effect.

Eric coined the phrase, "Leisure is the new infrastructure." You have to listen to every word he says and parse each one.

What he meant by that statement is that when cities, towns, villages and counties in the past wanted to spur economic development, they invested in infrastructure—things like roads, water mains, sewers, bridges and, later, telecom, cellular towers and wi-fi. They also invested in subsidizing foreign businesses as well as local ones.

Eric observed that communities are better off these days investing in leisure, art, design, entertainment, events, museums, learning, and meeting spaces. He noted that every visitor to Renfrew county, for example, would spend around $100 per person per day. In a place like Miami, it was $249. Trying to get that type of knock-on spending via a one-time investment in a sewer pipe is difficult. Most projects Eric worked on, even the most prosaic office building, will include some type of "leisure" space and activity.

It wasn't until I pulled into Sandi's Deli (on the way to giving a keynote speech on reanimating small towns, villages and counties by creating more sustainable and dynamic local economies) that the full import of "Leisure is the new infrastructure" finally dawned on me.

As long as zoning bylaws don't prohibit entrepreneurs from adding leisure aspects and other mixed uses to their properties, the cost to the township of this economic development activity is essentially zero.

I might slightly alter (heresy!) Eric's quote, "Leisure and learning are the new infrastructure." I suspect learning has as big a multiplier as leisure uses.

…

I was very sad to receive this note from Eric's office—

By now, many will have learned that Eric Kuhne died suddenly on 25 July (2016).

An architect by trade, Eric was a true visionary—a "Leonardo" of future city design. He wrestled with the philosophical, poetical and societal potentials of how people increasingly will live. To Eric, humanity's greatest work of art was the City, and the architectural studio he founded and ran for more than three decades radiated that ethos. That was clear from its modest, perfect name: <u>Civic Arts</u>.

Eric was an American who found his ideal home in London, crafting his design studio to perfection in Clerkenwell. Visiting Eric there was like stepping into a dream factory, decorated with impressive model ships, vintage planes hanging from the ceiling, a curious trove of bizarre and beautiful objects to tickle the mind, and a bewitching library of more than 14,000 books—unusually intriguing volumes, chosen to unstick one's imagination.

Eric's colleagues have published an <u>obituary</u>. To many who didn't know him but were swept up in his <u>scintillating Facebook stream</u>, he must have seemed like a fountain of eclectic and surreal musings. ...Eric was an effervescent, exuberant, omnivorous and ubiquitous presence. He drank up every drop of (knowledge) and, year after year, contributed behind the scenes with unflappable creativity and boundless enthusiasm. To those who knew Eric well, what is so shattering is that he had recently found greater happiness—both professionally, and personally. Projects were tumbling in that began to meet his lofty aspirations; and personally, he and Pamela were deeply in love and only beginning to embark on their adventure together. All of us who worked and played with Eric thought we would share so many more tomorrows than yesterdays. He was only 64.

…

ADDENDUM 5
How to Avoid Deal-Flopping Appraisals

You think appraisers work for you just because you pay them? No they don't.

They work for your lender, or at least they have the lender's best interest at heart not yours because they get a ton more work from lenders than they do from you.

Lenders want low appraisal values so they can argue it's not their loan-to-value ratio LTV mortgages that are to blame for the fact that your mortgage proceeds are lower than you expected. "It's your appraiser's fault."

mortgage proceeds = appraised value x LTV

Therefore, if your lender approves a LTV of 80% on a purchase price of $500,000, you'd expect mortgage proceeds of $400,000. However, if the appraisal comes in 10% lower, you only get 80% of $450,000 or $360,000 leaving you $40k short.

From the lender's POV, they now have effectively lowered their LTV without having to say to either the governor of the Bank of Canada or the chair of the Federal Reserve that they short changed Canucks and Yanks...

Anyway, here's how to avoid getting a low appraisal that'll crater your financing or refinancing:

-together with your lender, realtor, mortgage broker and lawyer, pick an appraiser who does not have a reputation as a deal flopper
-do your own CMA (comparative market analysis)
-provide that CMA and all supporting data (on a detailed spreadsheet showing <u>all</u> the renos and improvements you've made, many of which are invisible to an appraiser or building inspector plus details of your closing costs which are often non-negligible, also include good quality pro images cuz a (GOOD) picture is worth, well you know what it's worth) to the appraiser in advance or at least when they come on-premises
-if they refuse to accept your information, fire them on the spot/don't let them come into your building/after all, you are (usually) paying them not the bank
-maybe fire your mortgage broker and lender too if this persists
-accompany your appraiser on his/her property tour pointing out important facts including all the reasons why your property has additional value
-make sure your CMA covers as much as possible: list comparable sales, then calculate value using both an income approach, direct comparison approach and cost approach (replacement cost less depreciation)
-for commercial or income property, make sure you know all your income and expenses, have them available in a spreadsheet and find out what cap rate applies to your type of property (since value based on an income approach equals net operating income before debt servicing divided by this cap rate)
-you can be a bit vague about your rental program or the nature of occupancy because, frankly, you don't actually know—every project is an experiment until proven otherwise so, if you are asked, maybe it's owner-occupied for a while, maybe later on it's rented out via Airbnb or perhaps you'll have a few roommates—the thing is KISS, keep it simple
-be nice and pray

...

Postscript by Chad Robinson of BestInterest.ca:

-remember s/he who *orders* the appraisal owns the appraisal, not who pays for it.
-there are also a ton of different types of appraisals; for example, an appraisal with a value criteria of a sale within 30 days is different from one with a sale time frame of 6 months. Some lenders force appraisers to use unrealistic sale times therefore lowering value.

...

ADDENDUM 6
Buying Residential Property? Don't be Lazy

Here are a few tips for readers who are thinking about acquiring some residential rental property to consider before they do:

a) Get a property manager who carefully vets tenants. You are far better off to leave a place vacant than to rent it to a bad tenant. If you do have a poor tenant, an experienced property manger will know how to navigate the RTA or similar process to evict them.

b) Don't ever buy a property that doesn't cashflow. The idea that you can make up for monthly cashflow deficiencies by capital appreciation is flawed. It will also crater your IRR, internal rate of return.

c) Buy low/sell (or refinance) high. You make money in real estate when you buy not when you sell. So if you get in a competitive situation and get carried away and pay too much for that cool triplex or duplex, your battleship is sunk before you start.

d) Try to use all the leverage you can— financial institutions in Canada will still lend to people with good credit (ie, good Beacon/credit scores) with just 5% to 20% down. So rather than buy just one residential unit with 25% down, maybe you can buy more.

e) If you own five units and one becomes vacant, your vacancy rate has jumped from 0 to 20%, but if you only own one unit and it becomes vacant, your vacancy rate has leaped from 0 to 100%, which is bad.

f) By using beaucoup leverage, you will actually have more cashflow and more forced savings and more wealth effect provided you live in a stable economic environment (like, say, Ottawa, San Fran, Toronto, Vancouver, Austin, Sydney, Vancouver, Shanghai, Berlin or Boston and not Butt Place, Nowhereville) and provided you followed my earlier rule—buy low.

g) You or your property manager should visit each of your rentals, once per month or at least once per quarter. Tell your tenants in advance (some jurisdictions require you do this in writing) that you will be visiting on a regular basis to collect rent personally, to inspect the unit every time you visit and to fix any problems immediately. Don't be lazy, do it. If prospective tenants don't want this, no problem. They can rent somewhere else. Friends of mine owned a 5-bedroom home near Algonquin College in Ottawa that they rented out to students for $550 per room per month. They visited every month bringing dinner with them (kids are always hungry). They developed nice relationships with their tenants, monitored the condition of the place, never lost a single month's room rent, and even helped them with homework and personal problems when warranted.

h) When I owned a rental property in a tough neighborhood, I co-opted the locals including troubled teens by hosting a FREE BBQ and blocko (short for block party) every summer. I gave all the kids (some of whom were gang members no doubt) free burgers and flying discs, and told them if they needed anything to let me know. In the years I owned that shopping plaza, I had zero graffiti and vandalism—the locals looked out for it, for sure. The few hundred bucks it cost was way less expensive than higher insurance premiums. (Note: you can often get a permit to close a street for a blocko from your local municipality. They're usually free or ultra low cost. You can invite everyone in the area by the simple expedient of a flyer drop (in some neighborhoods like the one we were in, websites/mobile apps/email/Facebook/twitter/linkedin/online invitations just weren't going to work). Free food and beverages with some music and games (we liked Ultimate played on the street and Paddle Tennis) will bring people out for sure. But don't serve any alcohol—this leads to fistfights and opens you up to huge liability.)

i) You can add an in-home residential apartment to your principal residence. This has the useful advantage that you don't have to travel very far to keep an eye on the place plus part of your mortgage (if you still have one) becomes tax deductible since you are earning income from your home. In Canada, your principal residence is still capital gains tax exempt as long as the apartment is contained within the original footprint of the building, ie, in the basement or attic say. There has been government support for the cost of doing this in the form of CMHC and Ontario Renovates grants/loans (up to $25,000) but most of the in-home apartments that I've seen added over the years make financial sense even without soft loans or grants. Also, many cities and towns (eg, Ottawa) have legalized these. Ottawa's zoning by-laws were relaxed last decade to permit in-home apartments pretty much anywhere except for the village of Rockcliffe Park where Ottawa's upper crust live. We developed some innovative plans for new homes built with ready-made in-law (separate) suites. I lived in one of those when I was at UCSC many years ago and one of the granny flat plans we developed is a riff on that cool little place, located I still remember, at 1011 and ½ Seabright Avenue in Santa Cruz, Calif. If you would like to see some of our work, let me know via @ProfBruce.

j) If you build or buy a duplex/triplex/multiplex, make sure you sound, smell and fire separate your units and they comply with building, health and fire and safety codes. If you are purchasing an existing building, make sure you have a building inspector that knows these codes and can provide you with advice and costs estimates to make your units legal.

If you discover any surprises, it's best to find these out during your conditional period when you can either abandon the deal or ask for a price abatement from the seller before you waive your conditions or provide a notice of fulfillment of conditions to them. Fire separation is improved by adding an extra layer of drywall. If you add it so that sheet boundaries do not line up, you will not only improve fire protection, you will limit sound transmission and smells between units. There are lots of simple, inexpensive things that you can do that not only improve safety for your tenants; they make their lives more enjoyable. By not venting one unit into another one, for example, you've automatically reduced sound, smell and fire issues…

k) Residential real estate returns come in three pieces: monthly cashflow (aka cash-on-cash return) from rental and other income (like parking and multi media revenues) exceeding expenses, forced savings (every month you pay your mortgage, actually, where your tenant pays your mortgage, you end up paying a bit of the principal off) and wealth effect (which comes from capital appreciation—ie, when you sell for more than you paid or refinance under the same condition).

Almost no one I know can save their way to wealth but many can invest their way there.

My friends who owned that 5-bedroom student rental near Algonquin College made about $400 per month in free cashflow in the three years they owned their place. (The students all accepted 12-month leases even if they were from away so they would be sure to have place to live when they came back each fall.)

Their mortgage was paid down by $18,000 during that period (remember, it's really the students paying off their mortgage for them) and they made a capital gain (the wealth effect) of about $38,000 on the sale after all expenses were paid (eg, legal and REALTOR fees on completion of the transaction).

They originally financed 85% of the purchase price, so the cash they put down was around $40k of their own money.

Thus, over three years, they made $14,400 from their monthly free cashflow (cash on cash), $18,000 from paydown of their mortgage and $38,000 from capital appreciation. This represents a tidy $70,400 (before tax) profit/gain in three years on an initial investment of only $40,000. Try to match that by investing the same $40,000 in the stock market (at the same level of risk) or by buying GICs or T-Bills, which pay 0.5% to 2.25%, pa There's just no comparison.

But what's also interesting is that they don't have $70,400 at the end of three years—they have $70,400 (assuming they did not spend their monthly cashflow) plus their original equity of $40,000. So they actually have $110,400 of cash in hand (less whatever taxes they owe on the money they made—part of which are incomes taxes and part of which are presumably less onerous capital gains taxes.)

So they turned $40,000 into $110,400 in three years versus $40,000 into $41,827.13 if they'd "invested" it instead in a bank savings account at 1.5% for three years.

Now let's assume through some kind of modern miracle, my friends had instead managed to save the same amount during those three years that they made by investing in their rental property. They would have saved it by deferring gratification except here's the thing—people don't like deferring gratification so they would have probably spent the dough.

I mean most people who have a few bucks saved can't resist the opportunity to buy a new iPad 17 or iPhone 40 or new hybrid car or take a neat vacation (somewhere warm no doubt) or whatever… so even good savers are generally broke from time to time. If you read my Grassel story (below), you'll see that Mensa Ants, who are really good investors, own just about everything while savers have much less and Grasshoppers (who spend everything they make) have zip, de nada.

…

Grasshoppers, Squirrels and Ants in Grassel—Occupy Grassel Movement Picking up Steam/Government Planning Action

Introduction

French economist Thomas Piketty in his work *Capital in the Twenty-First Century* shows that r, return on capital (at a world level), has ranged over recorded history between 4.2% and 5.4% pa while g, growth of world output, has ranged from near 0% to as high as 3.5%, averaging around 1% to 1.5% pa. For all of that time r > g and for most of it, r >> g. Wages tend to track productivity, which is closely linked to g, overall growth, while wealth (asset values) tracks r; hence, the gap between rich and poor tends to widen over time. QED.

This effect is magnified if the wealthy use low cost borrowing to leverage their returns. For example, a 4.8% pa return on capital can turn into an 8.3% pa return via borrowing. See my example below.

It also happens that the wealthy are likely to have greater access to sources of low cost financing so the gap between poor and rich tends to grow much more quickly than a simple comparison between values of r and g would suggest.

Here is my sample calculation–

Case 1 No Leverage
Capital Value $10,000
Equity $10,000 100%
Borrowing $0 0% 35 years 1.40% pa
r 4.80% pa
ROI $480.00

Case 2 Leveraging
Capital Value $10,000
Equity $2,500 25%
Borrowing $7,500 75% 35 years 1.40% pa
Borrowing ($272.52) per year
NOI $207.48
ROI $829.91 4
r 8.30% pa
E&OE

Explained another way, investors almost always beat savers. In most nations, the top 1% controls a higher percentage of assets than they do national income although they control, in most cases, amazing percentages of both[149].

The Story

The population of Grassel is mostly made up of Grasshoppers, Squirrels, and Ants. Mensa Ants (a different class of ant[150]) account for just 1% of the population. These are groups that populate the *World of Grassel*, a land of 100 rows and 100 columns, viz:

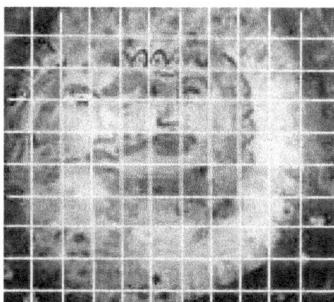

Grassel World, 100 Rows x 100 Columns

1. Grasshoppers are low wage earners who have to spend every cent they make just to survive. However, each Grasshopper starts life owning one square in Grassel with an asset value of $13,200. (All figures are in GD, Grassel Dollars.)

2. Squirrels are mid-income types and even though they have a lot more income than Grasshoppers, they somehow seem to spend all the Grassel Dollars they earn on current consumption. The amount they have left over each year for savings and investment? Zero. But they live on nicer squares in Grassel, each with an asset value of $19,800 each.

3. There is a minority population made up of Ants. They are an upper class folk who make many times what even Squirrels take home so they have some money left over for savings and investment! However, these Ants are very cautious and don't want to take any risks so they don't invest any of their hard-earned money—they save it instead and put it in Grassel state-backed treasury bills that pay interest at 2% pa.

---

[149] Depending on whom you believe (the Brookings Institution or Thomas Piketty's work); the top 1% of people in the US controlled 33% or 42% of US wealth in 2012 and 18% or 23% of income. The lower estimates are from Brookings. Source: https://www.theatlantic.com/business/archive/2016/03/brookings-1-percent/473478/.

[150] Named after Mensa, largest and oldest of high IQ societies.

4. Finally, we have a minority within a minority—Mensa Ants who make the same amount of money each year as the rest of their Ant class but they split their surplus cash between savings and investment. In fact, they place 90% of their surplus in investments; the balance they place in financial instruments. Since there is only one type of financial instrument in Grassel, they have some t-bills on which they get the princely sum of 2% pa in interest.

Grasshoppers and Squirrels are only too happy to sell the squares they own! Heck, they can use a boost to their cashflow. However, they don't save any of the extra cash they get from selling their squares. And they don't invest any either! THEY SPEND IT ALL.

The Ants won't sell the squares they own to Mensa Ants. They're into savings and they believe that owning a square is a form of savings for themselves and their famdamilies.

The Land of Grassel is 100 rows by 100 columns; ie, there are 10,000 squares of which: Grasshoppers own 3,333, Squirrels own 6,234, Ants own 333 and Mensa Ants 100 at time, t = 0. The 10,000 squares represent a total asset value of $170,060,000.

Every Grasshopper, Squirrel, Ant, and Mensa Ant start out with one square of Grassel land each. But the gods of Grassel are wondering if they come back a generation later (20 years on), what will have happened?

Well, after just 11 years, none of the Grasshoppers own any property and after 17, the Squirrels get wiped out too.

Of course, the Ants still own their properties since they refused to sell to Mensa Ants and they didn't need to so that they could maintain their lifestyle (like the Squirrels did) or just to pay for the necessities of life (like the Grasshoppers did). But they don't have much money either—their savings don't amount to much but at least they still have their squares.

This proves that in Grassel, you can't save your way to wealth, you have to invest your way there.

However, Mensa Ants have done very well. They have some savings/financial assets (in the form of fairly liquid T-bills[151]) but they own practically all Grassel property. In fact, although Mensa Ants only represent 1% of Grassel population, they own 95.5% of all assets (both squares and financial assets) after just 20 years. But what's even better for Mensa Ants is the fact that they have rents practically pouring into their Mensa Ant jean pockets in Niagara Falls-like proportions. (They have, being Mensa Ants, heard of Niagara Falls in a parallel universe.)

Ants (333 of them) start off with assets of $8,800,000 and, after a hard slog, 20 years later they have increased their holdings via savings to $15,084,361.60 which works out to $45,253.08 per capita. Not bad but a lot of hard work has gone into this by resisting current consumption—including tasty treats like buying a Samsung Galaxy 44.

But Mensa Ants (100 of them) who started out with just $2,640,000 in assets, end up, 20 years later, with a humongous portfolio worth $320,262,657.24 or $3,202,626.57 per capita by investing 90% of their surplus income while saving 10%. What's even better is that their passive income from owning nearly all the squares in Grassel is providing them with unearned rents of $51,958,095.46 or $519,580.95 per capita per year in year 20. How cool is that?

Investing has been a smart play for Mensa Ants, in part, because their return on investment (actually, their return on equity) is much higher than the interest rate on t-bills (22% pa versus 2%) and, in part, because they use leverage in acquiring squares—they are leveraging their equity (surplus cash) with a LTV (loan to value ratio) of 85%! Basically, they are borrowing from *savers* in Grassel to buy their squares from them or, put another way, savers are financing their own loss of property to Mensa Ants.

Their investment strategy has paid off so handsomely that, after 17 years, they have bought all the property they can in Grassel and must now look beyond their world for other opportunities. They have yet to figure out how to cross the border between Grassel and Niagara Falls but they're working on it.

What this shows is that without Grassel government intervention in the form of effective redistribution, practically all the assets of Grassel end up in the hands of a tiny minority of Mensa Ants. The Government is also thinking of introducing a tax on consumption to encourage Grasshoppers and Squirrels to save and also some education programs to teach Grasshoppers, Squirrels and Ants how to invest too. The consumption tax is thought to be regressive but, in fact, may be the only way that the Grassel government can get Mensa Ants to pay any taxes at all. Mensa Ants have such good tax accountants and tax attorneys that so-called progressive taxes on income are almost completely ineffective.

All of this is coming in response to the Occupy Grassel Movement which has seen Grasshoppers and Squirrels occupying squares much to the consternation of Mensa Ants.

The message is:

A) ALMOST NO ONE CAN SAVE HIS OR HER WAY TO WEALTH; YOU HAVE TO INVEST YOUR WAY THERE.

B) IN THE ABSENCE OF COUNTERVAILING GOVERNMENT EFFORTS, CONCENTRATION OF WEALTH WILL BE EXTREME AND GET WORSE OVER TIME.

---

[151] Debt instruments issued by the Treasury of Grassel.

By the way, a report from non denominational CBO, Congressional Budget Office, *Trends in the Distribution of Household Income Between 1979 and 2007* (http://cbo.gov/ftpdocs/124xx/doc12485/10-25-HouseholdIncome.pdf), published October 2011, showed that the top 1% more than doubled their share of national income after transfers and federal taxes during that period. This was, in part, due to less redistribution and partly due to most of the capital gains going to the top 1% of earners, which suggests that they, like Mensa Ants in Grassel, are doing most of the investing.

So a diversified financial strategy that makes sense to me for Canuck and American entrepreneurs and investors might involve a number of these elements:

a. owning some financial assets including secure t-bills and GICs.

b. also owning some mutual funds including some equities, possibly index based.

c. placing some of these assets in TFSA, Tax Free Savings Account, and RRSPs/401(k)s.

d. having some term insurance and possibly some life insurance especially if the latter is in seg funds which are protected by Canadian and US law (because they contain an element of insurance) from creditors[152].

e. having some cash and gold in a safety deposit box as a kind of "iron reserve."

f. owning some collectibles such as art or jewellry.

g. owning your own home (while treating it as if it were a rental, naturally, eg by adding a basement apartment or sideyard apartment (like the one we have) or a coach house…) and paying off your mortgage.

h. owning some other real estate investment assets—at least 4, 5 or 6 residential rentals, some land and maybe some small commercial holdings too like an industrial condo, a shopping plaza, or a mini storage place, anything that doesn't come into contact with the big players in real estate with their incredibly low COF (cost of funds) with which they can outcompete/kill you[153].

i. owning a Personal Business for Life, PB4L, an operating company that is your business with no partners and hopefully little or no debt.

i. owning a building that you can rent to your PB4L at fair market value.

This strategy has five main elements: financial assets, personal assets, insurance, real estate investing, and operating company. Canadians will also have access to the Canada Pension Plan and Old Age Security and Americans will have something similar to provide them with a modest base of income past a defined age. You may also want to consider setting up your own independent pension plan paid for by your company and a family trust, which may also provide you with some protection from creditors. Please note that the author is not making any recommendations here. But overall, I would keep things as simple as possible. Complexity is the enemy of success and everyone who listens to people who preach complexity to save a few tax dollars inevitably gets into trouble, in my experience.

…

---

[152] A type of pool investment that is similar to a mutual fund, but is considered an insurance product. Proceeds received by the insurance company are used to purchase underlying assets, and then shares of the segregated funds are sold to investors. Source: http://www.investopedia.com/terms/s/segregatedfund.asp#ixzz4qryimBtG

[153] Your minimum goal should be $10,000 to $12,000 in monthly independent income through real estate within 10 to 12 years, 15 if you are a bit slower off the mark. In Ottawa, if you owned seven homes (including your principal residence) at an average sale price as of March 2017 (which was $415,467 for residential houses, source:

http://ottawacitizen.com/news/local-news/ottawa-housing-market-gaining-momentum-as-average-price-jumps-5-3), you would have amassed nearly $3 million in real estate assets. Assuming you have at least two units per building (the main house and a basement apartment in each one), you'd have 14 rental units (including one you live in yourself.) If you rent your basement apartments for $1,230 a month (including tech package, of course) and the main homes for $1,875, you'll have total monthly revenue from your real estate portfolio of $21,735. If your vacancy rate is 5% and your expenses for things like property taxes, insurance, utilities, maintenance, repairs, contingencies and property management eat up 35% of your revenues, then you'll have an NOI (net operating income) of $13,421.36 a month. This means that after you have finished paying off all your mortgages, you're left with 13+ grand a month to live on, which sure beats the average CPP (Canada Pension Plan) payout of $550 a month (in 2015) by quite a margin. If you ever get in trouble or, say, one of your kids needs help, you can always refinance your portfolio in a New York minute with either a HELOC (home equity line of credit) or a mortgage. Remember, don't sell anything—refinance it and have your tenants retire that new debt for you. #Nice. My wife and I registered the name "Terrace Properties" for $61, which gives us a MBL (master business license) allowing us to open a bank account and run our properties under that name (giving us a last link to the first parent company of the NHL's Ottawa Senators). However, the properties, as you will recall, are owned, together with our children, in joint (personal) names as joint tenants not tenants-in-common.

ADDENDUM 7
How to Use Garden Suites to Add Value to Your Home and Community

As people who have followed my career already know, I like real estate projects that not only create private value but pay public dividends as well.

Developers realize that municipalities and community groups are going to demand additions to the public room and public benefits before approving most real estate projects these days.

It's not unique to real estate though—nations have been known to leverage public property like radio spectrum in return for, say, greater local content—but it's more regularized, in fact, built-in to the process of real estate approvals.

But what if providing public benefits could also boost private returns. That would be useful, right?

Influenced by California Design

Let me tell you a story.

When I was a young person, I lived with my girlfriend in a 1-bedroom "garden suite" or "granny flat" at 1011 and ½ Seabright avenue in Santa Cruz, California. My girlfriend was attending UCSC, and I was visiting her. The tiny home impressed me.

It was located in the backyard of 1011 Seabright avenue, in behind the *big* house where a lovely lady, an elder, lived by herself.

Our flat had its own laneway where we could park our Beetle and a wonderful flower garden. You entered into a front room, which served as living room and study.

At the far end was a dining area with a galley kitchen off to the side where a 2nd door led to a herb and vegetable garden, shared by big and little houses.

There was a single bedroom accessed off the living room plus a bathroom with pocket door. It was slab on grade construction.

Its floor plan looked something like this—

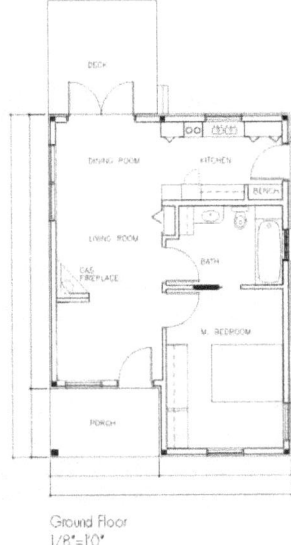

And here's a recent aerial photo courtesy of Google maps; the backyard coach house is still there… ☺

I asked our landlady why she'd built a granny flat in her backyard.

This is what she said, "Well, I like students. It can be a bit lonely you know at my age and they keep me company like you are doing now. Plus I feel a lot safer having people around."

Later, as I got to know her better, she told me she also needed the rent money and her own kids and grandchildren had basically forgotten about her.

Bringing California to Ontario

When I was in a position later in my career to do something about it, I created a subdivision called Briarbrook in Kanata (a western suburb of Ottawa).

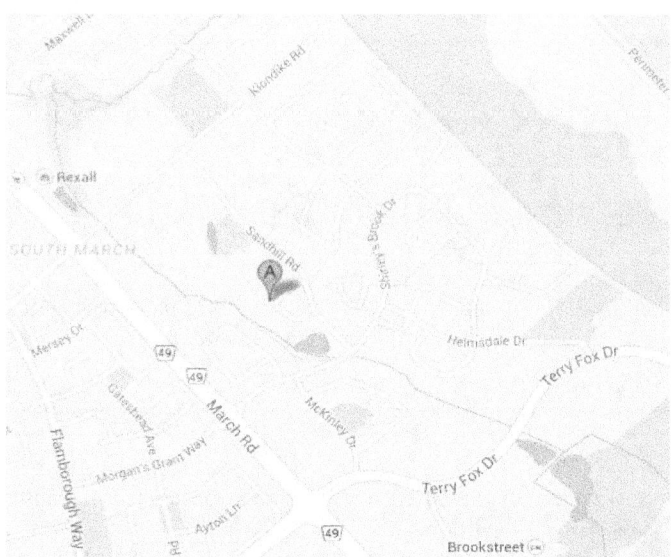

It permitted construction of granny flats in their backyards, thinking this was a way to improve ROI for homeowners plus allow elders to remain in their communities longer.

Every pie-shaped lot in Briarbook (ie, the biggest lots in the subdivision) allowed construction of these additional tiny homes.

I baked it into the zoning codes for that subdivision, which I wrote myself.

Social Return on Investment

So if a homeowner spent $100,000 building a two-bedroom, 1-bath granny flat in their backyard and rented it for, say, $1,375 per month (plus some sort of contribution for utilities, property taxes and multi-media package) to students or for that matter, adult children returning home to live with mom and dad (so far 3 of my 5 adult kids have returned to the nest to live with my wife and I) or grandmother or grandfather needing a place to live, then the homeowner is looking at a cap rate of around ($15,300 x .95 x .65)/$100,000 or 10.2% pa.

Not the worst result, wouldn't you agree, especially when compared to 1.2% on your "high interest" bank savings account or 1.7% on your GICs?

But it also serves a social purpose—it provides *quasi-independent* affordable housing for young people and elders alike and keeps elders out of those vertical warehouses for the nearly-dead called retirement residences.

From a family's point of view, the cap rate might in fact be much higher.

If it costs say $3,500 per month to put your mother-in-law into a retirement residence versus $1,375 a month in her own granny flat, you could argue that the simple ROI on your $100k investment is actually a much higher (($3,500 – $1,375) x 12 x .95 x .65)/$100,000 or 15.7% pa.

Adding granny flats also makes better use of existing *public* infrastructure like water and sewer mains, stormwater works, communications, roadways, schools, libraries and parks. All good so far.

Regulated Out Of Existence

Returning years later to Briarbrook for a Sunday afternoon stroll, I peeked in the backyard of a number of those pie-shaped lots. Nowhere did I see granny flats sprouting. How come?

One suspicious man, perhaps thinking I was casing his place, stopped me and asked what I was up to. Telling him I was the developer of Briarbrook (and Ottawa Senators founder) calmed him down and he became loquacious.

Why were there no granny flats?

Did he even know that these were allowed (I built permission for them right into zoning bylaws for the neighborhood, which, de facto, we wrote for the city)?

"Yeah, I'm aware we can build a granny flat in our backyard, but nobody in their right mind would do that," he answered.

"How come?" I asked.

"Well, the city said it's ok to build 'em but you can only get a temporary building permit—you've gotta tear them down after 5 years."

"No way," I said.

"Way," he replied. "Yeah, and I forgot to mention they also wanted to lever another development charge outta us to pay for additional infrastructure."

"What additional infrastructure? There is none."

"Exactly, it's just another tax," he answered.

"How much were they asking for?"

"$15,000 a door."

"Wow."

So no wonder no coach houses were ever built there. The city regulated them out of existence.

No one in their right mind would spend $100k for a cute little home plus pay a needless charge of $15,000 to the city only to have to tear it down five years later.

Oh, and by the way, they could only be inhabited by a family member—no rental to a third party was permitted so after granny packed up and left, you couldn't boost your income like my Californian landlady did by renting it to me and my girlfriend.

California Style... Redesigned

I was frustrated so I decided to build some myself with plans based on my California experience. Because this is Ontario, we added a full basement, which we turned into its own 2-bedroom apartment.

So our "granny flats" were actually high ranch bungalows on their own lot with one, 2-bed, 1-bath apartment on the main level (a ½ level up from street grade) plus a 2nd one in its lower level.

The latter had its own private door on the side of the building so the basement apartment could be accessed that way plus then it was only ½ level down, feeling less like a basement. We built eight of them.

What was cool about our updated design was that, with the removal of a single door separating the upper and lower levels, you could turn the place into a 4-bed, 2-bath single family home.

Put the door back in (a 3-minute job) and, presto, you were back to two apartments.

The flexibility of the design also allowed people to, say, use the lower level for their business with its own entry and address…

NIMBY, Not In My Back Yard

Back to Briarbook. Now why would the city of Kanata (long since absorbed by Ottawa) do such a thing, effectively regulating granny flats out of existence?

Well, if you know anything about municipal politics, the NIMBY movement and community associations, most of them are motivated by two things—fear and greed.

They are fearful that adding granny flats opens them up to low rent housing and undesirable elements invading their precious suburbs.

Greed enters the fray because they worry that such a trend would lower property values. No amount of rational argument will ever sway a mob of NIMBY'ites. Never.

I can speak from experience—I've been in public meetings in front of 450 angry homeowners yelling things at me like, "I know where you live!" or "I know what kind of car you drive!"

But there is a great deal of evidence that adding granny flats, in-home apartments, frontyard/sideyard parking, work-from-home businesses, small neighborhood shops, learning and entertainment options, community gardens to suburbia drives property values up not down, and makes them easier and quicker to sell, provided, of course, that public order is maintained.

People are right about that—you can't create *any* value in a lawless society (just ask Detroit's mayor about this) so Canada's value system and priorities—peace/order/good government—are spot on.

…

Here's a modern redesign of a coach house we have been working on, which you will have seen before in this work:

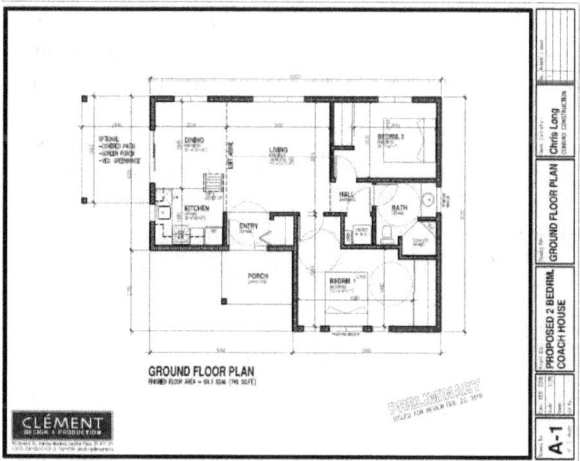
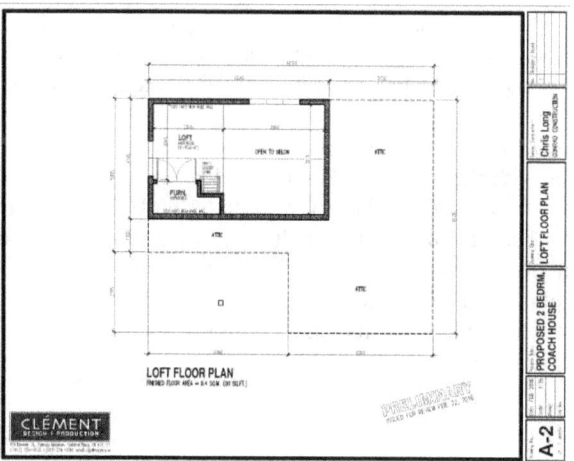

It's a design by architectural technologist Leo Clement together with input from Chris Long (owner of Conrad Construction and CoHouse) and moi.

The turning circles you see in the design are to show where wheelchair access is provided. To be considered an "accessible" home, it must, at a minimum, have a 0-step entry, wider doorway, and corridors (for wheelchair mobility) plus one accessible bedroom and w/c (water closet, aka bathroom) on the main level.

We provide 0-step entry via a landscape solution not by building those ugly wooden ramps you see from place to place, which stigmatize your building.

I can't figure out why more east coast builders aren't doing this. Roger Gervais, an expert in this field, tells me western-Canada or US based homebuilders are much more likely to adopt best practices. They seem less bound by past practices and designs.

Think about… a young woman or man pushing a baby carriage or carrying groceries, an elder with a walker or wheelchair. What's better? Steps to navigate to get in your front door or a 0-step entry?

And why would you ever want to exclude what CMHC (Canada Mortgage and Housing Corporation) says will be nearly 25% of your homeowner or renter market (seniors) by 2032, just 15 years from now? An aging population isn't just a Canadian problem. It's happening in Europe, Russia, Japan, even China, and the US.

The coach house Leo designed has two bedrooms—because by the time most couples are in their 50s or 60s, they are sleeping in separate bedrooms. Also, two bedrooms can attract roommates or a young couple with a baby so the market you will pull from is quite large. In addition, you get substantially more rent when you have two bedrooms.

Leo also added a loft bedroom (for the grandkids or other visitors) so we cheated—it's a 3-bedroom place, and, if you add a full basement, you can add still more rooms there…

Lastly, having some outdoor space is crucially important in cold weather cities where people are stuck inside for months at a time. I can't believe the number of new condo buildings, coop apartments, student residences, microsuite developments that are being built without any balconies or private outdoor space for their occupants. Stop doing that!

I don't care if you're cheaping out or your budget is too self-absorbed to allow for it or you're telling yourself it's expensive to maintain/replace/keep safe balconies. Let the people *breathe*. ☺

…

You've heard me say it before; we built better cities and towns and villages as well as individual structures in the 1930s, 40s, 50s, and 60s than we do now. It's true. I can prove it to you.

When I got my real estate brokers license after the Ottawa Senators went bankrupt and I was wondering how I was going to support myself and my famdamily (eight frigging courses and exams at that time), I took it upon myself to visit with more than a dozen Ottawa-based homebuilders.

My message? You're building the wrong product for the marketplace.

You can imagine the reception I got was pretty frosty, and I changed no one's mind (still haven't I am afraid to say even though I'm a good salesperson—hey, I convinced the NHL to give Ottawa a franchise while Canada was busy losing two of them—Quebec Nordiques (to Colorado to become the Avalanche) and the Winnipeg Jets (to Phoenix to become the Coyotes)).

I told them (more than decade ago now) that they should build new homes with basement apartments and new towns with them too. I talked about, for example, Brooklyn's experience with Brownstones[154] (many of them built in the period from 1890 to 1930 and still in use, in fact, prized) in places like Bedford-Stuyvesant.

They almost always included a basement suite (called "garden level" flat) with its own ingress/egress through a front door tucked under the front stairs and, hence, not visible from the street, an important consideration lest the neighborhood look "cheap."

Have a look at this image[155]; you'll see what I'm getting at:

---

[154] So called because they were faced with ancient (Triassic and Jurassic) sandstone.
[155] I took this photo from my TV so I apologize for its quality. For fans of *Homeland*, you will recognize Carrie Mathison (played by Clair Danes) mounting the front steps to her Brooklyn townhome while her occasional lover, the mysterious and quasi-heroic Peter Quinn (played convincingly by Rupert Friend) lurks below in the front door of her garden level suite.

[photo by author from television screen]

Now those lower level apartments were meant for gardeners, caregivers, nannies, teachers, tutors, housemaids, cleaners, handymen… not spies but they provided much-needed places for a whole raft of folks who could live close to employment opportunities in affordable units.

Today, with homes and towns being so expensive, why not give millennials a chance to purchase their own places by giving them an opportunity to earn extra income? Why not give elders a shot at having caregivers live not 20 miles away but 20 feet away?

I'm even trying to convince Habitat for Humanity to include these basement suites in the home they build so that their clients will have an opening to earn income from their house too. I mean, "Give a person a fishing rod not a fish," right? Then s/he eats forever…

…

So why did the industry reject my advice?
Here's what they told me:

1. we do things the way we do them because we've always done them this way so that's what we're going to do
2. we can't change our designs
3. things are fine the way they are
4. there's no demand for such things in our marketplace
5. it'd be a big hassle for not much reward
6. if we added a second unit, we'd have to pay the city a second development charge (DC)

Of all their reasons, the last one is the only one with any legs.

DCs are huge in Ottawa and probably a growing factor in your town or city too. In my opinion, DCs are just another tax on homebuyers, which falls disproportionately on first time buyers and benefits sitting owners (ie, most voters and councilors) who get a nice bounce in the price of their homes because the closest substitute for a new home is an existing one. So if your town levies a DC like Ottawa's (nearly $30k), the price of the existing housing stock will go up by nearly this amount. Great gig if you are already a homeowner (many of which, BTW, were built when there were no DCs).

I do have a few small builders and coaching clients who do this and the way they avoid paying two DCs is they file a building permit with the city for a *single-family* residence. The day after they get their occupancy permit, they apply for a renovation permit to add a (legal) basement apartment, which provincial policies (fortunately) forbid municipalities from levying DCs on[156]. Even though they might not like it, cities, towns, villages, townships and counties (in Canada) *must* follow directives like this from their direct senior level of government.

…

---

[156] Ontario provincial policy also thankfully prohibits cities from levying another DC on secondary dwellings, aka coach houses too.

ADDENDUM 8
Urban Catalysts and Anti Catalysts

Years ago, when I was working as a professor at Carleton University's School of Architecture, my students and I put together a list of urban catalysts—things you could do with cities, towns and villages to make them more successful places from an economic as well as environmental, community and investment point of view. These are things you could "sprinkle" like pixie dust on urban area, et voilà; green shoots will appear in their asphalt aprons…

I have great faith in humanity's ability to remedy problems, many of them self-inflicted. I believe that we could go into the most land intensive, wasteful, most boring and monocultured parts of suburbia and ex-urbia, and fix those places if was is political will and community agreement to do so.

So below is our list of urban catalysts. I add some "green for real" and home automation things you could do that seem to make economic sense as well as a few initiatives/events that might also be added to your community program.

Unfortunately, I also have a list of anti-catalysts—things you do that'll cause negative reactions to occur; ie, your town economy will crater and your most valuable resource (your kids) will head out down the road looking for more opportunity and a better place to raise their own children.

Neo Urbanism Catalysts

1. Add granny flats
2. Add in-home apartments
3. Add elder care in residences
4. Build-to lines[157]
5. Minimum heights
6. Minimum densities
7. On street parking allowed
8. No one-way streets
9. More not less ingress/egress
10. Use grided streets not curvilinear roads
11. Allow work from home with up to 5 employees
12. Density bonus for residential uses in commercial zones
13. Add corner stores/small plazas in residential zones
14. Add accessory residential uses to industrial/commercial zones
15. Use performance zoning where everything is permitted except that which is expressly forbidden
16. Allow outward expansion to drive up density in existing areas
17. Window on the world/at grade openings to the street/increase penetrations of buildings
18. Zero side yard setback
19. Uniform transition lines/step back of buildings at transition points
20. Neighborhood theming
21. Organized street trees
22. Boulevard design
23. Add leisure uses
24. Food trucks
25. Street art and performance art
26. Mural art, active signage, architectural signage
27. Micro farming
28. Mandate not just more density but more intense land use—mixing together of various uses on a single site
29. Use negative property taxes where warranted to allow less desirable uses to find a location (like group homes)
30. Exploit vertical rent curves as well as horizontal ones
31. Allow cities to expand outward to provide more diverse lifestyle options as well as pushing up rent curves at the centre
32. Zero tolerance for street crime and petty vandalism

---

[157] Instead of having setbacks in which you cannot build anything, build-to lines require you to build out to a line. This is to encourage building closer to the street, using a higher percentage of every lot, and creating a uniform streetscape with a more enclosed public room.

33. Add more patios and pop up stores to your streets as well as farmer markets and flea markets...

Being Green

All-off button
Get rid of grass/substitute local flora (xeriscape) or hard surfaces
Low flush toilets with two flow settings
Solar hot water
Solar panels
Solar air wall
Additional insulation
Heat recovery unit
Heat pump
Water-saving faucets
LED lighting
Intermittent spin washer
Low energy-consumption appliances
Install motion sensors to turn off lights
Get a programmable t-stat (thermostat) that doesn't require a PhD
Install blinds/keep closed at night
Caulk everything
Ceiling fans
Daylighting via skylights, light shelves, wall cuts, clerestory windows, light tubes, & light bottles
Rainwater capture/reuse
Go Green! Live closer to work
Work from home

Smart Home Automation

There is a lot of talk about smart home automation. However, a lot of it is crap, and some of it is very expensive crap.
Here're are a few things that make sense to me (in addition to tech/multi media packages and IT support)—

1. solar panels
2. solar hot water (which believe it or not has a decent ROI even in cold weather, northern shelf cities like Ottawa) for washing, hot water baseboards and in-floor radiant heating
3. smart t-stats (controlled from your phone or your tenant's phone or both)
4. security systems/monitoring/smartphone CCTV (again dead ending on your phone or your tenant's phone or both) with fall alert (for elders)
5. door locks either opened by your phone (or your tenant's phone) or at a minimum keypad locks where you can change codes via an app
6. all-off electrical switch (controlled from your phone or your tenant's phone or both) including control over lighting

That's about it.
The only other thing I'd probably do is use rainwater barrels for rainwater recycling, something like this—

Initiatives

a. Events
b. Festivals
c. Biz incubator
d. High School for the technological arts
e. Eyes on parks program
f. Project facilitators
g. Goodwill ambassadors
h. Casino
i. Hotels
j. Twitter guest moderators
k. Industrial park with accessory residential
l. Small parcel commercial development/own your own facility
m. Designate 1,000,000 sf MCF[158]s
n. Expand urban boundary
o. Google+/Google Maps registration
p. Creating Canada 2017 project (advice that is soon going to be pointless as 2017 ebbs away)
q. Paint color for sand mix in new asphalt

Anti-Catalysts

Common traits found within cities, boroughs, and communities, which have experienced serious urban decay include:

- Corruption in city or state government
- De-Industrialization
- De-Population- flight to gated communities and suburbia
- Property taxes levied on improved values instead of unimproved land values (a tax on renovation)
- Racial, Social, and Economic Segregation
- Crime ("Value can only be created when social order prevails")
- Neglect: 'holes' in the urban fabric
- Abandonment: land and buildings achieve negative value (rent curves are negative)
- Tax sales: city repossessions for unpaid taxes
- Obsolete, Oppressive and overly specific Zoning By-Laws
- "Broken Windows Syndrome"
- Rent Control
- Homelessness
- Neighborhood Pollution (ie, litter, air, water, soil, etc)
- Suburban Exile/Suburban Apartheid
- Lack of Adequate Public Transit System
- NIMBY Mentality
- Building OUT instead of UP
- Social/Economic Dependence
- Lack of Public Resonance, Concern or Civic Pride
- Low Development Density
- Shortage of Urban Infill
- Disinvestment by Public and Private Interests
- Lack of Basic Social Programs (i.e. Health, Education, Sanitation, Day Care, Recreational Facilities etc.)
- Tenements (aka "Towers in the Park") and derelict and abandoned buildings
- Unemployment
- Home invasions
- Criminal and disruptive elements living in neighborhoods and the 'next door' apartment
- absentee ownership

---

[158] Major community facility such as an arena, stadium, large tech complex, huge fulfillment center, airport... anything with significant traffic impacts or region-wide economic implications. Usually quite land-intensive use.

- failed renovations
- fraudulent speculators
- mortgages in excess of FMV (fair market value)
- shoddy workpersonship and incomplete work
- mortgage defaults
- tax liens and foreclosures

Defining Characteristics of Urban Deterioration[159]

- Overgrown, derelict sites
- Street lights out.
- Peeling Paint
- Broken windows
- Numerous "For Lease/For Sale" signs
- Prostitution
- Drugs
- "Panhandlers"
- Homeless
- Roaming Gangs
- Absence of police, or excessive police presence
- Graffiti
- Ports
- Heavy industry
- Air pollution
- Noise Pollution
- Abandoned cars
- Defended institutions and homes
- Razor wire, barbwire, security fencing, video surveillance
- Large recent immigrant population and those just starting out.

Bounding Characteristics of Urban Class Distinction

- Highways and freeways
- Railroad tracks
- Racial Segregation
- Parkland
- Waterfront access
- Elevations (higher elevations imply higher rents except where access to water and waterfront takes priority)
- Wind Directions… west side is usually the prosperous areas are located, while depleted areas are more commonly seen to develop on the east side. ("Go west young man, break bread in the new land…" First immigration began from the east and as people began to prosper, they generally moved west.)
- Car traffic directionality (well-to-do people live in the west end, drive to work later and drive home later to avoid glare from sun; industrial workers in the east end leave for work earlier and leave for home earlier)

…

---

[159] North American physical clues that distinguish areas of urban decay.

ADDENDUM 9
How a Behemoth Real Estate Developer Can Clobber You

I'd like to share an excerpt from my book, *Don't Back Down, the real story of the founding of the NHL's Ottawa Senators and why big leagues matter*, where I deal with a situation I faced upon taking over real estate development firm Terrace Investments Limited, the first parent company of the modern-era Ottawa Senators hockey team.

One of our partners was about to tumble into bankruptcy leaving Terrace, a small company at the time, in peril.

We had to face down a bankruptcy trustee, deal with a court proceeding, and fend off a large predatory real estate corporation about to devour a huge portfolio of valuable industrial and commercial properties including a half share of four buildings belonging to Terrace.

You know the old saying, "There are two chairs in heaven waiting for the first two partners to get there and still like each other."

Perhaps the best number of partners anyone can have in business is… zero?

Here is the excerpt…

Fixing Terrace meant first dealing with an imminent bankruptcy. Admiralty Enterprises, run by irrepressible entrepreneur Lawrence Freedman, was about to declare bankruptcy.

Lawrence was the guy who wanted to build a national chain of roller rinks, but his real strength was in construction of industrial buildings.

He knew how to lock up great sites, secure easy credit (in the 1970s and 80s), pop up cheap buildings, and sign tenants.

What he didn't know how to do was to control and manage his sprawling real estate empire, always a challenge to entrepreneurs who have the attention span of a minnow.

Four of his more than 80 industrial sites, were 50-50 co-ventures with Terrace Investments Limited. One of those was a roller rink.

Here's the thing you need to know—in bankruptcy, trustees are gods. They have incredible power, and courts are not keen on overturning or second-guessing them.

So if you put a trustee offside, you are not usually going to fair very well. That's just as true for bankrupt companies or individuals as it is for their creditors.

In this case, Terrace wasn't strictly a creditor; it was a joint venture partner on the ownership side.

When I visited the trustee, I told him, "We'd like to buy Lawrence's half of these four buildings we own together."

"I am not in a position to discuss this with you now. We are in the process of seizing control of all of his assets, his bank accounts, and notifying tenants that their rents are now to be paid to us. Just finding out what Mr Freedman actually owns is a challenge. Come back next month."

I didn't know it at the time, but the trustee was BS'ing me—he was already negotiating with Bob Campeau for the sale of the entire portfolio. This is what trustees do—look for the guy with the deepest pockets, and for the fastest exit.

Bob was a charismatic, angry, ambitious Franco-Ontarian from Sudbury who moved to Ottawa to become a major homebuilder in the 1960s and 70s. His homes were well-built and are still prized today in inner parts of the city.

His core team of executives was unusual in a small town like Ottawa—dynamic and dedicated, they loved their boss despite his mercurial personality.

They hunted and fished together in Robert's private northern Quebec camp; they were a very tight and impressive team. They branched out in the 1970s and 1980s to commercial real estate in Ottawa and Toronto.

By the late 1980s, Campeau Corporation upon the advice of US-banker Bruce Wasserstein used junk bonds to do a leveraged buyout of Allied Stores and Federated Department Stores. They scooped up Bloomingdale's, Abraham & Straus, Jordan Marsh and other beloved brands.

The problem was that while they knew how to run a real estate empire, they knew nothing about merchandising. It turns out that it greatly helps if you actually know something about the business you are in.

Department store sales along with the national economy stalled, costs were slashed but not fast enough, and cashflow declined. As a result, they were unable to pay punishing interest rates on their junk bonds and Campeau Corp teetered into bankruptcy themselves.

Campeau Corporation was in turn acquired by Olympia and York (owned by the Reichmann brothers) which later went bankrupt too—after London's Canary Wharf development proved to be their Waterloo.

So you are starting, I hope, to see a pattern.

Admiralty (successful real estate developer) → roller rinks → bankruptcy → Campeau (successful real estate developer) purchase of Admiralty → LBO Allied Stores and Federated Department Stores → bankruptcy → O+Y (successful real estate developer) purchase of Campeau → Canary Wharf → bankruptcy

Somewhere in there I could add:

Terrace (successful real estate developer) → NHL expansion franchise → bankruptcy

If there is a lesson in there, it's this:

1. Stick to what you know
2. Debt is a powerful tool
3. It can work for you
4. It can work against you
5. There is good debt (secured debt)
6. There is bad debt (unsecured)

Secured debt is debt that is secured against an asset, against which you are hopefully not upside down on equity.

For example, you don't have LTV (loan-to-value) ratios of 125% or more like so many of them did in those days (and would do again if their lenders, investors, and shareholders would let them get away with it)

Secured debt is supposed to go away when you sell the underlying assets.

Unsecured debt is like personal credit card debt—it is supported solely by your personal or corporate guarantee. If things go bad, this debt sticks to you as an individual or to your company.

The Reichmann brothers had a clever scheme—they would tell lenders that they had no secured debt on a vast office tower in Toronto or New York; ie, no mortgage.

They could raise unsecured debt (eg, a line of credit) based on the fact that their assets were not pledged to anyone and with a promise made not to pledge it to anyone.

In this way, they could, in effect, "leverage" the same building over and over again, raising billions.

It's perfectly legal, and ultimately deadly to your business if cashflow falters even for a quarter or two.

Former LA Kings owner, the charming Bruce McNall, did the same thing—he apparently pledged the same rare coin collections over and over again, only in his case, he didn't use negative pledging.

He gave each of his lenders a collateral mortgage. It'd be like you having five or six first mortgages on your home. He was sentenced to 70 months in prison for fraud.

…

You might think that the Reichmann's London project was a logical extension of their multi-billion dollar commercial real estate portfolio in New York and Toronto, but you'd be wrong.

Real estate is a hyper local business. What works in the mainly English side of Ottawa (its west end) may not work in a more French Vanier or Orleans (in its east end) and vice versa.

London's commercial property market is very different from anything the Reichmann's had seen before.

It's very City-focused; it's ultra conservative; it's snobby and hidebound; it's in a straight jacket of its own making—companies at the time signed 25-year leases.

No North American CEO would ever sign a 25-year deal, never. Things change far too fast in the local, national and international economy to ties your company to a physical plant for that long.

But it also meant lease-up took far too long at Canary Wharf—the Reichmanns could not shake enough financial companies loose from their longterm commitments to the City.

The whole situation was made much worse by the fact that the tube did not (at that time) serve Canary Wharf.

So figure out what you are good at, and then stick with that. It works.
Later on with the Sens, we believed that core competencies were these—

1. pro and amateur scouting
2. hockey program
3. player development
4. relationships with key stakeholders

That's the list. Everything else—like parking, food and beverage, security, cleaning—could be and should be done by someone else.

Anyway, here's what a New York Times editorial had to say about Bob Campeau at that time: "It took the special genius of Robert Campeau, chairman of the Campeau Corporation, to figure out how to bankrupt more than 250 profitable department stores. The dramatic jolt to Bloomingdale's, Abraham & Straus, Jordan Marsh and the other proud stores reflects his overreaching grasp and oversized ego."

But before he cratered his career, there was still the matter (seven years earlier) of acquiring the Admiralty portfolio at 20¢ on the dollar.

...

Shortly after our first and only meeting, the trustee unceremoniously announced that Campeau Corp was the successful bidder for all Admiralty properties.

As far as I could tell, they were the only bidder. I never got a call back from the receiver, who also refused to take any calls from me.

So I did something I don't usually do, I called a lawyer—Brian Hebert, a tough talking, funny, profane guy.

"Brian, I have this document signed by Admiralty and Terrace. It's called a joint venture agreement. It seems to suggest that if either party decides to sell its interest, it may do so provided that the other party is given a right to match said offer. Is that right?"

"Bruce can you fax me a copy of that agreement?" Brian proudly responded.

Proudly I say because Brian and I were among early adopters of facsimile machines, which were a wonder in those days. Imagine being able to send someone something without having to call a car or bike courier, in just minutes!

...

So after Brian confirmed that Terrace did indeed have a first refusal right, I called the great man himself in Toronto. It was a civil conversation. But Bob was adamant. He would buy the whole Admiralty portfolio or nothing.

When I mentioned having consulted a lawyer about Terrace's right of first refusal, the conversation derailed in a hurry.

I found out it's never a good idea to mention lawyers, even casually, if you are trying to reach a settlement.

"Why don't you want to be partners with the great and powerful Campeau Corporation?" he asked me in a scene taken from Dorothy's first visit to see the wizard of Oz.

I didn't want to tell him the truth. The fact is that when you are a small company, and you get into bed with a gorilla, you'll be crushed.

You see if the larger company has, say, a 100,000 square foot warehouse that they own 100% of down the street from another 100,000 square foot warehouse they own 50% of and you own the other half, it's profitable for them to take all the tenants from your building (since, guaranteed, they'll insist on operating control) to fill their vacant space.

Then after a couple of years of humongous losses, the larger company will call you up, and ask you, "Gee, we lost $2 million operating your building. When can we expect you to send us your share?"

Finally, a few months after you fail to pay your $1 million half of those losses, you'll get another call that'll go something like this.

"We value your half of the building at around a ½ million. But here's the thing. We're friends, right? We'll take your 50% ownership off your hands for nothing and call it even. OK?"

Instead I told Bob, "I think those buildings need local ownership, Mr Campeau. I'd like to try running them myself. Maybe see what I can do…"

He hung up on me.

The trustee was prepared to argue a concept in law apparently called the "greater good". Somehow, society would be better served by granting all these properties to Campeau Corporation, ignoring any legal rights purportedly held by small firms like Terrace.

It was in the best interest of the court, they argued, to support Campeau Corporation's all-or-nothing ultimatum.

Hogwash.

"So how much do you really want, Bruce?" Campeau Corp VP Andrew Jacob asked me ten minutes before the court hearing was set to begin. Bob Campeau was watching us from about 15 feet away, not deigning to make an approach himself.

"$2.1 million for our half, Mr Jacob. Same as I've said for the last 60 days."

"No, really? Come on, be reasonable."

"I am. Look those four buildings are worth $4.2 million. You know it. I know it. So our half is worth 2.1. You got Admiralty's half for $400,000, 20 cents on the dollar, Mr Jacob. If you pay us 2.1 and Lawrence 400, that means you get these four buildings for $2.5 million, that's 60 cents on the dollar. It's either that or I'm exercising our first right of refusal in ten minutes, and I'll own these buildings 100% for $400k."

"You can't win, Bruce," Andrew said to a 28-year old rookie developer.

"We'll see you in court, Mr Jacob."

At 2 minutes before the hour, after conferring with Mr Campeau, Andrew made an offer for our half at $2 million cash.

Right there and then, Brian Hebert made out a bill of sale by hand (in blue ink), which he had me and Mr Campeau sign (separately).

Then he walked into court and announced a settlement had been reached.

Terrace was on its way to a successful re-launch, thanks to Robert Campeau, the munificent.

...

Pretty much all that remains of Terrace Investments Limited after the Sens bankruptcy in the 2003/04 period is this plaque that I put on an outside wall of one of the properties we own and manage.

...

ABOUT THE AUTHOR

Prof Bruce

Bruce is an entrepreneur, real estate broker, developer, coach, urban guru, keynote speaker, Sens founder, novelist, columnist, peerless husband and dad.

Bruce M Firestone
B Eng (civil), M Eng-Sci, PhD
Century 21 Explorer Realty Inc broker
Ottawa Senators founder
Real Estate Investment and Business coach
1-613-762-8884
bruce.firestone@century21.ca
twitter.com/ProfBruce
profbruce.tumblr.com/archive
brucemfirestone.com

MAKING IMPOSSIBLE POSSIBLE

www.ingramcontent.com/pod-product-compliance
Lightning Source LLC
Chambersburg PA
CBHW082328220526
45470CB00008B/2435